Reaching the Goal

BUSINESS STRATEGY & MANAGEMENT

Can Two Rights Make a Wrong?
Moulton Reger ■ ISBN 0131732943

Developing Quality Technical Information, Second Edition
Hargis, Carey, Hernandez, Hughes, Longo, Rouiller, and Wilde
ISBN 0131477498

Irresistible! Markets, Models, and Meta-Value in Consumer Electronics
Bailey and Wenzek ■ ISBN 0131987585

Mining the Talk: Unlocking the Business Value in Unstructured Information
Spangler and Kreulen ■ ISBN 0132339536

Search Engine Marketing, Inc.
Moran and Hunt ■ ISBN 0131852922

The New Language of Business: SOA and Web 2.0
Carter ■ ISBN 013195654X

WEBSPHERE

Enterprise Java™ Programming with IBM® WebSphere®, Second Edition
Brown, Craig, Hester, Pitt, Stinehour, Weitzel, Amsden, Jakab, and Berg
ISBN 032118579X

Enterprise Messaging Using JMS and IBM® WebSphere®
Yusuf ■ ISBN 0131468634

IBM® WebSphere®
Barcia, Hines, Alcott, and Botzum ■ ISBN 0131468626

IBM® WebSphere® Application Server for Distributed Platforms and z/OS®
Black, Everett, Draeger, Miller, Iyer, McGuinnes, Patel, Herescu, Gissel, Betancourt, Casile, Tang, and Beaubien ■ ISBN 0131855875

IBM® WebSphere® System Administration
Williamson, Chan, Cundiff, Lauzon, and Mitchell ■ ISBN 0131446045

INFORMATION MANAGEMENT

An Introduction to IMS™
Meltz, Long, Harrington, Hain, and Nicholls ■ ISBN 0131856715

DB2® Express
Yip, Cheung, Gartner, Liu, and O'Connell ■ ISBN 0131463977

DB2® for z/OS® Version 8 DBA Certification Guide
Lawson ■ ISBN 0131491202

DB2® SQL PL, Second Edition
Janmohamed, Liu, Bradstock, Chong, Gao, McArthur, and Yip
ISBN 0131477005

High Availability Guide for DB2®
Eaton and Cialini ■ 0131448307

The Official Introduction to DB2® for z/OS®, Second Edition
Sloan ■ ISBN 0131477501

Understanding DB2® 9 Security
Bond, See, Wong, and Chan ■ ISBN 0131345907

Understanding DB2®
Chong, Liu, Qi, and Snow ■ ISBN 0131859161

RATIONAL

IBM Rational® ClearCase®, Ant, and CruiseControl
Lee ■ ISBN 0321356993

Implementing IBM® Rational® ClearQuest®
Buckley, Pulsipher, and Scott ■ ISBN 0321334868

Implementing the IBM® Rational Unified Process® and Solutions: A Guide to Improving Your Software Development Capability and Maturity
Barnes ■ ISBN 0321369459

Project Management with the IBM® Rational Unified Process®
Gibbs ■ ISBN 0321336399

Software Configuration Management Strategies and IBM® Rational® ClearCase®, Second Edition
Bellagio and Milligan ■ ISBN 0321200195

Visual Modeling with IBM® Rational® Software Architect and UML™
Quatrani and Palistrant ■ ISBN 0321238087

LOTUS

IBM® WebSphere® and Lotus®
Lamb, Laskey, and Indurkhya ■ ISBN 0131443305

Lotus® Notes® Developer's Toolbox
Elliott ■ ISBN 0132214482

OPEN SOURCE

Apache Derby—Off to the Races
Zikopoulos, Baklarz, and Scott ■ ISBN 0131855255

Building Applications with the Linux® Standard Base
Linux Standard Base Team ■ ISBN 0131456954

Performance Tuning for Linux® Servers
Johnson, Huizenga, and Pulavarty ■ ISBN 013144753X

COMPUTING

Autonomic Computing
Murch ■ ISBN 013144025X

Business Intelligence for the Enterprise
Biere ■ ISBN 0131413031

Grid Computing
Joseph and Fellenstein ■ ISBN 0131456601

Inescapable Data: Harnessing the Power of Convergence
Stakutis and Webster ■ ISBN 0131852159

On Demand Computing
Fellenstein ■ ISBN 0131440241

RFID Sourcebook
Lahiri ■ ISBN 0131851373

Service-Oriented Architecture (SOA) Compass
Bieberstein, Bose, Fiammante, Jones, and Shah ■ ISBN 0131870025

Reaching the Goal
How Managers Improve a Services Business
Using Goldratt's Theory of Constraints

John Arthur Ricketts

IBM Press
Pearson plc

Upper Saddle River, NJ • Boston • Indianapolis • San Francisco
New York • Toronto • Montreal • London • Munich • Paris • Madrid
Cape Town • Sydney • Tokyo • Singapore • Mexico City

ibmpressbooks.com

IBM Press Program Managers: Tara Woodman, Ellice Uffer
Cover design: IBM Corporation

Associate Publisher: Greg Wiegand
Marketing Manager: Kourtnaye Sturgeon
Publicist: Heather Fox
Acquisitions Editor: Greg Wiegand
Development Editor: Kevin Howard
Managing Editor: Gina Kanouse
Designer: Alan Clements
Senior Project Editor: Lori Lyons
Copy Editor: Lisa Thibault
Senior Indexer: Cheryl Lenser
Compositor: Bronkella Publishing LLC
Proofreader: Gayle Johnson
Manufacturing Buyer: Dan Uhrig

Published by Pearson plc
Publishing as IBM Press

IBM Press offers excellent discounts on this book when ordered in quantity for bulk purchases or special sales, which may include electronic versions and/or custom covers and content particular to your business, training goals, marketing focus, and branding interests. For more information, please contact:

U. S. Corporate and Government Sales
1-800-382-3419
corpsales@pearsontechgroup.com.
For sales outside the U. S., please contact:
International Sales
international@pearsoned.com.

Library of Congress Cataloging-in-Publication Data

Ricketts, John A. (John Arthur), 1952-

  Reaching the goal : how managers improve a services business using Goldratt's theory of constraints / John Arthur Ricketts.

      p. cm.

  ISBN 0-13-233312-0 (hardback : alk. paper) 1. Customer services—Management. I. Title.

  HF5415.5.R5944 2008

  658.8'12—dc22

                                                              2007025839

  ISBN-13: 978-0-13-233312-2

  ISBN-10:   0-13-233312-0

Text printed in the United States on recycled paper at Courier Westford in Westford, Massachusetts.

First printing September 2007

To Grayson, Jenna, and Chris

Contents

Foreword

It was a winter's day in an IBM® conference room in Philadelphia when I first met Dr. Eli Goldratt, the creator of the Theory of Constraints (TOC). I was meeting with Eli to discuss a substantial business dilemma we were facing in our Integration Services business at the time. In the aftermath of 9/11 and the burst of the dot-com bubble, the growth of our Integration Services business had slowed. We were working to address a rapid decline in our growth rate and the resulting pressures it was creating on our profitability. The challenge was that our traditional tactics for addressing such a situation weren't adequate to address the impact on our financial results. We needed some fresh thinking.

A few years earlier I'd read Eli's book *The Goal*, and it had captured my attention because it brought such a different perspective to traditional business issues. Eli's unique approach of teaching business improvement through the form of a novel is quite effective. However, while I thought I had an understanding of how to apply TOC to business, my success to that point had been limited. The fundamental elements of TOC are compelling when you read *The Goal*, but converting them into sustained performance improvement can be elusive.

As Eli and I got to know each other that day, he said something that caught my attention. We were talking about his work on TOC and how it came to pass that he went from a PhD in physics to a business performance guru. His reply was that he had a fundamental belief that the key to business improvement is the application of the discipline of the hard sciences. By this he meant that new insights in physics have to be proven and repeatable. There must be a clear and demonstrable cause-and-effect relationship between action and result. Eli believes that we are still at a very early stage in the development of our understanding of how businesses operate and that we can truly move to a point where our understanding of business will have the same rigor as the hard sciences. However, there is a pervasive need in large businesses to achieve a much better understanding of the true cause-and-effect relationships between actions and results.

The fundamental insight at the core of TOC is that optimization of performance at a lower unit level will eventually result in a degradation of performance to the overall process. While we all understand the simple logic that the weakest link determines the strength of the entire chain, we often fail to also realize that the act of strengthening the other links will have no impact on improving the chain. As leaders, we give all the units under our command the direction to continue to work to improve the strength of their link while we ignore that most of them are not the limiting factor or constraint. Hence, many of these actions yield no improvement in the overall performance. In essence, we ignore the discipline of the hard sciences and fail to understand the cause-and-effect relationship between the actions our units may have taken to improve their individual results and whether it will improve the overall result. The challenge then becomes identifying the true constraint and focusing management attention on lifting its performance while limiting attention to the nonconstraint resources.

Motivated by the urgency of our business challenge, and inspired by the compelling logic of Eli's Theory of Constraints, our team embarked on a quest to find ways to use TOC to unlock the trapped potential of our services business. This wasn't about a solution looking for a problem; it was about relearning the services business from the ground up, with a focus on getting to the truth of genuine cause-and-effect relationships between the elements of our business and the management system we deployed to drive its improvement. My team and I had a deep faith in this direction, and we shared excitement and conviction that TOC could be widely applied in our business and would lead us to substantial business improvements.

The team and I went through Jonah training, which teaches the techniques that are critical to successfully implementing the Theory of Constraints. Through the training, we became increasingly convinced that we were on the right path. We quickly chose to focus on the resource and capacity management processes in our business. This is a critical arena for any services firm because it relates to maximizing the productive use of the practitioners in the firm.

John Ricketts was a critical member of the team. He has an uncanny ability to take concepts and turn them into tangible deliverables. His first contribution was the development of a simulation game that we used to teach our resource deployment teams the concept of Replenishment. John also was invaluable in giving structure to the ideas and energy of the team as we worked to achieve the paradigm shift of our old resource management concepts to Replenishment. His contributions were essential to the successful rollout of the Replenishment for Resource Management program that we implemented. The program was critical to improving our profitability and revenue growth through dealing with the dilemma that is discussed in this book. Through our successful rollout of replenishment in the U.S., we later expanded its implementation to the other Integration Services units worldwide. Replenishment concepts are now being adopted in IBM's worldwide Workforce Management Initiative.

John extended our application of TOC by developing Throughput Accounting concepts for our services business, which enabled a more effective assessment of the financial linkage between our available staff and actions that could improve the pace of task completion in our project portfolio. He also developed and implemented education programs based on the Critical Chain application of TOC for project management.

As we began building our Managed Business Process Services (MBPS) business, John was brought in to develop frameworks for applying TOC to this emerging business area. This business is predicated on productive application of resources across a wide range of client business processes, such as finance and administration, human resources, procurement, and customer relationship management. His insights into TOC were widely applied in enabling our MBPS teams to deliver high value to our clients while ensuring a productive and profitable business for IBM. His thought leadership was critical to the rapid growth of this business in IBM.

All of us in professional services suffer a bit as the cobbler's children, often able to help others more than ourselves. John's book is an excellent tool that provides a foundation for leaders of services firms to unlock improvements in client service and improve revenue growth while also driving gains in profit. The techniques that John brings to light in this book are the bridge from the vision of Dr. Goldratt's work to the successful implementation in a range of services firms.

Erik Bush
Vice President
IBM Global Services

Preface

W hen I was young, my school had a sign above the chalkboard. It said simply, "THINK." Sounded like good advice. I heard the sign came from a computer company, which I imagined must be a place where people took thinking seriously. Years later I joined IBM, where they still do.

This book is the result of thinking, but not the conventional kind. My colleagues and I have been working on problems that afflict the majority of enterprises around the world. However, the most widely used solutions were invented some time ago, during different eras, so they aren't always well-suited to those problems. In contrast, the solutions presented in this book are targeted specifically at those problems, but they run counter to quite a bit of conventional wisdom.

The problems in question concern services: those tasks we have others do on our behalf because they can do them better, faster, cheaper—or we just wouldn't have the capability to do them ourselves even if we wanted to. Examples include legal, accounting, engineering, architectural, consulting, scientific, and technical services. These are tasks best left to the experts.

Many services benefit from innovations created during the Industrial Revolution. Consequently, service providers have the industrial technology and know-how to do repeatable services pretty well. Likewise, some services benefit from innovations created during the Information Revolution. Service providers can direct powerful information technology onto semi-repeatable services until they yield to the same old solutions, even if we don't always know how.

Things fall apart, however, when services can't be driven into submission with technology alone. At that point, everything depends on know-how, no matter how tenuous it may be. Yet complex, highly customized services are where the highest value sometimes lies, tantalizingly within sight but just beyond reach. Fortunately, we may be on the verge of a revolution in services.

IBM Global Services is one of the world's largest and most respected professional, scientific, and technical service providers. This services capability is pertinent because the Professional, Scientific, and Technical Services (PSTS) sector is the proving ground for the methods introduced in this book.

In the years since IBM entered the services business in earnest, services have come to account for more than half its revenue. This is a worldwide trend affecting many product-based enterprises. What's more, IBM has simultaneously transformed itself into one of the world's largest people businesses.[1] Even though IBM has completed hundreds of thousands of services projects, this book is not about IBM. It's about services innovations and the people who use them.

IBM has a history of fostering innovations. As far back as the 1950s, IBM helped launch computer science, now an accepted academic field. Recently, IBM helped launch Services Science, Management, and Engineering (SSME), an emerging academic field. IBM also hosted the Founder's Conference for the Theory of Constraints International Certification Organization (TOCICO), a professional organization for people applying the body of knowledge from which this book springs.

The genesis of this book was real-world problems that service providers and their clients regularly encounter. The less a service provider is like an industrial company, the less industrial-strength management solutions apply. And no service providers are less like industrial companies than those in the PSTS sector.

The solutions we eventually settled on are an extension of a body of knowledge whose principles seem like they ought to apply to every enterprise, regardless of whether it's producing goods or delivering services. Yet, like so many other innovations that work well in an industrial setting but hit the wall in services, that body of knowledge hadn't penetrated much beyond the realm of semi-repeatable services.

---

[1] *Felix Barber and Rainer Strack, "The Surprising Economics of a 'People Business,'"* Harvard Business Review, *83:6, June 2005, pp. 80–90.*

None of the experts we talked to knew how to overcome the constraints that kept it out of complex, highly customized services.

So we began to think about those constraints ourselves. That was appropriate because the body of knowledge we were investigating goes by a somewhat forbidding name: *Theory of Constraints*, often abbreviated as TOC. In scientific circles, theories are treasured because they guide research. Unfortunately, elsewhere theories are disparaged as just impractical notions.

Despite its name, TOC is composed entirely of practical principles and methods, not abstract theories. For example, the central idea behind TOC is that every system—every enterprise—is limited by its constraint. So to make any system or enterprise do more, its constraint has to do more. Could it really be that simple? No, but it was a fine place to start. And so began the investigations culminating in this book. Constraints were the way to crack the code on what we now call *TOC for Services*.

This book is written so that you don't have to know anything in advance about services or TOC. If you do, however, you can just review the "Foundations" part faster. The "Applications" and "Implementation" parts present the new solutions, so even if you're already familiar with services or TOC, you'll want to proceed at a normal pace there.

It might seem strange that a book from IBM Press covers management before technology, but there's a good reason: For technology to create the most leverage in services, it can't support only industrial solutions—it has to support services solutions. Thus, the technical issues covered in the "Implementation" part make sense only after the services management methods are laid out in the "Applications" part.

It might also seem strange that a book from IBM Press focuses on complex, highly customized, labor-based services rather than technologies such as Service Oriented Architecture (SOA) or Software as a Service (SaaS). SOA enables enterprises to build their software as collections of components that can be changed rapidly to accommodate evolving needs. SaaS enables software vendors to provide the functions of their software via subscriptions over the Internet. SOA and SaaS thus are enabling technologies rather than services per se. Enabling technologies are vital during implementation, of course, but that is a topic for another book.

Though the ideas explained in this book are presented as a set of holistic solutions, this book is essentially an interim progress report. That is, the ideas are complete enough to be shared publicly, yet there is still much work to be done. Hence, this book is the first word on TOC for Services, but we hope it won't be the last. Perhaps one day services scientists will look back and say it coincided with the leading edge of the Services Revolution.

Acknowledgments

If you've never experienced Theory of Constraints (TOC), it's hard to imagine the impact it can have when everything comes together. Unsolvable problems become solvable. Complicated solutions become simpler. Elusive goals become reachable.

The road an enterprise travels to TOC is never easy, however. So imagine how hard it is when there is no road, much less a roadmap. None of us expected to be pioneers when we began, yet it quickly became apparent that we were indeed pushing past old frontiers and into uncharted territory. Many people deserve recognition for their contributions.

Erik Bush was first to realize that traditional TOC applications had to be adapted in order to work with complex, highly customized services. While the rest of us were stuck on reasons why those applications wouldn't work on such services, he broke the deadlock by pointing out that if the problems were different, the solutions had to be different, too. It seems obvious in retrospect, but it was key to getting unstuck many times thereafter. Furthermore, Erik recognized that paradigm constraints are strongest in enterprises where everyone is an expert in his or her field. The buy-in process therefore has to vanquish prevailing paradigm constraints—but those paradigms have more lives than a sack of cats.

Steve Kagan was relentless in challenging policy constraints. For example, his insistence on back-to-back contracts to align subcontractors with client needs helped us identify an entirely new class of constraints for TOC. Likewise, his quest for applied analytics throughout sales and delivery of services steered our search for a consistent, yet simple, measurement system. And more than once he uncovered the folly of conventional process improvement notions that translate loosely as "we know we're headed in the wrong direction, but we're going to turn things around 360 degrees."

George Fioto led the first adaptation of a TOC application specifically for complex, highly customized services. His respect for deep skills and genuine talent reminded us that such services are fundamentally a people business—and the difference between partly cloudy and partly sunny is just attitude.

Steve Moore consistently championed and frequently demonstrated how TOC changes the nature of project management in services. Where medieval alchemists once struggled in vain to turn lead into gold, TOC practitioners can turn projects from leaden to golden without setting anyone's hair on fire.

Wayne Cerny led the plunge into marketing and sales of complex, highly customized services with a TOC mind-set. Much as most people are instinctively wary of learning how to swim by jumping in the deep end of the pool, the deep end is precisely where you need to be when learning to dive off the high board.

Howard Hess frequently reminded us that implementation is as much about changing business rules as technology. Nevertheless, untangling legacy systems without crashing the business is at about the same level of difficulty as changing tires while traveling at highway speed during inclement weather.

Chad Smith skillfully guided our initial foray into traditional TOC for manufacturing and distribution. In a later turnabout, as managing partner of a service provider, he was a savvy audience for services innovations. You know someone's a TOC professional when his fascination with evaporating clouds has nothing whatsoever to do with meteorology or daydreaming.

Carol Ptak provided advice and encouragement at every stage. As someone steeped in both TOC and technology, she noted that technology is necessary but not sufficient because even new technology can perpetuate old business rules. Consequently, introducing services innovations has all the exhilaration of being shot out of a cannon and then realizing the safety net opens only on impact.

Finally, Eli Goldratt deserves credit for inspiring a worldwide community of TOC practitioners—and for encouraging TOC researchers to examine their own constraints. Though he was with us briefly at the outset, it's doubtful even he could have foreseen where our TOC expedition would ultimately lead.

About the Author

John Arthur Ricketts is a distinguished engineer in IBM Global Services. As a consulting partner and technical executive, he deals with business and technical issues every day. His recent experiences range from Managed Business Process Services to Maintenance and Technical Support Services.

He began his career in manufacturing, where he saw firsthand the problems that Theory of Constraints was created to solve. While in graduate school, he managed a research laboratory studying computer users, and he developed decision support software for the U.S. Department of State. His graduate degrees are in information systems, with supporting fields in computer science and behavioral science.

After graduate school, John became a professor, teaching mostly MBAs and PhDs. He also taught in advanced information systems faculty development institutes. His publications have appeared in *MIS Quarterly, Interface, Information & Management, Journal of Software Maintenance, Informatica,* and *Computer Programming Management.* The IEEE Press, Wm. C. Brown, and EDP Auditor's Foundation have published his monographs.

After a decade in academia, John returned to the business world, where he led research and development of software reengineering products for a large consulting and systems integration firm. He later became director of software engineering at a major telecommunications firm.

Since joining IBM, he has worked in solution development, service delivery, new ventures, professional development, intellectual capital development, and asset development. John has dozens of patents pending. He has received awards from the Decision Sciences Institute and the Association to Advance Collegiate Schools of Business, as well as IBM.

PART I

Foundations

1

Introduction

We are all avid consumers of services, yet we seldom think much about where those services come from. Services are often like background music: Most are barely noticeable unless disrupted. How much we rely on services becomes painfully evident when the power goes out, planes stop flying, phones go dead, paychecks are late, hospitals are filled, day care is closed, water is shut off, Internet connections are lost, restaurants are closed, mail isn't delivered, 911 emergency lines are jammed, or automatic teller machines are down. When a disaster causes multiple service disruptions for an extended period, life gets really hard, really fast.

In developed economies, service providers are by far the largest employer, yet surprisingly few employees have a deep understanding of what it takes to provide services. When we pay close attention to complex services, they are like a concert performance: Musicians and dancers each play their part while the audience experiences the performance, but only the composer and director really comprehend what makes the entire performance. The performers and stage-hands don't experience it from the audience's perspective. Conversely, even an astute audience can't tell what is done off-stage and during rehearsals. And so it is with complex services.

Services that seem straightforward can be immensely complicated beneath the surface. Consider simple calls to customer service. To customers, calls to customer service can be frustrating because it seems like they should be quick and easy, but they often aren't. After all, the service provider just has to answer the phone and either solve the customers' problems or grant their requests, so how hard can it be?

Of course, the service provider's view isn't simple at all. What if 1,000 customers call at once? What if they speak a dozen different languages? What if they can't identify themselves and their purchases accurately? What if they can't describe their problems correctly? What if they request services that aren't provided in their area or goods that are out of stock? How many agents does the service provider need? What level of expertise should they have? What call routing and queuing technology is needed? Does the database cover thousands of products, parts, and services? Does the knowledge base accurately cover thousands of problems and corresponding solutions? What activation and authorization policies are needed to prevent theft, fraud, and injury? What information must be gathered to comply with legal and regulatory requirements? How will the cost of customer service be paid for? And so forth.

When you add it all up, seemingly simple calls to customer service can easily cost 100 times more than it costs for customers to accomplish the same inquiries or transactions by themselves via kiosks or the Internet. No wonder service providers love customer self-service.

Of course, some services are difficult or impossible to accomplish via self-service. Complex services may require special tools and materials, but they often require expertise. For example, professional services include medicine, law, engineering, architecture, accounting, and finance. Scientific services cover biology, chemistry, physics, astronomy, sociology, and psychology. And technical services include installation, maintenance, repair, and operation.

Professional, scientific, and technical services are the most highly customized of all services, which means that demand for these services is not easily predicted, and service delivery is not easily automated. Here are some fundamental questions that professional, scientific, and technical service providers face every day:

- How many people do we need, and what skills should they have?
- What is the best way to perform one-time projects?
- What is the best way to perform ongoing processes?
- What information do we need to manage our services?
- How should we market and sell our services?
- How can we devise a good strategy and convince others that the changes are beneficial?
- How should we implement those changes, and what technology do we need?

Conventional answers to these questions rely heavily on lessons learned in manufacturing. After all, the Industrial Revolution produced incredible benefits. However, the further services depart from industry, the harder it is to apply industrial methods. What we need is a comparable revolution in services.

The Rise of Services

Services are a rising if not dominant force in many economies today. In the U.S., services are about 80 percent of employment. In Europe, it's as high as 75 percent. In Australia, it's 76 percent. And in Japan, it's

67 percent. Overall, 65 percent of employment in developed countries is in some form of services.[1]

Even in recently industrialized economies, where employment in agriculture is still large, the services sector is significant. In China, services are 28 percent and growing rapidly because the burgeoning industrial sector and emerging consumer class demand better transportation and utilities. In India, it's 26 percent and rising because services based on information technology require less infrastructure than industry does.

Services-based economies are represented in the bottom-right corner of Figure 1-1, where the services band sweeps out wider and wider swaths from both agriculture and industry—and per-capita income rises markedly.[2] This trend has implications not only for developing economies but also for the developed ones, because their services now face global competition. Some services are inherently local because they require direct customer contact, but a growing set of services can be provided from virtually any location worldwide via information technology and efficient transportation systems.

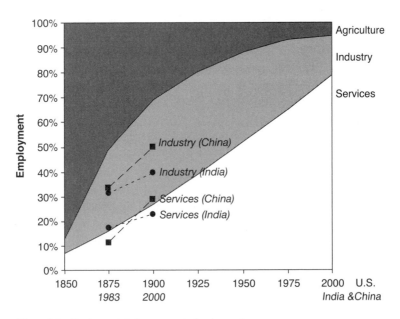

Figure 1-1   Employment during economic development

Today's developed economies made the journey from agrarian to industrial to services economies over a period of 150 years or more, first on the back of the Industrial Revolution, and then the Information Revolution. The Industrial Revolution started in England, later expanded to other European countries and the U.S., and eventually to Russia and Japan—but employment structure followed the same basic pattern everywhere. The current wave of up-and-coming economies is doing it far faster, however, because so much of the heavy lifting is already done. With the right social, educational, legal, and economic climate, developing economies can now come bounding into the services sector in just a couple decades.

Furthermore, developing economies are growing differently today. Until recently, economic development meant slow urbanization of small populations, but developing economies today are experiencing rapid urbanization of large populations, which stimulates demand for services as never before. As shown in Figure 1-1, services employment in China and India today is at about the same level as in the U.S. 100 years ago— yet industrial employment in China and India today is about half what it was in the U.S. at that stage.[3,4] Once the Industrial Revolution began in the U.S., it took nearly 100 years for services employment to exceed industrial employment. In contrast, China, India, and other developing economies are already there.

Despite this rise of services, the services management field is still based largely on foundations that can be traced back to the industrial era. Where there are clear parallels, such foundations are a natural fit. But as the services sector has grown in size, it has also grown more diverse, more distributed, and considerably more complex. Enterprises in the services sector now face challenges—and opportunities—that have no clear precedents in industry. Management foundations from the earlier era thus are showing their age.

In general terms, this book is about an updated approach to services management that embraces diversity, distribution, and complexity. In specific terms, it's about the adaptation of a highly regarded management approach from its roots in industry to the furthest corner of the services sector. That management approach is *Theory of Constraints*. The furthest corner of the services sector—services least like industry—is Professional, Scientific, and Technical Services.

Theory of Constraints

Theory of Constraints (TOC) gets its name from the fact that all enterprises are constrained by something. If they weren't, they could grow as large and as fast as they wanted. But one has to monitor Wall Street or Main Street for only a moment to know that for the vast majority of enterprises growth is really hard. Constraints are why.

So the first step in applying TOC is to figure out precisely where the constraints are. In enterprises with professional managers, it seems fair to assume that they must know where the constraints are. In fact, many don't have a clue. That's because lots of things seem like constraints but aren't. Most managers are surprised to learn that factories and offices each may have just one constraint. Everything else is noise insofar as identifying the constraint goes. So what separates constraints from noise? A constraint limits what can be produced by the factory or office as a whole. Everything else is a nonconstraint. For example, in an office processing insurance forms, the one step that's the perennial bottleneck is the constraint because it limits production of the entire office. In the final analysis, it doesn't matter how much any nonconstraint produces if the constraint can't keep up.

The second step in applying TOC is to utilize the constraint to its fullest extent. If that constraint in the insurance office is a machine that's often broken or a worker who's often absent, a more reliable machine or worker must be found because the productivity of the entire office depends on this. Note that the machine or worker in question doesn't have to be the most expensive or highest-profile. An ancillary machine or entry-level worker can be the constraint, despite their apparent insignificance in the office hierarchy.

The third step in applying TOC is to make sure that nonconstraints keep the constraint busy—but otherwise stay out of the way. Often this means that the nonconstraints have to be dialed down. This probably seems counterintuitive: The way to increase overall productivity may require cutting back production on everything but the constraint? It's counterintuitive only if you believe that every machine and worker determine overall productivity—but we've already established that they don't. For example, at the end of the day, it doesn't matter how many forms the office processed if they just piled up at the postage machine rather than going out the door.

The fourth step in applying TOC is to improve productivity of the constraint because lifting its performance is the only way to lift the office's performance. For instance, if the worker tending the postage machine now keeps it running continuously during business hours, yet forms continue to pile up ahead of it, the only way to improve the office's productivity is to improve the constraint's productivity. Ways to do this include running the machine outside business hours, replacing it with a faster model, getting a second machine, switching to e-mail, or eliminating some forms altogether. Once this is done, the nonconstraints can be dialed up, and the office's overall productivity will rise.

The final step in applying TOC is to repeat the previous steps. This step is more important than it might seem at first, because the foregoing steps may have caused the constraint to shift. That is, with a few tweaks, the postage machine may now be fully capable of keeping up. And if there are times when the postage machine sits idle because it has no work to do, it may no longer be the constraint. If so, where is the constraint? To answer that question, we must look for piles of work elsewhere in the office. If the piles are ahead of insurance underwriters, for instance, they're the new constraint. However, if there are no piles of work anywhere, and everyone is struggling to find work at times, the constraint is no longer within the office. It's outside, with insurance agents, claims adjusters, or customers. How could any of these roles be the constraint if they're outside the office? They're the constraint if they sell, adjust, or buy less than the office can produce.

Theory of Constraints thus gets its name from the central role that constraints play in determining overall production. Yet people sometimes react to that name in contradictory ways. Academics complain that there's no theory in Theory of Constraints, while managers dismiss anything called a theory because it sounds so disconnected from the real world. Fortunately, neither viewpoint is entirely correct. TOC is grounded in the real world because it has evolved based on what actually works in practice. A simple web search yields more than 100,000 hits for "TOC," with plenty of testimonials by managers. Though TOC hasn't been formalized in the way most theories are, it offers plenty of testable hypotheses, and refereed journals are well populated with TOC research.[5] So if you're put off by theory—or the lack of it—do what others have done, and refer to TOC as constraint management. Anyone familiar with TOC will know what you mean.

Professional, Scientific, and Technical Services

Although TOC originated in industry, constraints affect every enterprise, including those in services. TOC therefore has been readily applied to services that sufficiently resemble industry. TOC has not yet, however, penetrated into all corners of the services sector because plenty of services do not sufficiently resemble industry.

One fundamental difference between industry and services is that services cannot start until the customer arrives. Of course, some preparations can be made without a customer, but the service itself can't. For example, a restaurant can prepare certain foods in advance, and perhaps even distribute dishes to multiple venues from a central kitchen, but the core service doesn't start until a hungry customer shows up. This contrasts with industry, where many workers rarely if ever meet consumers of their products.

Another difference concerns inventory. In industry, inventory issues are pervasive: Figuring out the right amount of raw material inventory to hold, the right amount of finished goods inventory to manufacture, and where it should be distributed are core problems. In contrast, there can be no inventory of completed services because as soon as there's something to ship, it's more like a product than a service. For example, when a manufactured product breaks under warranty, manufacturers often prefer to exchange it for a remanufactured unit instead of performing a repair service because such services require different management. Even when manufacturers do offer repair services, those services may actually be provided by subcontractors, business partners, or a separately managed services unit within the manufacturer's enterprise.

A third difference between industry and some services is less often discussed: customization. In industry, customization of products makes it harder to manage constraints, so a preferred TOC strategy is to serve as many distinct market segments as possible with as few product variations as possible. Many services, such as health care and education, also benefit from standardization for constraint management and other purposes, such as quality control.

On the other hand, Professional, Scientific, and Technical Services (PSTS) are always customized to some degree. When a client engages an advertising firm to devise a new campaign, hires a research firm to conduct a scientific study, or utilizes an information technology services firm to build a web site, it's counting on those service providers to meet its unique requirements. So at the very least, the deliverables have be different from previous deliverables. But the projects or processes the service providers use to produce those deliverables often have to be customized, too. This customization makes it hard for service providers to find one constraint, marshal the nonconstraints around it, and keep the constraint from floating. This has largely kept TOC out of PSTS.

One place where TOC has found direct application in PSTS is in project management. Using the TOC application known as *Critical Chain*, PSTS enterprises can use TOC to manage the constraint within individual projects. Moreover, with a multiproject form of Critical Chain, PSTS enterprises can use TOC to manage constraints across several projects with a common constraint. Yet when no common constraint exists—as happens with highly customized projects in PSTS—multiproject Critical Chain just doesn't work. And when the services a PSTS enterprise performs include ongoing business processes, rather than discrete projects, even single-project Critical Chain doesn't apply. At the enterprise level, something is missing.

Therefore, to make TOC broadly applicable in services, we must identify the unique characteristics of PSTS enterprises and adapt TOC accordingly. If the nature of PSTS constraints is different, how they can and can't be managed will be different, too. But if TOC can tackle some of the most vexing problems in PSTS, it should also become more useful in other services sectors.

Organization of This Book

This book is organized into three parts, plus appendixes. First, there's the "Foundations" part you're reading now. The next chapter in this part, "Services On Demand," compares PSTS to other services, discusses unique attributes of PSTS, and discusses the implications of becoming an on-demand service provider. The "Theory of Constraints" chapter surveys TOC applications as they are routinely employed in industry and compatible services. This will make it easier to understand the adaptations needed for PSTS.

Part II, "Applications," is about TOC applications in PSTS. It begins with the "Resource Management" chapter because PSTS relies heavily on skilled resources. The application for Resource Management is known as *Replenishment for Services*. Chapter 5, "Project Management," covers an application known as *Critical Chain for Services*, which is a method of project management enabled by Replenishment. Chapter 6, "Process Management," covers an application known as *Drum-Buffer-Rope for Services*, which is a method of dynamic capacity management. The "Finance & Accounting" chapter illustrates an application known as *Throughput Accounting for Services*, which is a method of management accounting. The "Marketing and Sales" chapter then uses *Throughput Accounting* for services mixing, pricing, ranking, and other decisions.

Collectively, these applications are called *TOC for Services* (TOC$_S$) to distinguish them from traditional TOC applications, which are called *TOC for Goods* (TOC$_G$). As you will see, enterprises that offer goods as well as services can use both TOC versions as appropriate.

Finally, the "Implementation" part of this book is about implementing TOC for Services. The "Strategy and Change" chapter is about setting a course and getting buy-in. It uses Throughput Accounting for resource mix and investment decisions. Chapter 10, "Implementation and Technology," is about building TOC infrastructure, plus the information technology needed to support the strategy enabled by that infrastructure. For instance, if the strategy is to become more of an asset-based PSTS provider, the technology has to support the necessary assets. The last chapter then assesses whether the adaptation of TOC for PSTS is more broadly applicable in other sectors.

How to Read This Book

This book is organized so that later chapters build on earlier chapters. Unless you're already familiar with TOC and PSTS, the chapters are probably best read in order. Just skim or skip what you already know.

This book is written so that you don't need prior knowledge of TOC or PSTS. Hence, it always reviews the basics before delving into deeper topics. You may wonder how deep the rabbit hole goes in some chapters, but don't give up easily on the tough parts. They're there because you'll need them to understand how and why TOC can be adapted for services. Furthermore, some chapters have corresponding appendixes that delve more deeply into selected topics, so you may want to take a side trip occasionally.

If you're already a TOC practitioner, you may find portions of this book controversial because they violate some long-standing TOC principles. For example, traditional TOC categorizes constraints as either internal or external, but TOC for Services recognizes a third category of constraints. Traditional TOC assumes that capacity is relatively rigid, but TOC for Services makes capacity flexible. Traditional TOC says that if the constraint is internal, it should be carefully managed so that it won't float, but TOC for Services acknowledges that floating constraints are unavoidable at times.

Fear not, however. This book abides by—indeed reinforces—the majority of TOC principles. At the individual contract level in PSTS, TOC practitioners will see that familiar principles still hold. Nevertheless, as the subject shifts up to the business unit level, TOC simply won't work in services if you insist that every original TOC principle must always hold. Some services businesses really are different, and information technology really does change how services can be managed. So keep an open mind and read on.

Endnotes

1. "Comparative International Statistics," *Statistical Abstract 2004–2005*, U.S. Census Bureau.

2. "Growth of the Service Sector," *Beyond Economic Growth: Meeting the Challenges of Global Development*, World Bank, 2000, p. 51.

3. Sukti Dasgupta and Ajit Singh, "Manufacturing, Services, Jobless Growth and the Informal Economy: Will Services Be the New Engine of Indian Economic Growth?", *Conference on the Future of Development Economics*, World Institute for Development Economics Research, June 17–18, 2005, p. 8.

4. Ming Lu, Jianyong Fan, Shejian Liu, and Yan Yan, "Employment Restructuring During China's Economic Transition," *Monthly Labor Review*, August 2002, p. 26.

5. Victoria J. Mabin and Steven J. Balderstone, *The World of the Theory of Constraints: A Review of the International Literature*, St. Lucie Press, 2000.

2

Services On Demand

Basic differences between goods and services are easy to see: *Goods* are tangible and can be consumed now or later, while *services* are intangible and cannot be produced in advance. Of course, many purchases consist of a mix of goods and services. Restaurants are roughly balanced. Gasoline purchases are 99 percent goods if you count the occasional once-over with a squeegee as a service. Airline flights are 99 percent services if you count refreshments as goods. So pure goods and pure services are just end points on a continuum of possibilities.

If you've ever been unable to get an appointment when you want it, languished in a waiting room or holding on the phone, been told you can't get a sandwich without mayonnaise, or had your change request denied because customer service is closed, you weren't getting services on demand. In a nutshell, *services on demand* simply means getting service when, where, and how you want it. That may not sound hard if you're a customer, but it can be ferociously hard if you're a service provider.

Physical limits no doubt explain some slow and inflexible service. After all, there are only so many hours in the workday, seats in the theater, cooks in the kitchen, and so forth. But more and more service providers are coming to realize there can be competitive advantage to delivering services on demand. The central questions are how to manage it and how to make it pay off.

One of the most surprising findings from Theory of Constraints (TOC) is that the hardest constraints to change aren't physical at all. They're the policies we set. For instance, why must every patient in a doctor's office suffer the accumulated delay from all previous patients that day? If appointments run late day after day, the cause isn't unpredictability—it's capacity (a physical constraint) or scheduling (a policy constraint). First-in/first-out may seem simple and fair—and it certainly keeps the doctors busy—but it's not a scheduling method that necessarily optimizes wait time, quality of care, or patient satisfaction. And keeping doctors busy is not the same as optimizing what they can produce.

Imagine how different your office visit would be if information technology coordinated the scheduling, your arrival time, and the entire medical staff's availability so that you could be welcomed into an examining room within moments of your arrival, no matter whether you were the first or last appointment of the day. That may sound far-fetched, but some rental cars, limousines, museums, hotels, buses, hospitals, and parking garages have this level of coordination today. So if you're wondering why professionals, scientists, and technicians can't work the same way, you're not alone. In fairness to those groups, however, they do face some unique challenges, even when compared to other services industries, as we shall see shortly. Yet with the right tools, those challenges aren't as insurmountable as they may seem at first.

An on-demand enterprise can respond rapidly and flexibly to customer demands, market opportunities, or external threats. Why does this matter? On-demand enterprises earn more gross profit and have higher earnings growth than the median for their industries.[1] Even in Professional, Scientific, and Technical Services, the standard of excellence is rising.

Services Sectors

In the previous chapter, economies were divided into just three broad sectors: Agriculture, Industry, and Services. With the rise of services, however, census bureaus around the globe have further divided services into more specific sectors and even more specific industries.

Canada, Mexico, and the United States use the North American Industry Classification System (NAICS), which groups enterprises that use like means to produce goods or services. Other geographies have similar classification schemes. Sixteen of 20 sectors in NAICS are services-based, but only about half of the 1,170 industries included in those sectors are services-based. More services industries are planned for the NAICS revision in 2007, however, to better represent the continuing diversity of services.

Table 2-1 shows five NAICS sectors that help explain why the Manufacturing sector and the Professional, Scientific, and Technical Services (PSTS) sector occupy opposite corners of the goods-services space. Of the 16 services sectors in NAICS, the three closest to PSTS are included for comparison. Like PSTS, the Information, Educational Services, and Health Care and Social Assistance sectors generally require workers with higher education and specific experience.

Table 2-1   Selected NAICS Sectors and Representative Industries

Sectors	Representative Industries
Manufacturing	Apparel Manufacturing
	Food Manufacturing
	Wood Product Manufacturing
	Chemical Manufacturing
	Fabricated Metal Product Manufacturing
	Computer and Electronic Product Manufacturing
Information	Newspaper, Periodical, Book, and Directory Publishers
	Motion Picture and Sound Recording
	Radio and Television Broadcasting
	Internet Publishing and Broadcasting
	Telecommunications
	Internet Service, Web Search, and Data Processing
Educational Services	Elementary and Secondary Schools
	Technical and Trade Schools
	Junior Colleges
	Colleges, Universities, and Professional Schools
	Business Schools and Computer and Management Training
	Educational Support Services
Health Care and Social Assistance	Offices of Physicians
	Outpatient Care Facilities
	Medical and Diagnostic Laboratories
	Hospitals
	Nursing and Residential Care Facilities
	Social Assistance
Professional, Scientific, and Technical Services	Legal, Logistics, Human Resources
	Accounting, Tax, Bookkeeping, and Payroll
	Architecture and Engineering
	Computer Systems Design
	Management, Scientific, and Technical Consulting
	Scientific Research and Development, Testing Labs

Table 2-2 lists characteristics of each sector. All sectors contain profit-seeking enterprises, but Educational Services and Health Care and Social Assistance also contain a substantial percentage of not-for-profit enterprises. Although some measures differ, the original TOC applications work in both for-profit and not-for-profit enterprises. So for our purposes, this is not a distinguishing characteristic of the sectors.

Table 2-2   Characteristics of Selected NAICS Sectors

Characteristics	Sectors				
	Manufacturing	Information	Educational Services	Health Care and Social Assistance	Professional, Scientific, and Technical Services
Goal of organizations in sector	For-profit	For-profit	For-profit and not-for-profit	For-profit and not-for-profit	For-profit
Primary input	Capital	Varies	Labor	Labor	Labor
Primary output	Goods	Information	Service	Service	Service
Educational degrees are generally required	No	Maybe	Yes	Yes	Yes
Reliance on machines, materials, or facilities	Very high	High	High	High	Very low
Reliance on intellectual capital	Low	High–low	Low	Low	Very high
Primary entity that is sold	Goods	Information	Knowledge	Service	Expertise
Customization for specific customers	High–Low	High–low	Low	Low	Very high
Repeatability of processes	Very high	High–low	Moderate	Moderate	Very low
Workers work on assignment	No	No	No	No	Yes
Workers work on teams	Varies	Varies	Seldom	Sometimes	Frequently
Delivery requires contact with consumer	No	No	Yes	Yes	Yes
Inventory of main product/service is possible	Yes	Yes	No	No	No

On the other hand, the primary inputs to and outputs from each sector are distinguishing characteristics. The degree of capital intensity is highest on the left in Manufacturing, while the degree of labor intensity is highest on the right in PSTS. Likewise, the proportion of goods in a sector's outputs is highest on the left, while the proportion of services is highest on the right. The Information sector is least distinct on these characteristics because its capital-labor and goods-services mixes are each widely variable.

Similar patterns can be seen in educational requirements, with Manufacturing less often requiring higher education in its workforce than services sectors. Conversely, Manufacturing places highest reliance on machines, materials, and facilities. The PSTS sector as a whole is most different on this characteristic because it places significantly less reliance on machines, materials, and facilities than any other sector. On the other hand, PSTS also places much higher reliance on intellectual capital than any other sector, except for perhaps the Information sector.

Even though the table includes mostly services sectors, the primary entities they sell are quite different. The information sold by the Information sector is as diverse as publishing, recording, broadcasting, and computer software. Educational Services sells various levels of knowledge, ranging from primary through graduate and professional schools. Health Care and Social Assistance sells medical and welfare services. PSTS, however, sells expertise. That is, to win business, PSTS enterprises must more often differentiate themselves via unique capabilities than any other sector.

The main reason for this emphasis on expertise in PSTS is that its services generally require extensive customization for specific customers. Clients want lawyers to win their case, scientists to study their problem, and technicians to fix their equipment. Even when compared to flexible manufacturing and tailored information services, the degree of customization in PSTS can be markedly higher than in other sectors. Consequently, in PSTS repeatability of processes is lower, workers work on assignment to a specific customer far more, and the work is more often team-based than with any other sector.

Finally, the Manufacturing and Information sectors share a couple of characteristics that distinguish them from the other services sectors. Delivery in the Manufacturing and Information sectors does not generally require contact with consumers, while some amount of contact is mandatory in Educational Services, Health Care and Social Assistance, and PSTS. Likewise, while an inventory of the main product is typical of Manufacturing and Information, the other services sectors cannot create inventories of completed services.

Figure 2-1 depicts all NAICS sectors. The size of each bubble represents the size of that sector. The center of each bubble represents the dominant position of that sector on the goods-services and repeatable-customized axes. Of course, within each sector there can be enterprises that differ from what's typical. For instance, some manufacturers do customize their processes, not just their products. This figure shows, however, that some services sectors as a whole tend to do more custom work.

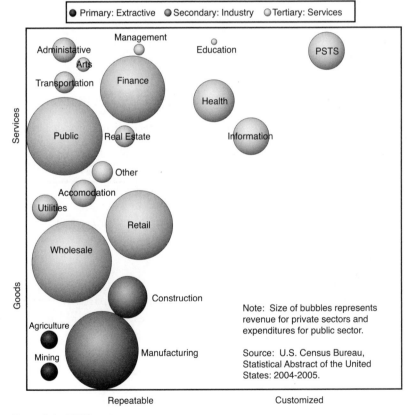

Figure 2-1   NAICS sectors

In particular, the PSTS sector is unique even among services sectors because it's the only sector where:

- The primary output is services, but sales are made on expertise.
- Workers are typically assigned to serve specific clients.
- The degree of customization for specific clients is extremely high.
- Reliance on intellectual capital is quite high.
- Repeatability of processes is relatively low.

That's why Manufacturing and PSTS occupy opposite corners of the goods-services and repeatable-customized space. If TOC can be adapted to PSTS, however, it should be applicable across the entire services space. Subsequent chapters focus first on PSTS, and then the last chapter assesses how TOC applies in other sectors.

Services as Available Versus Services On Demand

Much of the published research on services management pertains to highly repeatable, transaction-oriented services such as retailing, banking, food, hospitality, transportation, and public services. There is some coverage of semi-repeatable, case-oriented services such as health care, social assistance, and education. Less common, however, is published research on services management for highly customized, project-oriented services such as consulting, engineering, architecture, accounting, and research.

Typical services management topics include

- Setting services strategy
- Developing new services
- Designing processes
- Forecasting demand
- Planning capacity
- Solving queuing models
- Designing and locating service facilities
- Assuring quality

If it can be said there is a science to services today, it is in such topics as they relate to highly repeatable services. The repeatable nature of those services enables managers to plan and oversee sales and delivery where demand is relatively predictable, requirements are generally consistent, and clients are willing to wait for service if necessary.

Though there are many services where these conditions hold, there are plenty of others where they do not, never have, and probably never will. The nonrepeatable nature of such services means demand can be influenced but not predicted accurately, requirements are seldom consistent, and clients may not be willing to wait for service. Managing such services is more art than science because, well, there is no science yet. In those arenas, services management comes from experience, judgment, risk-taking—and occasionally just muddling through the inevitable rough patches.

An on-demand enterprise has several defining attributes:

- **Responsive**—The enterprise can sense and respond because it has an integrated view of its customers, employees, suppliers, business partners, and competitors.[2]
- **Variable**—The enterprise can alter its productivity, costs, marketing, and finances as conditions change because it has flexible processes and resources.
- **Focused**—The enterprise concentrates on its core competencies while using strategic business partners to handle its noncore tasks.
- **Resilient**—The enterprise readily handles changes and deals with threats because it has a flexible operating environment.

Notice that these attributes apply regardless of where an enterprise is in the goods-services space. Indeed, even some governmental units are moving to deliver more of their services on demand. For instance, motor vehicle licensing no longer requires all citizens to endure long lines, automatic toll collection is becoming commonplace, waste management can be done by subcontractors if they do it more efficiently, and emergency services are dispatched fast and flexibly via 911 emergency systems.

Though attributes of an on-demand enterprise are the same across the goods-services space, what it takes to attain those attributes can differ across sectors. And even within sectors, there can be various strategies. For example, one strategy for becoming an on-demand manufacturer is to build or retrofit factories so they can rapidly and frequently switch to manufacturing different products. But it is neither affordable nor practical for all manufacturers to reconfigure their batch shops, assembly lines, and continuous flow production to support mass customization.

Fortunately, responsiveness is largely in the eye of the beholder—the customer. If customers get what they want, when they want it, it doesn't matter whether the manufacturer actually switches production more often. Therefore, an alternative approach, often recommended by TOC, is to become more responsive to customer needs by changing distribution rather than production. That is, most changes are made downstream in warehouses, transportation, and the backroom of retail stores rather than in the factory itself.

The TOC application that accomplishes this change is known as *Replenishment*. Details will be covered in later chapters, but the essence of this application is to stop pushing large batches of products into the distribution chain in anticipation of sales and start letting actual sales pull small quantities of products through the chain more often. Although this change may feel counterintuitive because it violates long-standing notions about the efficiency of large batches, it has the advantages of reducing overall inventory and decreasing the probability of stockouts while simultaneously improving responsiveness. And it accomplishes all this without a radical change in manufacturing facilities, machinery, workforce, or process.

The TOC approach to problem solving is thus to act on *leverage points*, which are places where a modest change in constraint management has a major effect on throughput. Such an approach can be an effective way to become an on-demand business, because it targets changes where they will do the most good with the least investment. This makes the transition easier and faster.

Using leverage points to enact change is a departure from conventional improvement initiatives that attempt simultaneous changes across many business functions or *silos*. By targeting leverage points, TOC resolves conflicts that otherwise arise as each business function attempts to optimize its own operations, often at the expense of other business functions. Thus, TOC can be the means to become an on-demand manufacturer. As you will see in later chapters, TOC can also be the means to become an on-demand service provider.

Table 2-3 compares characteristics of services as available versus services on demand. These are, of course, end points on a continuum.

Table 2-3   Services as Available Versus Services On Demand

Services as Available	Services On Demand
Rigid capacity	Flexible capacity
Narrow capabilities	Broad capabilities
Internal constraint	External constraint
Provider's schedule	Client's schedule
Repeatable	Customized
Cost-based	Value-based

When a service provider has relatively rigid capacity and narrow capabilities, its clients receive services as available. That is, the provider generally has an internal constraint, which forces its clients to accept the provider's schedule, go elsewhere, or do without. Services as available is an effective way to deliver highly repeatable services when clients care more about cost than timeliness and the provider has more than enough demand to utilize its capacity.

In contrast, when a service provider has flexible capacity and broad capabilities, its clients can receive services on demand. That is, the provider generally has an external constraint, which enables the provider to accommodate the client's schedule, lest the clients go elsewhere. Services on demand can be an effective way to deliver complex, highly customized services when clients seek high value and the provider has enough capacity to meet demand.

Roles

As a services enterprise moves from services as available to services on demand, many things have to change, including the way people perform their jobs. To appreciate roles, however, it's helpful to understand a few other terms used in PSTS:

- **Project**—A set of finite-duration tasks that must be performed in a specified sequence to produce a desired result within a prescribed time and budget, such as building an information system.
- **Deliverable**—Things created by projects, such as consulting reports or computer software.

- **Process**—A set of activities performed continuously or on a frequently recurring schedule over an indefinite period, such as preparing paychecks.

- **Service Level**—The results of a process, such as its cycle time, quality, and cost.

- **Client**—A customer of a service provider.

- **Solution**—A combination of products and services that solve a client's problem.

- **Engagement**—An agreement (contract) between a client and service provider to deliver solutions.

- **Practice**—A unit within the service provider that specializes in delivering particular solutions or serving particular clients.

Though a large services enterprise can have hundreds of specific job titles, this book lumps them into a limited set of roles. Individuals may fill more than one role at once, which is especially prevalent in small service providers.

First, the majority of resources deliver services:

- **Professionals**—Lawyers, accountants, engineers, architects, consultants, veterinarians.

- **Scientists**—Biologists, physicists, astronomers, geologists, chemists, sociologists, psychologists.

- **Technicians**—Installers, operators, repairpersons, programmers, analysts, testers.

- **Practitioners**—A collective term for professionals, scientists, and technicians.

- **Staff**—Another name for practitioners.

Second, there are resources who sell services:

- **Partners**—Owners in a partnership (or equivalent rank in a corporation).

- **Sales Professionals**—Sell products as well as services by industry, territory, or solution.

- **Solution Architects**—Determine how to customize services (and products).

Third, some resources have management responsibilities:

- **Resource Managers**—Plan and oversee resources.
- **Project Managers**—Plan and oversee projects.
- **Process Managers**—Plan and oversee processes.
- **Program Managers**—Manage sets of related projects and processes.
- **Finance Managers**—Plan and oversee finances.
- **Marketing Managers**—Plan and oversee marketing.
- **Sales Managers**—Plan and oversee sales.

Fourth, other resources have leadership responsibilities:

- **Practice Leaders**—Responsible for sales, delivery, and investment in a specific practice.
- **Lead Professionals**—Senior professionals who guide other professionals.
- **Lead Scientists/Researchers**—Senior scientists who guide other scientists.
- **Technical Leaders**—Senior technicians who guide other technicians.
- **Managing Partners**—Senior partners who guide other partners.

Finally, these resources have executive responsibilities:

- **Sales Executives**—Oversee sales and maintain relationships with clients.
- **Delivery Executives**—Oversee delivery and maintain relationships with clients.
- **Officers**—Chief executive officer (CEO), chief operating officer (COO), chief financial officer (CFO), chief information officer (CIO), chief technical officer (CTO), and so on.

For the most part, the roles just listed fall within a given service provider. Sometimes, however, roles are filled by other enterprises:

- **Business partner**—Another enterprise that a service provider works with to sell or deliver services, such as a software vendor that relies on service providers for installation and technical support.

- **Subcontractor**—Another enterprise that a service provider (the primary contractor) uses to provide resources or perform specific tasks.

- **Third party**—Another enterprise that has an indirect relationship with the service provider, such as the vendor of products that the client engages the service provider to operate and maintain.

Viewpoints

To grasp why TOC can be useful in PSTS enterprises as they move toward services on demand, several viewpoints must be considered. Let's begin with clients.

If clients already expect PSTS enterprises to provide experts who can deliver complex, highly customized services, one might wonder what more there is to becoming an on-demand service provider. But client concerns are straightforward:

- Submit a bid or proposal that quickly solves one or more of the client's core problems.

- Start work when the client wants, instead of when resources become available.

- At least finish predictably, if not precisely when the client wants.

- Adapt readily to changing requirements, especially changes in scope and direction.

- Make sure there are enough experts with all the required skills.

- Collaborate well with the client's people.

- Coordinate well with third parties.

- Meet service-level agreements.

- Apply intellectual assets and thought leadership that bear directly on the problem at hand.

- Use the right kinds and amounts of technology.

- Deliver value that any stakeholder can appreciate at a price she considers fair.

Within a PSTS enterprise are people in various roles who collectively have a mirror image of client concerns, except with a how-to orientation. When a PSTS enterprise strives to become an on-demand business, here are some of its concerns:

- **Professional**—How can I create customized deliverables without starting from scratch?
- **Scientist**—How can I keep the research on time and within budget?
- **Technician**—How can I achieve high utilization and still maintain my skills?
- **Practice Leader**—How can I bid when the market price is below my cost plus margin?
- **Lead Scientist**—How can I design timely research that clients value highly?
- **Technical Leader**—How can I use technology to alleviate the client's constraint?
- **Resource Manager**—How can I manage experts when supply is volatile?
- **Project Manager**—How can I manage projects when so many tasks are uncertain?
- **Process Manager**—How can I manage business processes when demand is unpredictable?
- **Finance Manager**—How can I manage investments when their impact is unclear?
- **Partner**—How can I sell services that will maximize profit and client satisfaction?
- **Executive**—How can I find the leverage points in my own enterprise and get buy-in?

Anyone familiar with PSTS will recognize that these are not new issues.[3] However, the move to services on demand gives them fresh urgency and challenges the viability of some venerable services management techniques. For instance, if every practice leader, lead scientist, and technical leader optimize their services contracts, does that mean the enterprise as a whole is optimized? Probably not. The more contracts there are, and the more services that have to be delivered on demand, the less likely it is that local optimization leads to global optimization. Hence, services are poised to move from art to science.[4]

Conflict Resolution

One way TOC uncovers leverage points is to identify and resolve fundamental conflicts. We saw a fundamental conflict in manufacturing earlier: Efficiency requires large batches while responsiveness requires small batches. In the face of a seemingly unsolvable conflict such as this, improvement initiatives often are based on compromise. The factory could, for instance, run batches based on average weekly open orders. But this recalls the old statistician's joke that a man with one foot in boiling water and the other in a block of ice should be quite comfortable on average. Alternatively, the factory could calculate optimal batch sizes that incorporate both efficiency and responsiveness into one objective function. But because efficiency and responsiveness are actually different objectives, trying to find a single batch size that optimizes both really optimizes neither.

Compromise thus seems like an eminently fair solution, yet it leads an enterprise to oscillate between sides of a conflict. In the case of the factory, arguments about batch sizes could be frequent and heated. TOC therefore resolves conflicts in ways that do not require compromise. For instance, Replenishment allows a factory to produce large batches efficiently while becoming more responsive to customers by distributing small batches. No compromise is required.

Services enterprises have fundamental conflicts, too. So identifying and resolving them is an essential part of adapting TOC for services. Here, for instance, are a handful of services conflicts that will be resolved in later chapters. The first of them is the services counterpart to the manufacturing conflict just described.

- **Resource Management**—Efficiency requires high utilization, but responsiveness requires resources on the bench, available for immediate assignment.

- **Project Management**—Clients value projects that start and finish on time and within budget, but unique projects are inherently unpredictable.

- **Process Management**—Ongoing business processes are regulated by service-level agreements, but the service provider has little or no control over demand.

- **Finance and Accounting**—Expense control optimizes individual contracts, but the enterprise will sacrifice future performance if it fails to invest sufficiently.

- **Marketing and Sales**—Taking on riskier contracts increases revenue, but it also may increase troubled projects, which lead to higher costs and lower client satisfaction.

- **Strategy and Change**—Experts who advise others on strategy and change can have blind spots when it comes to their own enterprise's strategy and change.

- **Implementation and Technology**—One of the biggest obstacles to implementing new technology is the large installed base of old technology.

As you will see, these services conflicts can be resolved without compromise. However, the context, inner workings, and relationships between TOC applications are all different in PSTS.

Summary

Just as industry produces a bewildering variety of goods nowadays, service providers deliver quite an assortment of services. Across all services sectors, many services are repeatable, if not routine. On the other hand, the PSTS sector is unique in the degree to which its services are customized to specific client needs. Moreover, clients increasingly seek not just customized services, but services on demand, which adds timeliness and flexibility to the requirements.

PSTS is thus a sensible proving ground for the adaptation of TOC to services. If TOC will work in PSTS where the requirements are extreme, it's likely to work in other services sectors, too. Before we adapt TOC to PSTS, however, it will help to know more about traditional TOC applications and their use in services. That's what the next chapter is about.

Endnotes

1. IBM, *On Demand Business Impact Research Analysis*, December 2004.
2. Stephan Haeckel, *Adaptive Enterprise: Creating and Leading Sense-and-Respond Organizations*, HBS Press, 1999.
3. David Maister, *Managing the Professional Service Firm*, Free Press, 1993.
4. "Services Science: A New Academic Discipline?," *IBM Research*, 2004.

3

Theory of Constraints

Theory of Constraints (TOC) is one of the best-known management approaches you may never have used, even if you're a professional manager or executive. The most widely acclaimed book about TOC has sold millions of copies, and its lessons have been widely influential in industry.[1] Several dozen other books and hundreds of articles about TOC have since been published. Nevertheless, far more TOC references apply to industry than services. So if you're in a services sector, TOC may not be on anybody's agenda yet. That's understandable, because TOC was invented to address chronic problems in industry. From its origin in operations, however, TOC has been extended into other business functions in industry, including distribution, engineering, finance, marketing, sales, strategy, and change management. Moreover, it has been adopted occasionally in various services enterprises. This chapter briefly surveys TOC applications for industry because that foundation will be helpful in understanding how and why the TOC applications for services in this book are different.

There's also a branch of TOC known as the *Thinking Process*, which is applicable in any problem-solving situation. Though this book is a result of that Thinking Process, there's nothing about the Thinking Process itself that requires special adaptation for services. Thus, no chapters in this book are devoted to it. If you're interested, however, it's covered in most other TOC books, including some that are dedicated to the Thinking Process.[2,3]

In published cases of TOC usage in services, a common approach is to start with the Thinking Process and then use it to figure out which TOC applications from industry might apply. Here are some of the best-documented cases of TOC in services:

- Performing agricultural services[4]
- Changing the hiring process in a police department[5]
- Scheduling patient services in a hospital[6]
- Managing software engineering[7]

In each case, the authors were able to apply TOC because they were dealing with services delivered via relatively repeatable processes.

Software engineering is arguably the least repeatable. Yet unlike pure services, software inventories must be managed, so the software business is more like manufacturing in that way.

The rest of this chapter covers standard TOC applications. The terminology and examples come from industry, but each application has also been used in services to varying degrees. If you're already familiar with TOC, you may want to skip this chapter or skim selected sections because the coverage is more broad than deep. Conversely, if TOC is new to you, you may also want to explore the endnotes for more information. In either case, be aware that this chapter lays the foundation for the adaptation of TOC for Services in subsequent chapters.

All TOC applications spring from a common premise: If an enterprise is viewed as a chain, the enterprise as a whole can produce only as much as its weakest link will allow. That weakest link is, of course, the constraint. But the chain analogy has another implication: Pulling a chain is a lot more effective than pushing it. So switching enterprises from push to pull is a key ingredient in every TOC application.

Drum-Buffer-Rope

Drum-Buffer-Rope (DBR) is the TOC application for operations.[8] It's often used to plan and manage discrete manufacturing, but DBR has also been used by service providers as diverse as landscapers and hospitals, even though their services are perishable.

DBR gets its name from the roles that specific elements play during scheduling and management of production. To appreciate those roles, it helps to know the problems DBR was originally intended to solve. For that we need a quick review of the state of the art in manufacturing when DBR was invented.

A simplified manufacturing process composed of just five steps is illustrated in Figure 3-1. Of course, actual manufacturing processes are often composed of many steps in complex configurations shaped like a V, A, T, I, or some combination thereof. But a simple sequence of steps is sufficient to illustrate the essential elements of DBR.

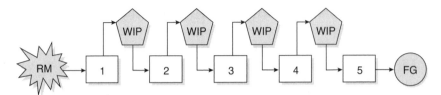

Figure 3-1   Traditional manufacturing

The steps are numbered 1 through 5. Assume that each step in this illustration is performed by a different machine type. RM stands for raw materials, WIP stands for work in process, and FG stands for finished goods, which are all forms of inventory.

One problem with traditional manufacturing is immediately apparent in the figure: There's a lot of inventory before, during, and after production. That's a problem because inventory is a significant investment, and it doesn't generate revenue until it's sold.

Another problem is that excess inventory impedes the production process. That is, as the shop floor becomes crowded with WIP, it gets harder to monitor due dates and ensure that the most urgent jobs are done first. The busier the shop gets, the less effective expediting becomes.

Thus, a third problem is that it's hard to predict when each job will be completed. Once jobs are released into the shop, they are hard to control. Some jobs may finish early, but too many finish late, which leads to customer dissatisfaction and missed sales. So as production slows, jobs may be started earlier, thereby further increasing WIP, slowing production, and perpetuating the push cycle.

Work also gets pushed into and through the factory by the desire for high utilization, a measure of how long each machine and each worker are actually performing tasks in the production process. The underlying assumption is that anything less than high utilization on every machine and every worker represents a lost opportunity for production.

Though appealing, that assumption is flawed. For one thing, producing goods that customers won't buy is wasteful, no matter how high it drives utilization. Yet even when customers will gladly buy what's produced, the push for universally high utilization overwhelms the constraint.

Somewhere in that production process is a step that cannot produce as many units per time period as the rest of the steps. That's the constraint. You can't see it in the figure, and neither can most managers in an actual manufacturing plant managed the traditional way. Fortunately, the constraint is hiding in plain sight, and with a little detective work it can be found.

What's far harder to do is change the perception that high utilization everywhere is a good thing. The belief that local optimizations somehow add up to global optimization is strongly held. Until this policy constraint is broken, however, the physical constraint cannot be managed.

The same five-step manufacturing process as before is illustrated in Figure 3-2, but it also includes the elements needed for DBR. Solid lines represent product flow. Dashed lines represent information flow. In an actual factory with many products and a variety of routings, there can be more than one constraint. To illustrate DBR, however, one will do.

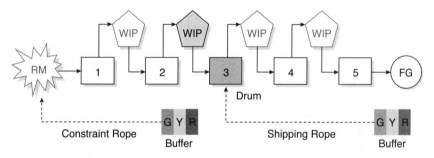

Figure 3-2   Drum-Buffer-Rope (DBR)

Step 3 is the constraint. It's also called the drum because it sets the pace for the rest of the steps. That is, upstream steps will occasionally be idle—have less than full utilization—so they won't overwhelm the constraint with work. And downstream steps will likewise occasionally be idle because they're waiting for the constraint to complete its step. But if all goes well, the constraint itself will have consistently high utilization, excess WIP will disappear, and more orders will ship on time.

When this happens, the factory is producing as much as it can, subject to the current constraint. This level of production is typically much more than it ever could produce under traditional manufacturing when the constraint was invisible. So managers in a factory adopting DBR may go from wrestling with insufficient capacity to having ample capacity.

A likely place to see WIP is ahead of the constraint, because it can produce less than any other step, by definition. Therefore, that WIP is sometimes mistaken for the buffer, but the drum buffer is actually all work scheduled on the constraint, even if it's currently at an earlier step. That is, the buffer is measured in time, not physical WIP units. So a view of the true buffer is typically contained in an information system nowadays.

If all jobs ahead of the constraint are early or on schedule, the amount of work needed to keep the constraint busy is adequate, and the buffer is said to be in the green zone. However, when some jobs are behind schedule and the possibility that the constraint could run out of work becomes significant, the buffer is in the yellow zone.

Because normal variation causes some jobs to run early at the same time that others run late, it's possible that the constraint won't actually run out of work. Hence, a yellow buffer does not automatically trigger action. However, when many jobs are behind schedule and it becomes clear that the constraint will indeed run out of work without action, the buffer is in the red zone. Upstream steps then have to sprint to refill the buffer, and thereby keep the constraint busy, while downstream steps may have to sprint to finish late jobs on time.

In addition to the drum buffer, which contains WIP, the shipping buffer contains FG. Because the market is the ultimate pacesetter, the shipping buffer protects customers from late delivery, just as the drum buffer protects the constraint from overloading.

The third and final element of DBR is the ropes, which govern when gating events occur. The shipping rope governs work on the constraint needed to meet market demand and keep the shipping buffer green. The constraint rope governs the release of raw materials to start new jobs that should keep the drum buffer green.

Under DBR, jobs are released much closer to their due date than in traditional manufacturing because they will spend less time waiting between steps. Like the buffer, the length of ropes is measured in time, and the ropes are actually contained in an information system.

An information system that supports DBR leads to global optimization by optimizing the constraint rather than every step in the production process.[9] Buffer management thus keeps the process in control without requiring constant attention and fine-tuning. If a factory has more than enough capacity to meet market demand, the constraint is said to be *external* or *in the market*. In this case, the shipping buffer, not the drum buffer, then regulates when jobs are released into the shop because the internal constraint no longer limits production. If a factory has enough capacity to meet market demand during normal and slack periods but not during peak periods, its dominant constraint is in the market even though it occasionally has an internal constraint.[10] In this case, a simplified form of DBR can be implemented that makes sensible trade-offs between keeping the constraint busy and satisfying customer demand in order to protect future sales. In both cases, when the constraint is external, no step has full utilization, including the internal constraint, but this is what keeps the factory from producing excess inventory that cannot be sold. The next section covers another TOC application that specifically addresses a market constraint.

Whenever the constraint shifts (due to changes in machines, people, process, products, or demand), DBR has to be reconfigured accordingly. This is a nontrivial effort, and it's why capacity in a DBR shop is deliberately unbalanced to prevent floating constraints.

Placement of the drum, however, should be strategic, not accidental. That is, when DBR is first implemented, the constraint location may not be correctly aligned with respect to profitable market opportunities. If so, rather than implement DBR around this previously unseen constraint, it generally makes more sense to adjust capacity so that the control point represented by the drum is relocated to a position where the factory will be better able to produce goods that meet market demand profitably.

DBR is also known as *Synchronous Manufacturing*. In a nutshell, here's how it compares to two other widely used production management approaches:

- In their pure forms, Enterprise Resource Planning (ERP) assumes infinite capacity and schedules all steps, while DBR assumes finite capacity and schedules just the constraint. Some ERP software can schedule to finite capacity, but it does not have other essential capabilities of DBR software. For instance, ERP prohibits late release of materials, while DBR prohibits early release because it increases WIP. Moreover, ERP drives material requirements all the way through the bill of materials (BOM), regardless of stock on hand, while DBR takes existing stock and buffers into consideration. Thus, ERP and DBR are fundamentally different solutions.

- Lean/Just-in-Time (JIT) seeks to optimize individual steps, while DBR optimizes the entire process around the constraint. They are fundamentally similar, but Lean/JIT doesn't work as well in job shops as flow shops because job shops have more diverse and changeable routings.

The benefits of DBR are substantial. One literature review found the following average improvements across 82 companies:[11]

- 70 percent reduction in lead time
- 65 percent decrease in cycle time
- 44 percent improvement in due-date performance
- 49 percent reduction in inventory
- 63 percent increase in revenue

A central benefit of DBR is to change the production process from push to pull: Nothing gets produced unless there's a market for it. Market pull through the internal constraint then optimizes production while minimizing inventory.

Because the market is the key driver of DBR, how demand ripples back through the distribution chain from customers to factory affects DBR. This connection leads to the next TOC application.

Replenishment

Replenishment (R) is the TOC application for distribution.[12] It was originally invented to manage distribution of goods, but it can be used by service providers who deliver goods along with their services, such as those in the Accommodations and Food Services sectors.

Replenishment is also called the TOC supply chain solution because one enterprise's distribution chain is often another's supply chain. Of course, calling them "chains" is not entirely accurate because they are increasingly complex networks. Nevertheless, where one enterprise's distribution network and interlocks with another enterprise's supply network, they are essentially the same elements viewed from different perspectives.

Replenishment gets its name from the specific manner in which goods are distributed or supplied. As with the previous TOC application, it is easier to appreciate Replenishment in the context of the problems it was originally intended to solve. Hence, we'll do another quick review of the state of the art, only this time it'll be in distribution, as of the invention of Replenishment.

A simplified distribution chain is illustrated in Figure 3-3. A real enterprise might have far more factories, warehouses, and retail outlets in its distribution chain, of course. And a real supply chain can look like a mirror image of this figure, with many sources funneling into a central location. Furthermore, the individual elements might be owned by a single enterprise or many different enterprises. Although it can be harder to implement a common solution across enterprises, Replenishment itself doesn't depend on who owns each element. Thus, this simple scenario is sufficient to illustrate Replenishment.

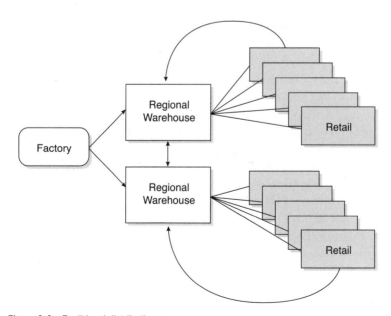

Figure 3-3 Traditional distribution

With traditional distribution, goods produced by the factory are immediately shipped in large batches to regional warehouses. Each regional warehouse in turn periodically ships smaller but still sizable batches to retail locations. Thus, most inventory is pushed through the chain to retail locations on the assumption that it will eventually be sold. This method is intuitively appealing, because only retail outlets make sales to consumers.

Unfortunately, variability in sales is highest at retail locations. This has several undesirable effects. First, some retailers may have an abundance of some products at the same time that others have none. Second, there's seldom an easy way to move inventory between retail locations to reduce overstocks and cover stockouts. Finally, when stockouts occur, if the time required to restock a retailer from the warehouse is longer than customers will wait, stockouts turn into lost sales, not backorders.

Thus, retailers with excess inventory return it to the warehouse, while those with no inventory lose sales while waiting for shipments. And when cross-shipments between warehouses are needed to cover shortages, those shipments may be delayed by the desire to ship large batches in order to save shipping costs.

Furthermore, whenever new products are introduced, retail locations—if not the entire distribution chain—tend to be filled with old products. So as new products are pushed through the chain, the old products must be discounted to clear them from retailers' inventory. And those discounts cut into sales of the new products, too.

The size and timing of batches pushed through the chain depend mainly on whether the factory follows traditional manufacturing or DBR/Lean/JIT. Traditional manufacturing is driven by sales forecasts. Yet when products are pushed through a traditional distribution chain, sales forecasts are notoriously inaccurate. So a vicious cycle is at work: The bigger the batches and the less frequently they're distributed, the longer the horizon on sales forecasts, which in turn makes forecasts even less accurate, which calls for bigger batches, and so forth.

Therefore, the net result of inaccurate forecasting and pushing large batches through a distribution chain is low reliability even when the chain is filled with excess inventory. This is another example of local optimization not leading to global optimization.

As in the previous section, the constraint may not be immediately obvious, but it's hiding in plain sight. It may be tempting to conclude that transportation or warehouse capacity is the constraint, but because inventory tends to pile up ahead of the true constraint, that's the clue we need. The amount of product that should be distributed is ultimately limited by sales to customers, so the constraint in a distribution chain is usually external or in the market.

The best way to break a sales constraint is simply to sell customers what they want, when and where they want it, at a price that corresponds with perceived value. Hence, to get the right products in the right amounts to the right locations at the right time, the solution has to be an alternative to sales forecasts, big batches, and infrequent shipments. Indeed, Replenishment turns traditional distribution completely on its head by eliminating sales forecasts and shipping small orders quite frequently.

The same distribution chain as before is illustrated in Figure 3-4, but it also includes the elements needed for Replenishment. Solid lines represent product flow. Dashed lines represent information flow.

Rather than being located only adjacent to the constraint, however, the biggest Replenishment buffer is located at a better leverage point. That is, most inventory is held in the factory warehouse buffer for reasons discussed next. Only a single factory warehouse buffer is shown in the figure for illustration, but each product actually has its own buffer. Likewise, each regional warehouse and retail location have buffers for each product.

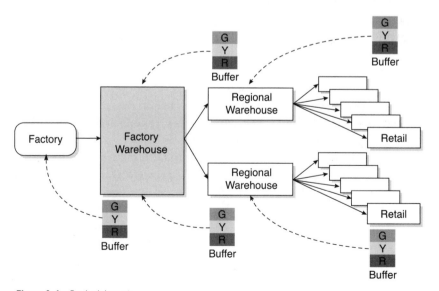

Figure 3-4 Replenishment

Buffers are divided into green, yellow, and red zones that correspond to no action, replenish, and expedite. But rather than being measured in time periods as in DBR, Replenishment buffers are measured in physical units of inventory.

Replenishment relies on *aggregation* to smooth demand. That is, demand at regional warehouses is smoother than demand at retail locations because higher-than-normal demand at some retail locations is offset by lower demand at other ones. Likewise, demand at the factory is even smoother than demand at the regional warehouses. Therefore, goods produced by the factory are stored in a nearby warehouse and are not shipped elsewhere until they are needed to replenish goods actually consumed by sales. The factory warehouse may be owned by a distributor rather than the manufacturer, but the effect is the same.

Because sales occur daily, shipments occur daily, too. And the quantities shipped are just sufficient to replace goods sold. At first glance this might seem to increase shipping costs over what could be achieved by shipping large batches less frequently, but the net effect on total shipping costs is that they usually go down, not up. Stopping the shipment of obsolete goods and reshipment of misallocated goods more than compensates for increased cost created by smaller shipments of saleable goods. Furthermore, the ability to capture sales that would otherwise be lost due to insufficient inventory makes Replenishment a much better alternative.

Thus, Replenishment is driven by actual consumption, not sales forecasts. As sales are made, the buffer levels at retail locations drop, eventually triggering Replenishment from a regional warehouse. Similarly, as buffer levels at regional warehouses drop, this eventually triggers Replenishment from the factory warehouse. The buffer zones at the factory warehouse are set, however, so that they trigger a manufacturing order that should resupply this buffer before it runs out.

Buffer sizing is based on both variability and time to resupply. That is, the more variable consumption is, the bigger the buffer must be to cover that variability. Likewise, the longer it takes to resupply, the bigger the buffer must be to cover demand during the wait. Therefore, as aggregation reduces variability and DBR reduces resupply time, the required buffer size decreases accordingly.

In addition to being used subsequent to DBR, Replenishment can be combined with DBR. That is, the Replenishment techniques that work in an external distribution chain can also be used internally within a manufacturing plant. This is appropriate when the same materials, parts, or subassemblies are used in multiple products. Rather than keeping separate buffers of the common items for each product being manufactured, keeping a central buffer and replenishing common items as they are consumed leads to higher reliability with less total inventory.

Furthermore, strategically placed replenishment buffers enable a manufacturer to reduce end-to-end production schedules. DBR software with replenishment capabilities is required, however, because ERP systems drive requirements all the way through the BOM, regardless of stock on hand or replenishment buffers.

If a manufacturer's business is predominantly design-to-order or make-to-order, using Replenishment to distribute its primary products is not as appropriate. However, even in those types of manufacturing, spare parts are usually make-to-stock, and Replenishment is quite applicable to them. Because spare-parts inventory for a large enterprise often represents an investment of hundreds of millions of dollars, a significant reduction in that inventory frees capital for reinvestment in other areas.

Several Replenishment outcomes are noteworthy:

- Reliability is significantly increased by replenishing goods based on actual consumption.
- Inventory is substantially decreased by keeping the bulk of it where demand varies least.
- Sales can be significantly increased by reducing delivery time and eliminating stockouts.
- Shipping large batches to save shipping costs is false economy.

The benefits of Replenishment can be striking. A traditional distributor that is 85 percent reliable can increase its reliability to 99 percent while reducing its inventory by two-thirds when adopting Replenishment. Furthermore, the average time to resupply retail locations typically drops from weeks or months to about one day.

A central benefit of Replenishment is thus to change the distribution chain from push to pull: Nothing gets distributed unless there's a market for it. Market pull, the external constraint, then optimizes distribution while minimizing inventory.

As seen in the previous section, when DBR unleashes latent manufacturing capacity, the enterprise's constraint often moves from internal to external. Conversely, when Replenishment unleashes latent distribution capacity, if there is sufficient demand, the constraint can move back from external to internal. The internal location may be engineering of new products rather than manufacturing, however. This connection leads to the next TOC application.

Critical Chain

Critical Chain (CC) is the TOC application for project management.[13] It was originally invented to manage engineering projects in a manufacturing environment, but it has since been used by enterprises in virtually all goods and services sectors.

Critical Chain gets its name from the specific manner in which projects are planned and executed. As with the previous TOC applications, it is easier to appreciate Critical Chain in the context of the problems it was originally intended to solve. Some aspects of Critical Chain have been widely adopted and are no longer distinctive, but most still struggle to gain acceptance. The following review of the state of the art compares Critical Chain to the older and still dominant project management method, *Critical Path*.

A simple project plan based on the Critical Path method is illustrated in Figure 3-5. Each block represents one task. The width of each block against the timeline at the bottom shows its planned duration. Adjacent blocks have a finish-start relationship: The task on the left must be finished before the task on the right can start. Where more than one task must be completed before another can start, this precedence relationship is shown with arrows. Precedence arrows between adjacent blocks are implied rather than explicit.

Each task is numbered, but the numbers are merely identifiers. They do not imply sequence. Subscripts on the task numbers indicate which resource is assigned to each task. Assume in this example that only one resource is assigned to each task.

Red tasks are critical, which means that if any of them are completed late, the entire project will be late unless some other critical tasks are completed early. Yet early task completions rarely happen. Thus, the set of all red tasks is the critical path.

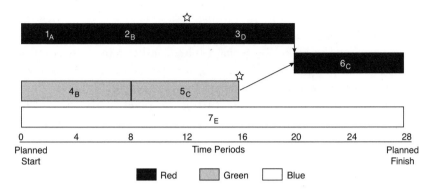

Figure 3-5   Critical Path

Green tasks are noncritical, which means that they have slack time. *Slack* is represented by the horizontal component of the arrow to their left or right. If they exceed this slack time, they too will make the project late. Hence, they are pushed leftward to indicate they will start as early as possible in order to preserve the slack. Task 5 could finish as early as Period 16 or as late as Period 20, and the project overall could still finish on time.

Blue tasks are *elastic*, which means they are based on the duration of nonblue tasks, so they expand and contract with the rest of the project. Thus, even if they have no slack, they cannot make the project exceed its planned duration. They can, however, make the project start late if an appropriate resource is not available. Project management itself is an example of an elastic task. Such tasks are usually omitted from plans for internal projects because they don't affect the critical path, but they are often included in plans for services projects to make project managers' and partners' tasks visible to the client.

Stars represent *milestones*, which are significant events or deliverables. Milestones are often used to mark the end of project phases, and thus serve as interim progress indicators. Some methodologies require at least one milestone per month.

Real projects generally have many more tasks and a web of precedence relations, of course. Nonetheless, even this simple project is sufficient to compare Critical Chain to Critical Path.

In contrast to previous TOC applications where the constraint was hidden, the constraint in this project plan may seem obvious. The critical path appears to be the constraint because it determines the shortest time in which the project can be completed if all goes according to plan. However, resources are a far less obvious constraint hiding in plain sight on many project plans. For example, unless people examine a separate resource view of the plan, many don't notice that two tasks in this project must be performed simultaneously by Resource B.

Frequent shifting between multiple tasks in order to create the appearance of simultaneous execution is called *multitasking*. A widespread assumption is that it increases productivity, but this assumption is faulty for a couple of reasons. First, it takes time to switch between tasks. More significantly, however, resources are sometimes assigned more simultaneous tasks than they can possibly complete on time. Bad multitasking occurs when the resulting productivity drain or overload are significant enough to cause tasks to fall behind schedule. This can cause the critical path to shift multiple times during a project, so frequent replanning is common.

In this example, Task 4 has some slack, but not enough to eliminate multitasking by rescheduling that task to its latest start time. If another resource with the same skills as Resource B can be assigned—a technique known as *crashing*—neither task will need to be rescheduled. On the other hand, if no other suitable resource is available, one of the tasks must be rescheduled, and the overall project duration will be longer. *Resource leveling*, as this adjustment is known, is now considered a best practice, even in the Critical Path method, but it was not common when Critical Chain was invented.

Another problem exists in the planned duration of individual tasks. Traditional project management includes a margin for *contingency* in every task estimate because individuals giving those estimates are held accountable if their tasks are completed late. On the other hand, they are also held accountable for the accuracy of their estimates, so they have a disincentive to complete tasks early. Hence, if a project due date isn't chosen arbitrarily—independent of scope—it is most likely based on inflated task estimates.

Despite these margins for contingency embedded throughout, projects too often finish late. One reason is that tasks completed early rarely compensate for tasks completed late. That is, late completions tend to be cumulative. Thus, protecting commitments on every task with contingency does not protect the project due date. This is yet another example of how local optimization everywhere does not create global optimization.

Finally, traditional project management often measures project status according to the percent of the project completed. This measure is misleading, however, because most of a typical project's tasks are not critical, which means they have no bearing on whether the project will actually be completed on time. Hence, projects that reach the 90 percent-completed stage early are often still in danger of finishing late. As the due date approaches, it may be necessary to compromise on one or more of the project commitments by reducing scope, increasing budget (by adding resources), or accepting late completion.

Figure 3-6 illustrates a Critical Chain project plan with the same scope, tasks, resources, and deliverables as before, but it is literally not the same project.

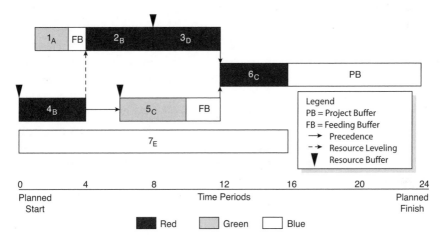

Figure 3-6 Critical Chain

The Critical Chain plan differs from the previous plan in these ways:

- All estimated task durations have been cut in half.

- Resource contention has been resolved via resource leveling.

- Tasks do not start until needed but must be completed as soon as possible once started.

- A project buffer has been added at the end of the project.

- Feeding buffers have been created where noncritical tasks precede tasks on the critical chain.

- Resource buffers have been inserted to remind resources of upcoming tasks.

- The critical chain includes a task not on the critical path, and vice versa.

- Overall project duration is shorter, both with and without the project buffer.

The Critical Chain is the longest set of dependent tasks, taking both precedence and resources into account. If there were no resource contention, the Critical Chain and the Critical Path would include the same tasks. But whenever resource contention exists, as in this example, tasks on the Critical Chain may differ from those on the Critical Path. Furthermore, real projects may have many potential Critical Chains, so computer software is required to find the best resource-leveling alternatives on all but trivial projects.

Even though there is no precedence relation between Tasks 2 and 4 in this example, Task 4 is rescheduled to finish before Task 2 because these tasks are assigned to the same resource. This resource leveling causes Task 4 to become part of the Critical Chain because it now affects overall project duration.

Task durations are cut in half because most individuals give task estimates that they have at least an 80 percent chance of meeting, and a task estimate that's 80 percent reliable is roughly twice as long as one that's 50 percent reliable. In addition to anticipating significant multitasking, an 80 percent estimate anticipates that managers will cut the estimates during planning—and during execution, many tasks will be late even before they start. As you will see, however, these additional concerns are addressed, during both planning and execution of projects.

In the aggregate, task estimates that are 50 percent reliable are sufficient to complete the project on time if there is no bad multitasking, because early task completions can offset late task completions. Furthermore, a portion of the contingency that used to be embedded in the task estimates has been moved into the project buffer, where it now protects the entire project rather than individual tasks.

Feeding buffers protect the Critical Chain. If noncritical tasks are completed late (as they will be about half the time because the plan is based on estimates with 50 percent reliability), the feeding buffers usually prevent accumulated delay from passing into the Critical Chain. Conversely, feeding buffers also allow early completions on the Critical Chain to be immediately followed by early starts on the Critical Chain.

Resource buffers are early reminders to resources with tasks on the Critical Chain that they must start their assigned tasks as soon as previous tasks are complete. That is, an early finish on one task must be followed by an early start on subsequent tasks unless resource contention prevents it.

Note that this project plan has no milestones because they encourage local optimization. Furthermore, because milestones are a commitment to the project sponsor or client, they need their own completion buffers, which could lengthen the project.

Projects managed according to Critical Chain are more likely to finish on time, in part because their status is measured differently. A key measure is the amount of the project buffer used relative to the amount of the Critical Chain completed. For example, if the Critical Chain is 50 percent complete and only 10 percent of the buffer has been used, the project is in excellent shape. But if the Critical Chain is 50 percent complete and 70 percent of the buffer has been used, the project is in danger of consuming the entire buffer and thereby missing its due date.

In general, estimated project duration based on Critical Chain can be up to 25 percent shorter than an equivalent traditional project. However, a traditional project has a high probability of being late, while a Critical Chain project has a high probability of being on time. Therefore, the actual difference in duration can be even larger than this difference in estimates.

Nevertheless, the committed due date in Critical Chain is always the planned finish date at the end of the project buffer, not the finish of the last task on the Critical Chain. This is a crucial distinction because the probability that the last task on the Critical Chain will be completed on time is no better than 50 percent. The probability that the entire project will be completed by the end of the project buffer is better than 90 percent.

A central benefit of Critical Chain is thus to change project management from push to pull: Rather than starting every task as early as possible and pushing every task for on-time completion, Critical Chain starts tasks at just the right time and lets buffer management pull the entire project to on-time completion. Furthermore, better estimating, work rules, and progress measurement optimize due-date performance while minimizing project-wide work effort. In other words, the purpose of Critical Chain is not just to create a better plan, but to change behavior during project execution. Critical Chain projects are thus like a relay race: Each task on an active chain starts as soon as its predecessors are complete instead of when they were originally planned.

Several Critical Chain outcomes are noteworthy:

- It allows more projects to be completed without increasing staff.
- The Critical Chain is more stable than the Critical Path, so replanning is not as common.
- Buffer penetration provides an unambiguous indicator of whether the project is on schedule.
- Eliminating bad multitasking makes individuals more productive and less prone to burnout.
- Knowing which tasks cause buffer penetration creates a clear priority for project managers.

Project managers must have more than passing familiarity with Critical Chain to use it effectively, but resources working on Critical Chain projects do not need to understand all the details. It is vital, however, that they understand the reasons behind the changes that Critical Chain brings to their jobs. For example, without such understanding, cutting task estimates in half will be perceived as exploitation that creates immense professional risk. On the other hand, understanding that resource leveling reduces overtime, that buffers protect the entire project, and that measures establish clear priorities is a route toward buy-in.

When an enterprise conducts multiple projects with shared resources, resource leveling should extend across projects. Otherwise, cross-project multitasking can increase markedly, thereby endangering timely completion of more than one project. Enterprises facing this challenge are likely to have both resource managers and project managers interacting via matrix management, which is considerably more complicated than a single-project environment and rife with opportunities for conflict.

Critical Chain has been extended to handle multiple projects with shared resources, but the prevailing method does not adequately address constraints in all services enterprises. Therefore, discussion of the multi-project extension will be deferred to a later chapter, where an alternative method for services is compared to the prevailing method that arose in industry.

As explained in Chapter 2, "Services On Demand," as TOC applications are first adopted by an enterprise, constraints can often be identified with a bit of informal detective work. As TOC applications are deployed, however, effective management of constraints requires different kinds of information than the enterprise has ever used before. That is the purpose of the next TOC application.

Throughput Accounting

Throughput Accounting (TA) is the TOC application for finance and accounting.[14] It was originally invented for use in a manufacturing environment, but has since been adapted for use in the computer software industry, as explained in Appendix C, "Throughput Accounting for Software." TA has been the subject of many books and articles, so the collective body of knowledge runs thousands of pages. Only portions relevant to this discussion are summarized in this section, however.

TA gets its name from the specific way financial measures are calculated and used for decision making. As with the previous TOC applications, it is easier to appreciate TA in the context of the problems it was originally intended to solve. The following review of the state of the art compares TA to the older and still dominant management accounting method, *Cost Accounting* (CA).

Figure 3-7 illustrates selected elements of CA. When CA arose in the early 1900s, labor costs dominated manufacturing, and workers were paid by the piece. Hence, it was reasonable at that time to allocate overhead expenses to products on the basis of direct labor costs for purposes of preparing financial statements.

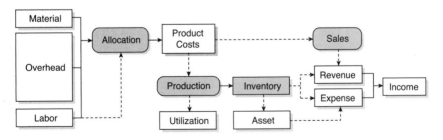

Figure 3-7 Cost Accounting

Ever since automation came to dominate manufacturing and workers came to be paid by the hour, however, allocation of large overhead expenses on the basis of small labor costs has created distortions. When re-aggregated at the enterprise level, product cost distortions do not affect financial statements. Yet if prices are computed as product cost plus standard gross margin, the prevailing method, product cost distortions carry into product pricing. Hence, some products may appear profitable when they are in fact unprofitable—and vice versa.[15]

Activity-Based Costing (ABC) is a relatively recent variant of CA, designed to be a better way to allocate costs. For example, a product manufactured in large batches requires fewer setups and inspections, so it gets allocated less overhead. Unfortunately, ABC does not consider that customers may not want to buy such products.

> *"Published studies demonstrate an overwhelming tendency for companies to use cost-driver information to do efficiently what they should not be doing in the first place. To achieve competitive and profitable operations in a customer-driver global economy, companies must give customers what they want, not persuade them to purchase what the company now produces at lower cost."*[16]

A second problem with CA is it can encourage factories to produce excess inventory beyond what is really needed to fulfill customer orders. As noted earlier, pressure for high utilization of every machine and worker is a frequent cause of excess inventory. In addition, inventory accumulation can be driven by the counterintuitive effect it has on earnings.

Rather than being expensed on the income statement in the period incurred, the cost of inventory goes on the balance sheet as assets. Consequently, an inventory profit may be generated, which a business can use to smooth reported earnings even though it has essentially nothing to do with real income. However, if that inventory cannot be sold, the accounting eventually unwinds: Inventory on the balance sheet turns into depreciation expense on the income statement and an inventory loss results. Moreover, excess inventory creates competitive disadvantage because it hinders production and ties up capital that might otherwise be used to generate real income.

A third problem with CA concerns management priorities. In most companies, the dominant measurements are not bottom-line measurements, except perhaps at the executive level. Operating expense tends to be managed closely because it is well-known and under direct control. In contrast, revenue tends to be viewed as less controllable because it depends on markets and customers, which are not under direct control. Inventory tends to be a distant third in management priorities because reducing it has an adverse effect on reported income.

As explained earlier, however, inventory actually has a substantial impact on the ability of a business to compete. And although revenue is not under direct control, it is not bounded in the same way that inventory and operating expense are. That is, there are limits on how much inventory and operating expense can be reduced and still have a viable business. Conversely, there is no upper limit on the revenue that a business can attain and still be viable.

TA addresses all these problems via a different measurement approach: It does not use product costs but eliminates incentives for excess inventory, and it reverses typical management priorities.[17] TA is not, however, a substitute for conventional financial reporting because publicly traded companies must comply with generally accepted accounting principles (GAAP). Fortunately, TA can be readily reconciled with GAAP reporting even though TA is a different approach to management accounting.[18]

Figure 3-8 illustrates selected elements of TA. Decision support is on the left; actual results are on the right. Some of the terms abbreviated in this figure will probably be familiar, but keep in mind that their computations are usually different from CA.

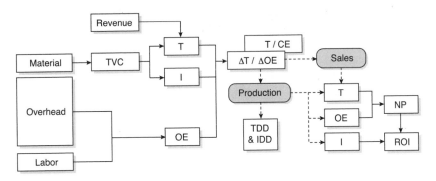

Figure 3-8 Throughput Accounting

TA begins with three financial measures:

- **Throughput (T)**—The rate at which money is generated through sales or interest. It is computed as revenue minus totally variable costs (TVC).

- **Inventory (I)**—All money invested in things intended for sale. It includes totally variable costs such as material, plus resources used in production such as land, machines, trucks, and computers. The more conventional term, Investment, is sometimes used instead of Inventory.

- **Operating Expense (OE)**—All money spent turning Investment into Throughput. It includes direct labor, rent, and labor, plus selling, general, and administrative (SG&A) costs.

T is maximized by selling goods or services with the largest difference between price and totally variable cost and by minimizing time between spending money to produce and receiving money from sales. Thus, T is determined by speed as well as magnitude, which is why the other TOC applications are designed to minimize delays.

Note that TA does not use labor costs to allocate OE. Furthermore, direct labor itself is not treated as a variable cost because enterprises do not adjust their workforce every time demand varies.

The financial measures are used to compute these performance measures:

- Net Profit: $NP = T - OE$
- Return on Investment: $ROI = NP / I$
- Productivity: $P = T / OE$
- Inventory Turns: $i = T / I$

An ideal decision increases T and decreases both I and OE. A good decision increases NP, ROI, Productivity, or Turns. Note that NP is net operating profit before interest and taxes.

Under TA, there are no product costs. Instead, there are constraint measures:

- Throughput per Constraint Unit: $T/CU = (\text{revenue} - \text{totally variable cost}) / \text{units}$
- Constraint Utilization: $U = \text{time spent producing} / \text{time available to produce}$

The way to maximize T is to maximize these constraint measures. Constraint utilization is important because each hour lost on the constraint is an hour lost by the entire factory or office. However, utilization of nonconstraints is not tracked because it encourages excess inventory.

Decisions based on T/CU include the following:

- Prioritizing use of the constraint (for example, choosing the best product mix)
- Deciding whether to increase the constraint's capacity via investment
- Selecting products to introduce or discontinue
- Pricing products based on the opportunity cost of using the constraint

Thus, for normal product decisions, T/CU is used to determine the mix that maximizes T. If producing less of one product in order to produce more of another product would increase T, for example, that's a good decision. But for major decisions that might shift the constraint or forfeit some T on current products, the following decision-support measure is better:[19]

- Change in Net Profit: $\Delta NP = \Delta T - \Delta OE$

The delta symbol (Δ) comes from mathematics and stands for "difference." It thus represents a comparison between alternatives.

Maximizing ΔNP ensures that major decisions improve profit across all products. And the following measure shows the impact of such investment decisions:

- Payback: $PB = \Delta NP / \Delta I$

To minimize unfavorable deviations from plans, these control measures should be minimized:

- Throughput Dollar Days: TDD = Selling price of late order $\times$ days late
- Inventory Dollar Days: IDD = Selling price of excess inventory $\times$ days unsold

TDD measures something that should have been done but was not: Ship orders on time. IDD measures something that should not have been done but was: Create unnecessary inventory.

The ideal value of these control measures is zero. The larger the value of either measure, the stronger the signal that corrective action is needed. Of course, if an enterprise uses a currency other than dollars, these measures can be recast as Throughput Value Days (TVD) and Inventory Value Days (IVD).[20]

In summary, TA is used to identify constraints, monitor performance, control production, and determine the impact of particular decisions. Yet the logic behind CA has been taught and practiced for so long that it can be hard to appreciate TA without an example.

Figure 3-9 compares CA to TA via a product mix decision. An actual decision could have hundreds of steps and thousands of products, which is one reason why redoing the analysis whenever the constraint moves is a problem. But this scenario consisting of just three products, with each product requiring the same three steps, is sufficient to illustrate key concepts. In this example, each product may require a different number of minutes per step, but the total time required by each product is the same. Furthermore, labor costs per minute are the same across all steps.

Product A has the highest price and lowest raw material cost per unit. Conversely, Product C has the lowest price and highest raw material cost per unit. Because the same workers will be used to produce any feasible product mix, the best mix would seem to be to produce as much of Product A as demanded, then B, then C. Following this priority, the factory will produce 100 units of A, 75 of B, and zero of C. Note that Step 2 limits enterprise production regardless of whether it's actually recognized as the constraint.

Operating expense includes rent, energy, and labor. When CA allocates operating expense to products based on their raw material costs, the resulting product costs confirm the expected priority: A has a lower product cost than B. Unfortunately, with this product mix, the enterprise generates a net loss. Because Product A appears to be profitable while B generates a loss, it's tempting to conclude that producing none of B would stop the loss. However, the operating expense covered by B would then have to be covered entirely by A, which would yield an even larger loss. Furthermore, if additional work were started in an effort to keep the workers at Steps 1 and 3 fully utilized, work-in-process inventory would grow. Therefore, by any measure, CA says this enterprise is unprofitable.

	Products				
	A	B	C	Have	Need
Demand	100	100	100		
Price	$105	$100	$95		
Raw Material	$45	$50	$55		
Step 1 Time	3	6	9	2,400	1,800 minutes
Step 2 Time	15	12	9	2,400	3,600 "
Step 3 Time	2	2	2	800	600 "
Total Time	20	20	20		

Cost Accounting	A	B	C	Total
Product Cost	$100	$111		
Mix	100	75	0	
Step 2 Used	1,500	900	0	2,400
Revenue	$10,500	$7,500	$0	$18,000
Raw Material	$4,500	$3,750	$0	$8,250
Gross Margin	$6,000	$3,750	$0	$9,750
Operating Expense	$5,455	$4,545	$0	$10,000
Net Profit	$545	-$795	$0	-$250

Throughput Accounting	A	B	C	Total
T / CU	$60	$50	$40	
T/CU / t	$4.00	$4.17	$4.44	
Mix	20	100	100	
Step 2 Used	300	1,200	900	2,400
Revenue	$2,100	$10,000	$9,500	$21,600
Raw Material (TVC)	$900	$5,000	$5,500	$11,400
Throughput (T)	$1,200	$5,000	$4,000	$10,200
Operating Expense (OE)				$10,000
Net Profit (NP)				$200

Figure 3-9 Cost Accounting versus Throughput Accounting

TA provides an entirely different perspective, however. TA ranks product profitability according to throughput on the constraint per minute (T/CU/t). And it does not allocate operating expense to products. Hence, Product A yields $4 per minute on the constraint, but B yields $4.17, and C yields $4.44. Therefore, TA says the priority should be to produce as much of C as capacity will allow, then B, then A. This is, of course, precisely the opposite priority seen previously. Because step 2 is the constraint, producing 100 units of C, 100 of B, and 20 of A is all that can be done.

With this product mix set via TA, the enterprise generates a net profit. Yet the only difference between CA and TA in this example is the product mix. All assumptions are precisely the same. Thus, CA does not optimize the enterprise. Indeed, this enterprise might not even survive if steered by CA.

Effective use of TA requires different information from CA, so new report formats must be implemented. For example, a TA earnings statement shows T, I, and OE relative to the constraint, while conventional CA reports are oblivious to constraints. Furthermore, just as CA and TA rank product profitability differently, they may also rank customer profitability quite differently.

Several TA outcomes are noteworthy:

- Financial measures reverse management priorities from OE, T, I to T, I, OE.

- Performance measures are not distorted by cost allocations.

- Constraint measures eliminate conflict between local measures (machine or worker utilization) and global measures (enterprise performance).

- Control measures remove incentive to build excess inventory and establish incentive to deliver on time.

Hence, previous TOC applications turned push into pull. TA tells the enterprise what to pull.

Implications for Services

Despite their obvious differences, industrial and services enterprise all have constraints. Thus, if the standard TOC applications summarized in this chapter are so useful in industry, it's reasonable to wonder why they haven't seen wider adoption in services. To be fair, each TOC application is used somewhere in services—but not widely. There are many reasons.

First, TOC is concerned with inventory, but what constitutes inventory in a services business can be harder to pin down. Is it billable hours, laboratories, software, servers, databases, equipment, methodologies, libraries, templates, deliverables, skills, or reputation? And if any or all of these constitute inventory, how would reducing them optimize a services enterprise? Even if we call those items investments rather than inventory, the optimal level of services investment isn't really addressed by conventional TOC applications. This is because services investments can be highly intangible and reusable, while industrial inventories more often are not.

Second, services in general are less repeatable than industry, and Professional, Scientific, and Technical Services are the most customized of all. When services and the steps they require change often, finding the constraint may require more than a little detective work. And by the time the constraint is located, it may hop elsewhere in the business. What's more, an enterprise that deliberately unbalances its services capacity to prevent a floating constraint may be committing itself to services that can't keep pace with what clients really want. So is it possible that floating constraints are unavoidable when services are delivered on demand?

Third, many services markets are moving away from services as available to services on demand. Even services businesses that historically operated with an internal constraint more often face a market constraint as technology and competition make alternatives plentiful and flexible. Where you once had to pick up your dry cleaning on Thursday, whether you wanted it then or not, now you can get it delivered in an hour. And cleaners are happy to accommodate you because they can charge you a premium price for expedited service that uses no more time on the constraint than regular service. Moreover, by capturing your request for service on demand, the provider prevents you from taking your business elsewhere or foregoing service entirely.

Finally, the degrees of freedom in delivering services can be greater than in manufacturing—particularly when the services depend on creativity. Resources with different skills and experiences can sometimes deliver services that are virtually indistinguishable when given the right tools and coaching. Resources aren't completely interchangeable, of course, but any sizable services contract can probably be configured in more than a hundred different ways to make the most of special talents and compensate for issues that arise unexpectedly.

The standard TOC applications have been used by service providers where their services sufficiently resemble industry. TOC hasn't seen widespread adoption in services overall, however, because innovations take time, and innovation adoption takes even more time. TOC has taken more than two decades to reach its current usage level in industry, and even today few enterprises use all the TOC applications. TOC in services simply hasn't reached the tipping point to wide adoption yet. Making it more widely applicable in services is, however, the purpose of this book.

Table 3-1 compares TOC for Goods (TOC_G) to TOC for Services (TOC_S). It thus provides a preview of the chapters ahead. Standard applications can be applied in essentially the same manner by any enterprise, while unique applications always must be tailored to a specific enterprise and its customers. Though every TOC_G application has a counterpart in TOC_S, every TOC_S application differs in significant ways.

Table 3-1 TOC for Goods Versus TOC for Services.

	TOC Application	TOC for Goods (TOC_G)	TOC for Services (TOC_S)
Standard	Drum-Buffer-Rope	DBR_G—manage manufacturing process	DBR_S—manage service process
	Replenishment	R_G—manage inventory	R_S—manage skilled resources
	Critical Chain	CC_G—manage multiple projects around strategic resource	CC_S—manage multiple projects using R_S
	Throughput Accounting	TA_G—manage finances around products	TA_S—manage finances around deliverables and service levels
Unique	Marketing and Sales	$M\&S_G$—use Buy-in to make customers want products because they solve core problems	$M\&S_S$—use Buy-in to make clients want services because they solve core problems
	Strategy and Change	$S\&C_G$—use Buy-in to bring about strategic change in goods producer	$S\&C_S$—use Buy-in to bring about strategic change in service provider *as well as clients*
	Implementation and Technology	$I\&T_G$—change goods producer's business rules, and then use technology to follow new rules	$I\&T_S$—change service provider's *or clients'* business rules, and then use technology to follow new rules

Summary

Drum-Buffer-Rope (DBR), Replenishment (R), Critical Chain (CC), and Throughput Accounting (TA) are four standard applications comprising Theory of Constraints (TOC) in industry. Each application solves a specific set of problems that otherwise prevent optimization of an enterprise.

DBR is the application for operations. By identifying one machine type or worker type as the constraint and scheduling production around it, DBR enables a factory to produce more than it can when every machine and worker are fully utilized.

R is the application for distribution. By distributing goods from a central warehouse in response to daily sales, rather than shipping large batches of goods to retail locations where sales are most variable, R increases sales at the same time it decreases inventory. Furthermore, R can be used within factories to much the same effect.

CC is the application for engineering. By managing resource contention as well as the precedence between tasks, CC eliminates bad multitasking, a significant productivity drain. Furthermore, by adopting estimating methods, work rules, and management procedures that focus on the constraint, projects managed with CC are not only shorter, but are more likely to finish on time and within budget.

TA is the application for finance and accounting. By focusing on Throughput before Operating Expense, TA reverses typical management priorities. By providing measures that show how to globally rather than locally optimize the enterprise, TA steers the enterprise toward its goal: to make money now and in the future (or produce goal units).

The common theme running through all TOC applications is constraint management. Because constraints are what keep an enterprise from reaching its goal, global optimization of enterprises has to address constraints.

Endnotes

1. Eliyahu Goldratt and Jeff Cox, *The Goal: A Process of Ongoing Improvement*, North River Press, 2nd Revised Edition, 1992.
2. H. William Dettmer, *Goldratt's Theory of Constraints: A Systems Approach to Continuous Improvement*, ASQ Quality Press, 1997.
3. Lisa Scheinkopf, *Thinking for a Change: Putting TOC Thinking Processes to Use*, St. Lucie Press, 1999.
4. Michael Spenser, "Theory of Constraints in a Service Application: The Swine Graphics Case," *International Journal of Production Research*, 38:5, 2000, pp. 1101–1108.

5. Lloyd Taylor, Brian Moersch, and Geralyn McClure Franklin, "Applying the Theory of Constraints to a Public Safety Hiring Process," *International Public Management Association for Human Resources*, Fall 2003.

6. R. Kershaw, "Using TOC to Cure Healthcare Problems," *Management Accounting Quarterly*, 2000, pp. 22–28.

7. David Anderson, *Agile Management for Software Engineering: Applying the Theory of Constraints for Business Results*, Prentice-Hall, 2004.

8. Kelvyn Youngman, "A Guide to Implementing the Theory of Constraints (TOC)," www.dbrmfg.co.nz, 2005.

9. Eliyahu Goldratt, Eli Schragenheim, and Carol Ptak, *Necessary But Not Sufficient*, North River Press, 2000.

10. Eli Schragenheim and H. William Dettmer, *Manufacturing at Warp Speed: Optimizing Supply Chain Financial Performance*, St. Lucie Press, 2000, pp. 151–152.

11. Victoria Mabin and Steven Balderstone, *The World of the Theory of Constraints*, St. Lucie Press, 2000, pp. 11–12.

12. Eliyahu Goldratt, *It's Not Luck*, North River Press, 1994.

13. Eliyahu Goldratt, *Critical Chain*, North River Press, 1997.

14. Eliyahu Goldratt, *The Haystack Syndrome*, North River Press, 1990.

15. H. Thomas Johnson and Robert S. Kaplan, *Relevance Lost: The Rise and Fall of Management Accounting*, Harvard Business School Press, 1991.

16. H. Thomas Johnson, *Relevance Regained*, Free Press, 1992, pp. 149–151.

17. Thomas Corbett, *Throughput Accounting: TOC's Management Accounting System*, North River Press, 1998.

18. Debra Smith, *The Measurement Nightmare: How the Theory of Constraints Can Resolve Conflicting Strategies, Policies, and Measures*, St. Lucie Press, 2000.

19. Eli Schragenheim, "Throughput Based Decision Support," *TOC Review*, 2001.

20. Tim Sullivan, Richard Reid, and Brad Cartier, *TOC ICO Dictionary*, TOC International Certification Organization, 1st Edition (draft), August 2005.

PART ## II

Applications

4

Resource Management

Resource management is a critical function in any labor-based services enterprise. Though equipment, supplies, and facilities may be necessary, they are insufficient without human resources who have the knowledge to use them effectively. Obviously, a hospital is just another building without doctors, nurses, and technicians.

Of course, some services are technology-based. Only a tiny percentage of telephone calls are operator-assisted nowadays, for instance. Nevertheless, installation, repair, and customer service are labor-intensive. So even in highly automated services enterprises, resource management can still be a vital function.

In Professional, Scientific, and Technical Services (PSTS), getting skilled resources when and where they are needed can be a constraint. Clients often want service to start as soon as a contract is signed—if not sooner. If the service produces deliverables, clients generally want them as soon as possible. And they often want resources with specific skills dedicated to their contract.

Hence, if the right resources aren't available, it may be impossible to close the sale. And if key resources are lost after the sale, it may be difficult to deliver the service and impossible to achieve client satisfaction.

In virtually all services enterprises, resources are thus key elements in the supply chain. Moreover, when one enterprise provides resources to other enterprises, as in subcontracting relationships, those resources are key elements in its delivery network, too.

Note that these resource supply and delivery networks are not the same as service chains. In a *service chain*, a series of services enterprises each perform their own service without distributing the resources that perform those services. For a single consumer transaction, separate enterprises might do the advertising, prospecting, sales, credit, rebate, transportation, installation, collection, warranty, repair, and recycling. So the central challenge in a service chain is to coordinate the services, not necessarily acquire resources. That challenge is addressed in later chapters.

As seen in the preceding chapter, Replenishment is the traditional TOC application for distribution and supply chains. It was invented for situations where time to resupply is longer than customers will wait for their orders, and reliable forecasting is impossible. Both conditions apply in services, too.

This chapter covers an application called *Replenishment for Services* (R_S). Traditional Replenishment will hereafter be referred to as *Replenishment for Goods* (R_G). As you will see, there are some clear parallels between R_S and R_G, but there are also some inherent differences.

Just as it was helpful in the previous chapter to know the problems that R_G solves, it will be helpful in this chapter to see the problems that R_S solves. For that, we need a quick review of the state of the art.

State of the Art

Prevailing methods of managing services capacity in PSTS include the following:

- **Hire-to-deal**—Individual leaders exercise discretion at the practice or departmental level and adjust resources as needed.
- **Hire-to-plan**—Capacity planning is done at the business unit level, where a business unit is composed of multiple practices or departments.
- **Supply-demand matching**—Capacity usage is optimized via priorities, scheduling, and pricing.

These alternatives are not always mutually exclusive. Some enterprises use a forecast for annual planning, which establishes a budget, and then leave it to individual leaders to hire within that budget. Unfortunately, leaders are sometimes tempted to hire as much as the budget allows, regardless of whether actual market conditions turn out as forecast.

Hire-to-deal can be highly responsive to conditions in both the services market and the job market.[1] But its effectiveness rests heavily on the ability of individual leaders to sense where the markets are headed and implement capacity changes accordingly. Therefore, scrambling to fill open positions or shed excess resources is not uncommon, and compromising on the fit between candidates and positions does occur. Moreover, one practice or department may be short on certain skills at the same time another has excess, so individual leaders within the same enterprise may be making opposing resource decisions without knowing it.

Hire-to-plan has the advantage of forecasting capacity changes far enough in advance to support large changes in capacity and achieve a good fit between candidates and positions, even for highly skilled positions.[2] The annual plan also allows delegation of some tasks to resource managers so leaders can focus on other tasks, such as selling and delivering services. Unfortunately, an enterprise can continue adjusting capacity per the plan long after a services market has headed in the opposite direction.

Supply-demand matching includes various methods to allocate available supply to prioritized demand or steer demand where capacity is available.[3] Methods include workforce scheduling, complementary services, self-service, cross-training, and price incentives. These methods are especially useful when resources are constrained by other factors, such as availability of laboratory facilities.

Hence, individual discretion fosters local optimization while forecast-based planning can be unresponsive to market conditions and supply-demand matching may fail to meet some demand. Hire-to-deal is based on the assumption that local optimization adds up to global optimization. Hire-to-plan is based on the assumption that forecasts are accurate and stable enough to produce global optimization. Supply-demand matching is based on the assumption that supply is either fixed or adjustable only in large increments.

The question is not whether hire-to-deal, hire-to-plan, or supply-demand matching can work. Obviously, they can. The question is whether they optimize the enterprise. Experience with R_S says they may not when services must be delivered on demand.

Supply and Distribution Chains

An examination of supply and distribution chains helps explain why R_S must differ from R_G. Figure 4-1 illustrates the context of supply and distribution chains in industry and services. The flows in industry are, of course, physical materials and goods, while the flows in services are intangible skills embodied in human resources.

In industry, raw-materials inventory is a buffer against variability in supply, and finished-goods inventory is a buffer against variability in demand. Thus, industrial demand and supply are decoupled by inventories. Services, however, cannot be stockpiled. In services, the bench, which is composed of resources without current assignments, is a buffer against variability in both demand and supply. This dual nature of the bench, plus the fact that it's composed of people rather than objects, means the bench must be managed differently than physical inventories.

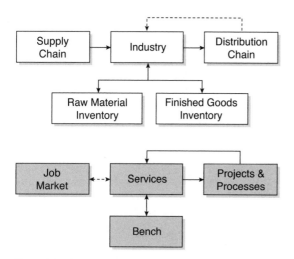

Figure 4-1 Supply and distribution chains in industry and services

If a services enterprise cannot afford a bench or chooses not to maintain one, it must have an internal constraint, flexible capacity via overtime and extended days off, or a workforce that's adjusted as demand rises and falls. With an internal constraint, delivery lead times lengthen as demand rises, which is incompatible with on-demand business. Flexible capacity and adjustable workforces are compatible with on-demand business, and are common in services that rely on day labor. But they are impractical in PSTS enterprises due to the lead time needed to make adjustments. Hence, having a bench is common, except in small PSTS enterprises.

In industry, returned goods are the exception; but in services, resources returning from assignments are the rule. Therefore, if industrial production is curtailed as demand falls, finished-goods inventory remains stable. But if services production is curtailed as demand falls, the bench naturally rises. The reverse is also true. Hence, services benches are prone to oscillation during normal demand and persistent under- or oversupply during abnormal demand.

In industry, resupply is driven by total demand. For instance, the sale of 100 units of finished goods should ultimately trigger resupply of a corresponding amount of raw material. In services, however, resupply is driven by incremental demand and attrition. For instance, if ten resources return from projects, one resigns, and 12 must be deployed to new projects, incremental demand plus attrition calls for acquisition of three additional resources.

In industry, demand for goods can be independent or dependent. For instance, sales of motor oil and salad oil are independent, but sales of printer ink and printer paper are dependent. In services, dependent demand is quite common. For instance, a project that needs a lead researcher also needs research staff with appropriate skills. A shortage of any resource type can eventually affect the others.

In industry, batching of raw-materials purchases and finished-goods shipments are long-standing practices with an economic objective, but batching is largely irrelevant in services. There is seldom much reason for a services enterprise to acquire resources in batches, except during acquisition of other firms or during the college recruiting season. Resources may be trained for, deployed to, and returned from projects in batches, but this is more often an artifact of scheduling than a conscious attempt to reduce expenses.

In industry, inventory literally just sits somewhere. In services, resources do not sit idly on the bench. Indeed, they are often extremely busy doing things they cannot do while on assignment, such as getting trained, mentoring other resources, developing intellectual property, and working on internal projects. Thus, while physical inventories create operating expense, a carefully managed services bench is an investment.

In industry, aggregation of demand at a central warehouse isn't necessarily easy. For instance, just 20 product options enable more than 1 million configurations, so reducing allowable configurations by *demand shaping*—steering consumers to buy configurations that can be readily assembled—is a key tactic. In services, aggregation can be just as difficult, but for different reasons. Some resources are not interchangeable due to physical constraints, such as education, training, location, and language. Other resources are not interchangeable due to policy constraints, such as regulatory, legal, cultural, or contractual reasons.

Overall, substantial differences between industry and services prevent direct application of R_G to services. And within PSTS, R_S must accommodate multiple resource flows.

Demand and Supply in PSTS

Figure 4-2 illustrates demand and supply for an enterprise in PSTS. Demand, of course, comes from the services market. Yet there can be three broad kinds of demand within that market, shown as dashed lines in the figure.

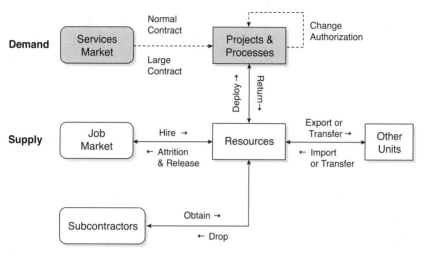

Figure 4-2 Demand and supply in PSTS

First, normal contracts have a short to moderate sales cycle of six months or less. They then require a small to moderate number of resources for a delivery cycle of one year or less. Normal contracts are plentiful enough that they create relatively steady demand when aggregated.

Second, large contracts have a long sales cycle lasting about 6 to 18 months. They then require a correspondingly large number of resources for a delivery cycle up to 10 years in duration. Though multiple large contracts may be signed during a year, they nevertheless create lumpiness in demand—and again in supply when resources return at the end. Smoothing via aggregation generally isn't possible because large contracts rarely end during the same period in which other large contracts are starting. Even when they do align in time, they rarely align in resource requirements.

The third and final kind of demand is *change authorizations*, which change the scope or timing of services. They vary in size, but most change authorizations are relatively small, even when they modify a large contract. In the aggregate, however, change authorizations are a significant source of demand.

R_S can be applied to any kind of demand, but it is most effective on normal contracts and change authorizations. Because large contracts have a long sales cycle, their resource requirements can be predicted and given special handling, if necessary.

Eight resource flows, shown in the figure as solid lines, are typical in PSTS. Those flows take place with the job market, subcontractors, other business units within the service provider, and projects or ongoing business processes performed for clients.

Half of the resource flows increase resource supply:

- Existing resources return from projects or processes.
- New resources are hired from the job market.
- Subcontractors are obtained temporarily.
- Resources are imported temporarily or permanently transferred from other units.

The other half of the flows decrease resource supply:

- Resources are deployed onto projects or processes.
- Subcontractors are dropped.
- Resources are exported temporarily or permanently transferred to other units.
- Resources are lost through attrition (voluntary separation) or release (involuntary separation).

In addition, atypical flows occur at times. For instance, a service provider may hire some of the client's resources with the client's approval, and clients may have the option to hire some of the service provider's resources. These actions are sometimes called *rebadging* because the resources continue their present roles for a different employer.

Replenishment for Services

Even though supply and distribution in services differ from industry, the basic principles behind Replenishment are still valid. First, aggregation reduces variation. Second, buffers sized according to average demand during time to resupply protect against shortage. Third, buffer zones provide a convenient reference that tells managers when action is required. Finally, buffer management driven by actual demand protects against shortage while avoiding excess.

The following sections explain how these principles apply in R_S. Skill groups aggregate demand for resources. Buffers are sized according to net resource consumption. Buffer zones guard against both resource shortages and excess. Finally, buffer management utilizes a wide variety of techniques for adjusting resource capacity.

Skill Groups

Deciding how to group resources is the first step in applying R_S because aggregation takes place at the group level, as illustrated in Figure 4-3. In general, aggregation of demand data increases its reliability. For example, the forecast for a resource group can be ten times more reliable than separate resource forecasts for 100 projects using the same type of resources.

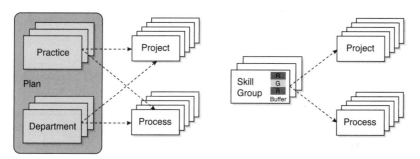

Figure 4-3   Prevailing resource management versus Replenishment for Services

Groups should be composed of resources that are as interchangeable as possible. Consequently, grouping resources by skills is usually the most appropriate method. For example, in an accounting firm, auditors, tax accountants, and advisors would be placed in separate skill groups. Of course, individuals with only unique skills won't fit neatly into any skill group.

Members of skill groups can be further distinguished by attributes such as specialty, education, geography, and performance. If another attribute in addition to skill type determines whether resources are truly interchangeable, the skill groups should be made more specific. For example, geography, language, and cultural differences often make it desirable to have separately managed clusters of skill groups for Asia-Pacific, European, Latin American, and North American geographies even though corresponding skill groups in each geography have the same core skill.

Each resource should be a member of one primary skill group for aggregation purposes, but that does not mean secondary skills and other attributes are unimportant. They can be used, for instance, to find an exact match with client requirements, such as a Spanish-speaking expert on Securities and Exchange Commission regulations.

Note that a skill group is not the same as a resource pool. Skill groups should be reasonably differentiated from each other, while resource pools are relatively undifferentiated. That is, a resource pool typically contains resources with such a wide variety of skills that its members are not necessarily substitutable without some significant compromise.

In PSTS enterprises organized by practices or departments, skill groups may cut across those organizational boundaries. Yet if skills are truly applicable across boundaries, managing resources by skill groups is less likely to create a skills imbalance. Thus, R_S may lead an enterprise from a hierarchical to matrix form of organization.

Buffer Sizing

Buffer sizing is the second step in applying R_S. Each skill group requires its own buffer because resources cannot readily be substituted from other skill groups, by definition, and patterns in demand and supply often differ between skill groups. Hence, for purposes of Replenishment, skill groups in services are roughly analogous to products in industry. Given the inherent differences between services resources and industrial inventories, however, it should be no surprise that R_S uses a somewhat different buffer sizing method than R_G.

The recommended buffer size in R_G is based on maximum forecast consumption within average resupply time, taking into consideration the unreliability of resupply. In other words, higher consumption, longer resupply time, and higher unreliability all require a larger buffer. For example, if an enterprise sells a maximum of 100 units per month of a given product, it takes one week to resupply, and that resupply is reliable, a buffer of about 25 units should enable the enterprise to meet demand without stockouts most of the time. Yet if demand rises to 125 units per month, resupply time rises to two weeks, and resupply becomes less reliable, a buffer of 75 units or more may be needed.

The recommended buffer size in R_S substitutes net consumption for total consumption. That is, resources returning for reassignment can often meet most, if not all, new demand, so only the difference matters. *Net consumption* can be computed as new demand minus available supply for a given period or total demand minus total supply for an entire skill group. Unlike total consumption of goods, which is usually only zero or positive, net consumption of resources can be zero, positive, or negative. Negative net consumption occurs when there are more resources returning from projects than there are resources being assigned to projects.

The recommended buffer size in R_S is also affected by different dynamics during average resupply time. In R_G average time to resupply is determined by the performance of internal processes and external suppliers. Decision time can be virtually zero if replenishment orders are issued automatically whenever the buffer falls below a trigger level. In contrast, average resupply time in R_S is determined by a diverse set of sources, including the job market, subcontractors, and other business units. Decision time is never zero, and replenishment orders are never automatic because the resource manager has to decide whether the current level of net consumption is transient or permanent. It doesn't make sense to initiate the process of acquiring new resources if there's a reasonable expectation that an equal or greater number will return shortly for reassignment.

Longer average resupply time can have opposite effects in R_G and R_S. In R_G, the longer it takes to resupply, the larger total consumption is because it's cumulative. But in R_S, the longer it takes to resupply, the more likely net consumption is to approach a stable value because surpluses in some periods cover shortages in others if the variations are random. Nevertheless, aggregating over any time longer than necessary is not desirable, because it delays buffer management. During seasonal cycles and economic upturns or downturns, net consumption deviates consistently from zero, and a shortage or excess of resources can accumulate. It's therefore helpful to bear in mind the distinction between systematic variability and random variability in net consumption while striving for shorter average resupply time.

In R_G, unreliability of resupply can be quantified by the standard deviation of resupply time, but how that should be factored into buffer sizing is open to interpretation. One simple rule of thumb is to increase the buffer size by 50 percent, which makes sense if the buffer is small and items within it are not too expensive. A computational alternative is to convert the standard deviation of resupply time into equivalent units of inventory. For example, if 5 units are sold each day on average, and the standard deviation of resupply time is two days, add 10 units to buffer size just to cover the unreliability of resupply.

In R_S, this rule of thumb can be expensive if every resource in the buffer requires a salary, benefits, and training. Standard deviation calculations are possible, but whether they really matter is open to interpretation. Suppose net consumption for a given skill group is one resource every 30 days and average project duration is 120 days. If average time to resupply a given skill is 90 days with standard deviation of 30 days, adding one resource to the buffer size just to cover unreliability is probably justified. But if resupply time is 30 days with standard deviation of five days, adding a resource to cover unreliability is harder to justify, and the inclination is to round down to zero and rely on overtime unless part-time resources are available.

Buffer sizing is illustrated in Figure 4-4 with R_G on the left. Average resupply time (μ) plus standard deviation of resupply (σ) are on the horizontal axis. Total consumption during average resupply time (t) and the buffer size (b) after allowance is made for unreliability of resupply are on the vertical axis. If μ or σ increases, the arrowheads move farther in the direction they're already pointing, so t and b rise. If total consumption during average resupply time increases, the slope of the arrows (m) becomes steeper, so t and b rise. Conversely, a decrease in μ, σ, or m causes t and b to fall.

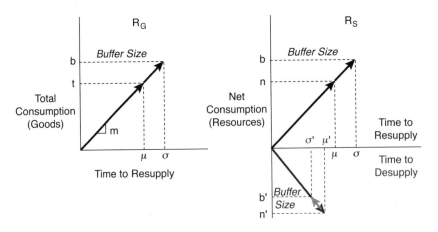

Figure 4-4   Buffer sizing

R_S is on the right in the figure. When net consumption (n) is positive, buffer size (b) is calculated essentially the same way as R_G. On the other hand, if average resupply time drops effectively to zero, as it can for some skill groups during an economic downturn, buffer size drops to zero, too. However, resupply time does not have to drop all the way to zero to have this effect. If resupply time plus allowance for unreliability is less than the amount of time clients will wait to start their contracts, buffer size drops to zero, because the enterprise can acquire exactly the number of resources it needs without delaying its contracts.

If net consumption (n') becomes persistently negative, R_S enters new territory. The horizontal axis becomes average time to desupply, and buffer size (b') is negative even after allowing for unreliability. In other words, buffer size is the number of resources by which the skill group should be reduced to match resources to declining demand and keep the bench from growing excessively. For example, ramping down on resources occurs when a service is discontinued, a skill becomes obsolete, or the peak season fades. Note that the arrowhead corresponding to b' points in the opposite direction from the arrowhead corresponding to n'. This prevents resources from being reduced too soon.

A negative buffer size does not necessarily imply that the bench itself—the actual buffer level—will fall to zero. It simply says that resources returning for reassignment will outnumber opportunities for reassignment, so something must be done to prevent the bench from growing excessively. And even if the buffer level does become negative, indicating unfulfilled resource requests, the necessary resources should be returning from completed assignments shortly.

Unless services replenished by R_S are in a total tailspin, a negative buffer size will be fleeting. Once the skill group size is adjusted in line with the services market, net consumption should again turn zero or positive, and the buffer size will return to a non-negative value that covers growth and normal variation.

Chapter 8, "Marketing and Sales," covers ways to keep net consumption from becoming persistently negative, even during an economic downturn. Hence, a negative buffer size may be avoidable. But even if it's not, the natural attrition rate on resources generally covers some, if not all, of the necessary resource reduction. Nonetheless, various methods for expanding or shrinking resources are covered in the following section.

Buffer Zones

While the buffer size determined in the preceding section is the target, the *buffer level* is usually the actual number of resources on the bench. If the buffer level is negative, however, its absolute value is the number of assignments that could be made if the bench weren't empty. For instance, if the buffer level is −3, three open assignments are waiting for the next available resources. Because resources sometimes join or leave contracts in progress, open assignments may or may not be disruptive. It depends on whether the skill group is the constraint, which is a topic addressed more fully in later chapters.

The buffer level naturally departs from the buffer size determined in the preceding section due to variability in net consumption. Note, however, that net consumption and the buffer level move in opposition. When net consumption is persistently high, the buffer level can become negative, thereby indicating that resources are needed but unavailable. When net consumption is persistently negative, the buffer level rises to excessive levels unless steps are taken to move the buffer level toward the intended buffer size.

Setting buffer zones is the third step in applying R_S. *Buffer zones* are predefined ranges that provide a convenient way for managers to know when action is required. In R_G, the inventory buffer is typically divided into green, yellow, and red zones, indicating no action, replenish, and expedite, respectively. Thus, buffer management in R_G is unidirectional. In R_S, however, buffer management must be bidirectional because neither shortage nor excess is necessarily self-correcting. In R_S, the buffer zones are therefore arranged around the buffer size.

Figure 4-5 illustrates buffer zones for R_S. For many skill groups, a simple rule of thumb that establishes symmetric zones is adequate. Appendix A, "Resource Optimization," explains how to optimize resource buffers, and that method may generate asymmetric zones.

With this rule of thumb, a normal (green) zone surrounds the buffer size. If net consumption is normally distributed, a normal zone one standard deviation above and below the buffer size covers the buffer level about 68 percent of the time. A shortage (red) zone one standard deviation below the normal zone and an excess (red) zone one standard deviation above will each cover the buffer level about 14 percent of the time. That leaves the buffer depleted about 2 percent of the time or overflowing about 2 percent of the time, but those conditions should be transient if net consumption is not in a significant upturn or downturn.

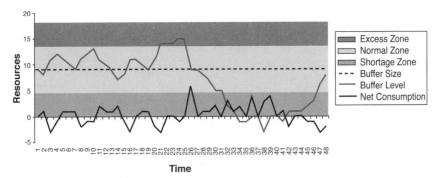

Figure 4-5   Buffer zones

Buffer Management

Buffer management is the fourth step in applying R_S. It is decisions made and actions taken to maintain an appropriate buffer level as net consumption varies.

Figure 4-6 illustrates buffer management in the larger context of R_S. Recall that in R_G, the buffer level is the entire inventory for a given raw material or product, but in R_S the buffer level is usually just the bench, not all resources in the skill group. Thus, in this figure the buffer zones are shown floating on top of base capacity and temporary capacity. *Base capacity* matches the growth trend of the skill group, while *temporary capacity* matches cycles.

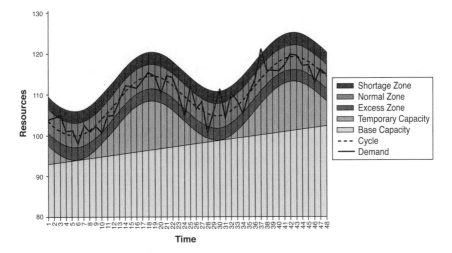

Figure 4-6   Buffer management

Note that moving averages or exponential smoothing usually don't smooth out the data enough to matter, so they are not included in the illustrations. Buffer zones are a better decision aid.

Indeed, it is not necessary to forecast the trend or cycles because R_S adapts to them automatically. With weekly buffer management, a buffer that's just 1 percent of a skill group can easily support a double-digit annual growth rate. However, it generally makes sense to staff seasonal fluctuations with subcontractors or seasonal workers if they are available.

Buffer zones in this figure are intentionally inverted from their orientation in the previous figure because the demand line shows total resources rather than net consumption. When the demand line punches through the shortage zone on top, resources are depleted and no one is left on the bench. Conversely, when the demand line falls through the excess zone on the bottom, the bench is overflowing.

As seen in a previous section, buffer size is determined entirely by net consumption, average time to resupply, and unreliability of resupply. A small skill group and a large skill group can therefore have comparable buffer sizes if the small group has higher net consumption, longer resupply time, or less reliable resupply. Thus, the width of buffer zones is unaffected by base and temporary capacity.

If buffer management is successful, nearly all variation in skill group size occurs within the buffer zones. So if buffer management under R_G is like trying to keep a ball in the air, buffer management under R_S is like trying to drive on a winding mountain road without running into the wall on one side or falling into the chasm on the other.

When done well, buffer management does not initiate opposing resource orders during consecutive periods. That is, if net consumption is generally positive, an occasional negative value will not trigger a resource reduction, but will instead be recognized for what it is—just random variation that will likely correct itself in successive periods.

When it becomes clear that resource changes are needed because the buffer size has changed or the buffer level has strayed persistently into a red zone, resource managers have many options. Hiring or layoffs are obvious choices, yet last on the priority list. Other actions to consider first include the following:

- Examine the services portfolio for large contracts that will start or end soon.

- Search for resources who will return for reassignment sooner or later than expected.

- Substitute resources between compatible skill groups, such as across geographies.

- Redeploy resources from noncritical to critical contracts.

- Reassign resources between skill groups, and schedule the necessary retraining.

- Expedite or postpone resources already in the inbound or outbound resource pipelines.

- Influence the attrition rate via incentives to stay or leave.

- Encourage or discourage sabbaticals and leaves of absence.

- Convert some resources from full-time to part-time, or vice versa.

- Acquire or release subcontractors.

- Temporarily export or import resources between business units.

- Permanently transfer resources between business units.

Thus, R_S does not assume skilled resources are disposable—quite the contrary. Steady growth is the ideal result of R_S.

Resource Management Cycles

As seen in the previous chapter, R_G ships just enough finished goods to replenish actual consumption each day. The frequency of buffer management is daily, and the amount of inventory shipped is small but variable.

R_S similarly performs buffer management on a fixed schedule, with relatively small but variable resource changes. However, daily buffer management is generally too frequent for R_S because net consumption is most unstable over short intervals. On the other hand, if buffer management is not frequent enough, the bench is more likely to be depleted or excessive because time to resupply or desupply limits how fast adjustments can be made. So an appropriate balance must be struck.

As a practical matter, buffer management under R_S typically works fine on a fixed weekly schedule, particularly if most resource assignments start and end on whole weeks. When net consumption is stable, R_S generates roughly the same resource orders every week. In addition to fulfilling those orders, however, resource managers must also be vigilant for changes in net consumption—especially turning points between positive and negative—and changes in resupply time or reliability.

Buffer resizing is often considered at the same time as buffer management, but buffer resizing actually occurs far less often. Buffer resizing is triggered by a noticeable change in net consumption, resupply time, or reliability. Hence, buffer resizing for a given skill group may actually occur only a few times each year, if at all.

Likewise, skill regrouping may be considered at the same time as buffer management, but it occurs even less often than buffer resizing. When skill regrouping does occur, it may consist of the establishment and dissolution of just a few skill groups. It may also involve splitting or merging existing skill groups. Thus, skill regrouping may actually occur only once or twice a year, if at all.

Decision Support

In PSTS, most resources are working at client sites, professional offices, laboratories, or shared service centers, so there's no way to tell by direct observation what the buffer level is when resources are scattered. Therefore, resource managers benefit from computer-aided decision support during resource management cycles.

To know how many resources are effectively on the bench, resources who will be returning shortly must be added to those without a current assignment, and those who are already reassigned must be subtracted. Current assignments can include training and internal projects. The resulting available-to-promise number, the buffer level, then drives buffer management. The relation of the buffer level to recent history, plus a view of future large contracts, drives buffer resizing, if necessary.

R_S has so many interacting variables, whose timing makes a difference, that the ability to compare alternatives can lead to better decisions. By combining information from outside and inside sources, what-if analysis answers questions like these:

- We are short on capacity for a noncritical skill, and some subcontractors are available quickly. Should we get subcontractors now, or can we afford to wait for incoming employee transfers so they won't be sitting on the bench after they arrive?

- During the next month we'll be short on a critical skill, but we expect some resources with that skill to be returning for a new assignment. Should we ride out the shortage or hire additional resources?

- Demand is rising, and the buffer level just fell into the shortage zone. If we decide to hire resources now, will they arrive before the buffer is depleted? If they'll be late, how late?

- Demand is softening, but the job market is stable, so if we stop hiring now, will normal attrition be enough to keep the buffer level out of the excess zone? What if the job market softens too?

- Average project duration is dropping but demand is stable. Is there any impact on net consumption? What if project duration continues to drop? Should we resize the buffer?

- We currently have excess capacity, and another business unit is willing to accept transfers. How many resources should we transfer to restore the buffer level?

- The job market has softened, average replenishment time is shorter, and reliability of resupply is higher. Should we reduce the buffer size? If so, by how much?

Virtual Buffers

A *virtual buffer* is a real skill group buffer plus available resources in other skill groups with a matching secondary skill code. The same information systems used for decision support may be able to depict virtual buffers as another view of the resource database.

Secondary skill codes capture the entire spectrum of skills possessed by individuals within PSTS enterprises. For many individuals, secondary skills are just as sharp as their primary skill. However, the proficiency level of resources with a secondary skill code isn't always as high as the primary skill group. In general, activating a secondary skill should not require retraining. It may just require a little extra time for individuals to get acclimated to their new roles and dust off skills they haven't used recently. Nevertheless, a specified level of proficiency can be used to select individuals for virtual buffers, if desired.

Virtual buffers work just like real buffers, except that virtual buffers have the highly desirable effect of moving resources to where the work is rather than leaving them on the bench in their primary skill group. Though primary and secondary skill codes are brought together in a virtual buffer for management purposes, primary skill groups still have adequate protection against variability because only their excess resources are eligible for inclusion in other skill groups' virtual buffers. Every primary skill group's real buffer remains intact.

During upturns and normal business conditions, virtual buffers create some supply-side risk because each resource can be counted in as many virtual buffers as they have secondary skill codes. But during downturns, the risk that a resource on the bench will be tapped from multiple directions at the same time is considerably smaller. And even if this does occur, a priority scheme based on constrained skills and relative buffer levels ensures that resources flow to the most urgent needs first.

Skill Group Categories

In PSTS, skill groups fall into three categories. First, *commodity skills* are plentiful, can be resupplied quickly, and never constrain the enterprise, so those skill groups usually have no buffer. Subcontractors to PSTS enterprises may, however, buffer commodity skills.

Second, skills that are not commodities, yet are rarely if ever the constraint, should have an appropriate buffer, and managing it is straightforward, because resupply is relatively quick and reliable. The majority of skill groups staffed with employees fall into this category.

Finally, skills that usually are a constraint should have an appropriate buffer, but managing that buffer can be anything but straightforward, because resupply is neither quick nor reliable. If constrained skills require expertise that can be gained only through higher education, lengthy training, or extensive experience, the target buffer size can significantly exceed what can actually be supplied from all sources. This is sometimes called the *Redwood problem*, because it takes just the right conditions and a long time to grow another constrained resource. Hence, other TOC$_S$ applications in subsequent chapters also address resource constraints.

Impact of Replenishment for Services

As noted at the beginning of this chapter, R_S (hire-to-buffer) was invented to solve problems with prevailing resource management methods in services: Individual leaders' discretion (hire-to-deal) fosters local optimization at the practice or department level, forecast-based planning at the business unit level (hire-to-plan) can be unresponsive to market conditions, and optimizing existing capacity (supply-demand matching) assumes that capacity is relatively fixed. Hence, no prevailing approach necessarily optimizes the enterprise.

R_S, on the other hand, does optimize skill groups across the enterprise, and it's responsive to conditions in both the services and job markets. In contrast to prevailing resource management methods, which push resources from practices or departments onto contracts, R_S pulls resources onto contracts from relevant skill groups based on actual market demand. This matching of supply to demand—and skills to requirements—enables better service with fewer resources.

Though several adaptations are required, the main characteristics of R_G remain evident in R_S, as shown in Table 4-1. Though R_G and R_S can be used independently, an enterprise that offers a mix of goods and services can use them concurrently.

Table 4-1   Replenishment for Goods Versus Services

Replenishment For ...	Goods	Services
Item being replenished is ...	Physical items	Skilled resources
Production can be done ...	In advance	Only after service request
Stockouts cause ...	Lost sales or backorders	Lost or late contracts Low service levels
Supply and demand are ...	Independent	Coupled
Buffer size is based on ...	Total consumption	Net consumption
	Resupply Time	Resupply and Desupply Time
	Resupply Unreliability	Resupply and Desupply Unreliability
Buffer level equals ...	Entire inventory	Bench (fraction of skill group)
Buffer zones are ...	Unidirectional	Bidirectional
Buffer management means ...	Ordering more goods	Increasing/decreasing resources
Buffer management is ...	Automatable	Not automatable

Moreover, just as members of a supply or distribution chain in industry can coordinate their replenishment, so can members of a supply or distribution chain in services. For instance, when one service provider commits to managing a resource buffer to a given service level, as a subcontractor might for its clients, other members in the chain who rely on those resources may choose to reduce their own buffers accordingly, thereby increasing the chain's efficiency. This is important because competition is increasingly between chains—or value networks—rather than individual enterprises.

Several R_S outcomes are noteworthy:

- Resource capacity is best managed by aggregation in skill groups, where demand varies least.

- Appropriately sized resource buffers are not likely to be depleted or excessive for long.

- Buffer management is more consistent than leader discretion, much simpler than annual planning, and more responsive than supply-demand matching.

- Service levels can be improved by replenishing resources based on net consumption and resupply time.

- Information systems can provide vital information to resource managers.

Though R_S assumes that individuals within skill groups are reasonably interchangeable, it does not assume that there are no individual differences, nor does it assume that resources are disposable. Everything you know about hiring, training, organizing, and motivating still applies. All R_S does is optimize the quantity and timing of resources needed for services on demand.

Summary

Replenishment for Services (R_S) is the TOC_S application for resource management in services. It solves the fundamental problem of figuring out how to manage resources according to market demand, both when the services market is rising and when it's not. R_S is simpler and more responsive than annual planning, and it optimizes the enterprise rather than individual practices or departments.

R_S requires that resources be organized in skill groups and that members of each skill group be reasonably substitutable for one another. For each skill group, a target buffer size is calculated from net consumption within average resupply time, taking into consideration unreliability of resupply. Buffer zones are then established around the target buffer size. When the buffer level strays and stays outside the normal zone, buffer management allows various actions to alleviate the shortage or excess of resources. If those actions are not sufficient, resources may be acquired or released in order to get the buffer level back within the normal zone.

R_S does not depend on a forecast, nor does it depend on the source of demand for resources. A project, for instance, is a set of finite-duration tasks that must be performed in a specified sequence to produce a desired result within a prescribed time and budget. In contrast, a process is a set of activities performed continuously or on a frequently recurring schedule, such as operating a data center or contact center, providing maintenance or technical support, and processing payroll or tax returns.

Resource requirements for a project are driven by the specific tasks within scope, so most resources have short-term assignments. On the other hand, resource requirements for a process are driven by the volume of work flowing through the process, and most resources have long-term assignments.

Despite these differences, R_S is just as applicable to processes as projects, because resource requirements are aggregated into skill groups. Indeed, R_S can serve projects and processes simultaneously if they have shared skills, as many service lines do. How R_S works with project management and process management is covered in the following chapters.

Endnotes

1. David H. Maister, *Managing the Professional Service Firm*, Free Press, 1993.
2. Bente R. Lowendahl, *Strategic Management of Professional Service Firms*, Handelshojskolens Forlag, 1997.
3. James A. Fitzsimmons and Mona J. Fitzsimmons, "Managing Capacity and Demand," *Service Management*, McGraw-Hill, 1994, Chapter 13.

5

Project Management

Among the Theory of Constraints (TOC) applications covered in this book, Critical Chain (CC) for a single project is perhaps the most readily adoptable in services. The reason is simple: Many services are delivered as projects, and CC can be used without modification on virtually any services project. This chapter is nevertheless devoted to project management because service providers rarely conduct projects in isolation. How a project management method handles multiple projects can be crucial in services.

Whenever multiple projects must be performed concurrently, single-project Critical Chain, as summarized in Chapter 3, "Theory of Constraints," provides no assistance in resolving conflicts or optimizing the enterprise. Fortunately, multi-project Critical Chain (MPCC), as summarized later in this chapter, addresses this need directly.

MPCC optimizes a set of concurrent projects with shared resources by scheduling projects around an internal constraint.[1,2] It therefore has a strong internal project orientation, as would be expected for a set of engineering projects within an industrial enterprise. Although such enterprises do augment their resources on occasion, they can be reluctant to adjust capacity to the point where any number of concurrent projects can be tackled on fully independent schedules.

Thus, if internal project sponsors are willing to wait for their projects—or they have no choice—scheduling around an internal resource constraint is workable. Likewise, if external clients are willing to wait for services as available, scheduling around the service provider's internal constraint is workable.

Then again, many clients of services enterprises are not willing to wait for their projects to fit into a service provider's schedule—and they do have a choice. Clients will gladly take their projects to another service provider who can march to their due date, or at least hope to do so. And internal project sponsors are not always obligated to use internal service providers. Outsourcing means even internal providers have external competition. Hence, as originally conceived, MPCC just doesn't support services on demand.

This chapter compares multi-project versions of Critical Path (CP) and Critical Chain (CC), so it's an extension of concepts covered in Chapter 3. In addition, it presents an alternative form of multi-project CC tailored for services on demand.

Just as it was helpful in previous chapters to know the problems those applications solve, it will be helpful in this chapter to know the problems that this alternative version of multi-project CC solves. For that, we need a quick review of the state of the art and project management issues specific to services.

State of the Art

When reading the professional and academic literatures, which both cover adroitly executed projects that succeed despite long odds, it's easy to be fascinated by advances in project management. Service providers monitor new project management techniques, of course, but until one demonstrates that it's more than a curiosity, most service providers will only use it experimentally.

CC is emerging from its early-adopter stage, but it's not quite at the tipping point for mainstream adoption. As evidence, dozens of professional and academic articles on CC have been published, and several commercial project management software packages or add-ons now support CC. Yet just 10 percent of professional project managers use CC extensively, and only another 30 percent make even limited use of it.[3]

It's also easy to be discouraged about the state of project management by reading the literature, which presents examples of ill-conceived and overreaching projects that failed, sometimes spectacularly. Surveys have pegged the success rate on technical projects at anywhere from 90 percent to a dismal 30 percent.[4]

The general project success rate is hard to pin down because the definition of success is multifaceted, and there are many shades of grey between abject failure and unmitigated success. Some projects are canceled for legitimate business or technical reasons. If the need goes away or the means to fulfill that need is no longer appropriate, there would be no point in completing such a project. Yet some surveys count this as a failed project. Moreover, some enterprises deliberately start more internal projects than they can finish, knowing that only the strong will survive.

For a service provider, however, anything less than a high project success rate is not sustainable, because it can take many successful projects to recoup the financial loss and damage to reputation on just one unsuccessful project. A service provider with a low project success rate, as measured by client satisfaction and follow-on business, is most probably on its way to going out of business.

Therefore, depending on who is surveyed, different viewpoints on project success emerge:

- **Project sponsor view**—Delivered by the due date with full scope and high quality

- **Project manager view**—Delivered on time, within budget, and with high satisfaction

- **Client stakeholder view**—Generates business value, stock appreciation, job security, and so on

- **Service provider view**—Strengthens the client-provider relationship and creates follow-on

A project can fail from any one of these viewpoints while succeeding on all the others. There is perhaps some solace in the fact that if the mission of projects could be easily accomplished to everyone's complete satisfaction, we wouldn't need something as elaborate as a project to do it.

Whereas project success rates are debatable, top-ten lists of reasons why projects fail are more consistent. Choice of project management method is rarely among them, but failure to follow the chosen method is consistently among them. In other words, a variety of methods can work in the hands of a skilled project manager, and any method is generally better than no method.

Because project management takes place in a larger context, related methods have evolved:

- *Program management* handles interlocking projects, usually via a program management office (PMO) that oversees multiple project managers.

- *Portfolio management* includes justifying, prioritizing, funding, and tracking of projects and programs throughout a business unit or across the entire enterprise, with oversight by an executive steering committee.

MPCC pertains directly to program management. Chapter 7, "Finance and Accounting," pertains directly to portfolio management.

Project Management in Services

Professional, Scientific, and Technical Services (PSTS) enterprises can use many of the same project, program, and portfolio management methods used on internal projects. Yet services projects are different in several ways, which can make some methods more suitable than others.

Obviously, services projects must address client requirements. If they don't, nothing else really matters. The more novel client requirements are, the more innovative services projects must be. Likewise, the more urgent client requirements are, the more timely services projects must be. When clients require both innovation and timeliness, highly diverse services projects result. Services projects therefore need management methods that are flexible enough to handle a wide variety of projects, plus the wide variety of resources they employ.

Projects are considered *repeatable* if they have comparable objectives, work breakdown structures, scopes, schedules, staffing, and deliverables. For instance, although products vary, product engineering projects often follow a standard template. PSTS projects, on the other hand, are highly customized. Any or all of the aforementioned project attributes can differ substantially between projects, so there may not be a template to follow. And even when a template is available, it's often just the starting point for customization. Services projects therefore need planning methods that cope with ambiguity and instability in tasks and deliverables.

A services project is likely to be estimated and bid before specific resources are assigned to most tasks. Indeed, some resources may not be assigned until a project is nearing completion. Estimating therefore creates a service provider commitment rather than a personal commitment by individual resources, as is more often the case on internal projects where resources make their own task estimates. Services projects thus need estimating methods that do not overcommit the provider or its resources to be assigned later.

Any project is susceptible to scope changes, but when services are delivered on demand, changes can occur at every status meeting. Indeed, the entire direction of a services project can change more than once, and scope can decrease as well as increase. Nevertheless, because milestones are visible to stakeholders, project sponsors often resist changing them, even when the tasks leading up to them have been considerably reconfigured. That's why milestones have a way of becoming millstones. Services projects thus need measurement methods based on something more flexible than milestones.

Terms and conditions in a services contract cannot be changed unilaterally by either the client or the service provider. Every change in direction, scope, staff, schedule, budget, deliverables, or acceptance criteria requires a project change authorization signed by the client and provider. For instance, if a services project cannot be completed until after the due date specified in the contract, that due date must be amended. When a service provider makes the start of some projects contingent on the completion of others, delays or accelerations ripple across projects—and perhaps across clients. Services projects thus need scheduling methods that decouple projects unless they have dependencies based on deliverables.

A services project draws resources from at least two enterprises: the client and the provider. And if subcontractors are involved, the number of enterprises can be three or more. Any of these enterprises can have resource constraints. For instance, on information technology (IT) projects, the provider's IT architects may be its constraint, while the client's acceptance testing resources may be its constraint. Scheduling around one enterprise's resource constraint can put a project in conflict with another enterprise's resource constraint. Services projects thus need communication methods to coordinate constrained resources across enterprises.

On a services project, the client always has responsibilities, even if they're just to sign off on the service provider's deliverables. Many times, though, the client's responsibilities are much more substantial. The client may, for instance, provide a co-manager, physical facilities, and half the staff. The service provider then provides its own co-manager, intellectual capital, experts, and subcontractors. As the project progresses, however, reassigning some responsibilities to another party may be beneficial. Services projects thus need replanning methods to shift selected responsibilities between the client, service provider, and subcontractors.

Quality assurance of services projects is an ongoing process that starts with the bid and proposal and doesn't end until the final project sign-off. Issues may include technical problems, people problems, and business problems. *Troubled projects* understandably get lots of executive oversight until their issues are resolved. Services projects thus need quality assurance methods that identify trouble without unduly burdening projects that are trouble-free, diagnose the cause of trouble, and apply a suitable remedy. Services projects are usually related to one or more of the client's ongoing business processes. The impact of problems on a services project can therefore affect the client and the service provider well beyond the duration of the project. For instance, if a provider is engaged to perform a business process on behalf of the client and a project is required to establish the necessary IT, delays in that project or defects in its deliverables can make it difficult to achieve service level agreements related to the business process. Services projects thus need *risk-management* methods that steer projects based on the larger business context.

The services projects with the highest potential business benefit for clients often require substantial up-front investments. For example, competitive pressures may force migration from legacy to modern IT, or a business breakthrough may require a client to integrate its IT better with other enterprises in its supply or distribution chains. Service providers may fund some of the investment and make their price contingent on attainment of certain business benefits. Doing so, however, entails risk. Services projects thus need risk-reward sharing methods so that the client and the provider both benefit when the client's needs are well-served.

A change in scope, time, cost, or quality on any project requires a compensating change in at least one of the other variables. From the client's perspective, a smaller, quicker, cheaper, and better project is often desirable. But from the service provider's perspective, a project like this usually means less revenue. So to grow revenue while delivering services on demand, service providers have to perform bigger projects, more small projects, or drive revenue from something other than just billable hours, such as software assets and business value. Services projects thus need assets, and service providers need methods to generate revenue from those assets.

Finally, service providers must simultaneously manage a portfolio of unrelated projects for multiple clients, programs of related projects for specific clients, and the service provider's own internal projects. Services enterprises can have thousands of projects under way concurrently, and they aren't all small projects with a lone project manager. Some are complex programs managed by teams of project managers, program managers, and executives. Services projects thus need professional program and project managers.

Methods for Single Projects

The prevailing project management method in both goods and services industries is still Critical Path (CP), but Critical Chain (CC) is winning converts. A more-detailed comparison was covered in Chapter 3. A summary comparison of CP and CC is shown in Table 5-1.

Table 5-1   Critical Path Versus Critical Chain for Single Projects

Single Projects Via ...	Critical Path (CP)	Critical Chain (CC)
Tasks are estimated with ...	80 percent confidence	50 percent confidence
Contingency time is planned ...	In every task	Only around the Critical Chain
Resource contention is ...	Sometimes ignored	Always managed
Resource leveling affects ...	Noncritical tasks	All tasks
Work rules allow ...	Bad multitasking	No bad multitasking
Planned duration is usually ...	Greater than CC	Less than CP
Early starts on gating tasks are ...	Encouraged	Discouraged
Replanning is done ...	Frequently	Rarely
Progress is tracked against ...	Milestones	Time buffer penetration
Late project completion occurs ...	Often	Seldom

CP and CC are both plan-based project management methods that tend to be used when scope is relatively fixed but the due date and budget are negotiable. They therefore are distinct from *Agile Project Management* (APM), a non-plan-based project management method that tends to be used when due date and budget are fixed but scope is negotiable.

APM has been used successfully on software projects where requirements are initially ill-defined, the client/users are actively involved, and an iterative approach is acceptable. It thus tends to apply to a different subset of services projects than CC. However, a hybrid approach to project management based on APM and CC has been used for product development.[5]

CC overcomes problems that can cause CP projects to be chronically late, but CC has its own critics.[6,7] They point out that CC requires a huge cultural change. It relies on rules of thumb rather than scientifically validated quantities, software occasionally generates suboptimal

CC project plans, and CC itself is sometimes ambiguous, such as when there is more than one critical chain. These criticisms come from theoretical and simulation studies, however, not case studies of actual projects. CC converts are not easily dissuaded by rules of thumb, nonoptimality, or ambiguity, because CC addresses some thorny project management issues—yet is simpler than CP.

Thus, the criticisms are useful in raising awareness, but none are a compelling reason to avoid CC. Indeed, there are thousands of CC projects worldwide.[8] Most are in industrial or government organizations rather than services, however.

If a service provider can make the cultural leap, CC can address some of the special needs discussed in the previous section. For instance, CC replaces project milestones with *buffer penetration* measures, CC always resolves resource contention, and CC includes communication to ensure that resources are available when needed. For services projects where estimates must be made before specific resources are assigned, however, CC must be supplemented with a standard estimating method that conforms to its estimating rules, especially 50 percent confidence and no multitasking.

Complex problems tend to require huge projects to solve them. Huge projects tend to be massively parallel, with lots of concurrent tasks and potential resource contention. And as complex project size grows, productivity often declines in a nonlinear fashion.[9] Nevertheless, CC has been used successfully on projects of more than 1 million person-hours—with the highly desirable effect of reducing work effort by a third.[10]

On the other hand, there's no reason to believe that CC in any way repeals Brooks' Law, which says "adding more people to a late project makes it later."[11] A corollary of this is when project size doubles, you can't just assign twice as many people to get it done according to the original schedule. Fortunately, because CC uses task estimates with no contingency and makes its buffers explicit, it mandates an increase in schedule or reduction in scope, which is consistent with Brooks' advice to "take no small [date] slips."

When project scope is fixed, the critical chain is known to be more stable than the critical path. Hence, replanning of CC projects is less common than on CP projects. But how CC performs on projects with variable scope has not been well-studied. Any project requiring information technology, research, or high creativity—such as advertising or architecture—has lots of uncertainty regarding what the final deliverables should be and how they should be produced. Because PSTS projects are customized at the outset and are volatile thereafter, the critical chain may not be as stable on services projects as it is on internal projects.

One way to cope with highly uncertain tasks is to enforce *time boxes*. That is, upper bounds on some task durations are set with the understanding that the results may not be as complete or polished as they would be with more time, but the advantages of rapid and predictable task completion greatly compensate for the potential loss. When task time is upper-bounded rather than totally variable, this should reduce the required buffer sizes in CC unless the risk just shifts to other tasks. However, using time boxes with CC is another topic that hasn't been well studied.

Despite the criticisms and unknowns, CC is following a typical innovation-adoption trajectory. Pioneers have demonstrated that it works, early adopters have jumped on board, and mainstream adopters are beginning to pay attention. Whether CC will see significant adoption in services, however, may depend on how well its multi-project version addresses more of the issues that service providers face. That's the topic of the next section.

Methods for Multiple Projects

Just as CP and CC handle single projects in different ways, they also handle multiple projects quite differently. Those differences have implications for everyone connected with those projects, including sponsors, managers, staff, and stakeholders.

CP handles multiple projects by treating them as subprojects of a super project. Specific tasks can be linked via precedence relations across projects, or entire projects can be collapsed into separate phases on the Multi-Project Critical Path (MPCP) plan, with precedence relations just between phases. Cross-project resource leveling is possible with the first approach, but not the second.

MPCP thus employs the same method and has the same characteristics as single-project CP: multitasking, delay accumulation, and milestones. Consequently, when resources are shared across projects in an MPCP plan, the actual duration of each project tends to lengthen, roughly in proportion to the amount of multitasking.

In contrast, CC uses separate but related methods for single projects and multiple projects. It handles multiple projects first by planning each of them according to single-project CC, and then it staggers their schedules and adopts work rules that keep resources focused on the highest-priority project until their tasks are complete.

Even though the methods differ, all the features that apply to single-project CC also apply to MPCC: no multitasking, no accumulated delays, no milestones. Consequently, when resources are shared across projects in a multi-project CC plan, the planned duration of each project is lengthened only by buffers within projects, while the planned duration of all projects is lengthened only by the offsets between projects.

Consider Figure 5-1, which illustrates various multi-project scenarios.[12] Each scenario is composed of three projects, and each project is composed of nine tasks performed by three resources. The tasks within each project must be performed in sequence, and each task is estimated to take one time period. The projects could each represent a scientific research study performed by a lead researcher, research assistant, and statistician, for instance.

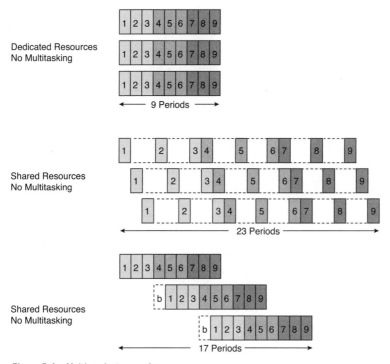

Figure 5-1   Multi-project scenarios

The first scenario dedicates resources to each project, so there is no cross-project multitasking. A change to one project has no effect on the others, because each project is separate. Each project's duration is thus nine periods. For this scenario to work, however, the enterprise needs three of each resource type. If it has fewer, another approach must be followed. One alternative would be to simply do one project at a time, which would take 27 periods. The other scenarios in the figure both do better than this, however.

The second scenario shares one set of resources across all projects via multitasking. Each task is completed across all projects before the next task is started. Consequently, there are periods between tasks on each project when no progress is being made because the resource is working on another project. And at least one resource is idle during any period. Each project thus takes more than 20 periods, or more than twice as long as a single project would without multitasking. Moreover, this scenario depicts no lost productivity due to project switching, as could occur if the projects were at different sites. If present, it would further delay each project, and because the projects are coupled, a delay on any project would delay the others, too. This scenario thus illustrates a not-quite-worst-case, yet all-too-common, outcome of MPCP.

The final scenario also shares one set of resources across all projects, but it does not allow multitasking, and the projects are staggered. Each resource works on one project until his or her tasks are complete, and then he or she moves to the project with the next-highest priority. Every project is therefore completed six to 12 periods sooner than its counterpart in the previous scenario. Indeed, this third scenario could complete nearly two additional projects with the same duration and resources as the prior scenario. Note that buffers ahead of projects decouple them from preceding projects, so a delay on one project would not delay the others unless the delay exceeded the buffer. This scenario thus illustrates what MPCC is intended to achieve.

CP projects are sometimes staggered, as in the final scenario. For example, a portfolio of computer software applications going through a conversion service are frequently staggered. But staggered projects are not explicitly part of the CP method, as they are in MPCC. So the size and position of buffers is rarely the same. In fact, CP more often relies on task-level contingency than buffers.

These scenarios are, of course, highly simplified representations. Actual MPCP and MPCC are often even more different than the figure suggests.

In an actual MPCP plan, there are practical limits to how much multitasking can occur before the planned due dates become untenable. And the complexity of a super project plan sometimes limits how many projects can actually be managed together. Critics contend, however, that much of the effort that goes into managing super projects involves details that don't really affect the outcome.

In an actual MPCC plan, the position of the buffers between projects often isn't at the start of each project. Instead, those buffers are placed ahead of tasks assigned to the constrained resource. Because the constrained resource type in MPCC is supposed to be a strategic decision, Figure 5-2 depicts strategic resources, who are assigned to strategic tasks, which are protected by strategic resource buffers. Thus, projects are staggered by creating interproject dependencies between strategic tasks performed on each project. For example, using this method, time to overhaul large transport aircraft was trimmed by a third, while the number of aircraft simultaneously undergoing overhaul was cut nearly in half, thereby keeping more aircraft productive.[13]

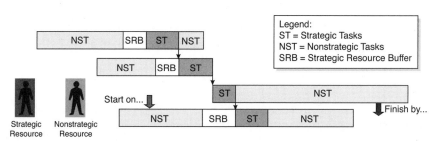

Figure 5-2 Multi-project Critical Chain with strategic resources

The *strategic resource* is often a resource type chronically in short supply, not readily available from outside sources, and slow to develop internally. In other words, strategic resources are generally the "redwoods" described in the previous chapter. If not, one resource type is designated as the strategic resource and is deliberately understaffed to ensure that the constraint does not shift to another resource.

The staggering of projects is designed to keep the strategic resource busy because it constrains the entire set of projects. The strategic resource buffer then prevents delays on preceding tasks from delaying the strategic task and allows early completion of one strategic task to be followed by an early start of the strategic task on the next project.

Unfortunately, this linkage of projects on strategic tasks means that project sponsors cannot dictate start or finish dates for their projects. The best they may be able to do is negotiate a change in the priority of their projects, which would move them earlier or later in the chain of staggered projects. Priority-setting is an essential function during portfolio management of internal projects, but it's unwise on services projects if clients can simply go elsewhere.

Furthermore, MPCC assumes that the enterprise has finite capacity overall, yet enough spare capacity among its nonconstrained resources that none of them will unduly delay a single project or impede the ordering of multiple projects. So at the same time it has a constrained resource, the enterprise usually has less than full utilization of its nonconstrained resources.

MPCP and MPCC are summarized in Table 5-2.

Table 5-2   Critical Path Versus Critical Chain for Multiple Projects

Multiple Projects Via ...	Critical Path (CP)	Critical Chain (CC)
Scheduling is done as ...	Super project	Staggered projects
Linkage between projects is ...	Tasks or phase precedence	Strategic tasks
Project schedules are protected by ...	Task contingency	Strategic resource buffers
Resource contention is ...	Sometimes ignored	Always managed
Work rules allow ...	Bad multitasking	No bad multi-tasking
Planned resource utilization is ...	High for all resources	High only for constrained resources
Actual resource utilization is ...	Variable for most resources	Moderate for most resources
Delays affect ...	Multiple projects	One project
Planned duration is usually ...	Greater than CC	Less than CP
Actual completion is often ...	Later than due date	Earlier than due date
Sponsors can negotiate ...	Planned start/finish dates	Project priority
Capacity is ...	Variable within limits	Fixed unless strategy changes
Enterprise constraint is ...	Internal resource budget	Internal constrained resources

The enterprise constraint for MPCP is internal in its budget for resources, so capacity is variable within limits. On the other hand, the enterprise constraint for MPCC is the strategic resource, so capacity is assumed to be fixed unless a change in strategy dictates a change in resources.

As noted earlier, CP is still the dominant project management method in services. Managing a program of related projects for a specific client as a super project via CP is practical, but managing a service provider's entire portfolio for all clients as a super project generally isn't as practical. Therefore, resources more often than not are dedicated to particular projects or programs. Services on demand can be delivered this way when time to resupply resources is short, as it generally is for subcontractors, or when there are ample resources on the bench, as occurs with forecast-based resource management.

Critical Chain for Services

The question then becomes whether MPCC is a viable, if not better, alternative for services. The prospect of single-project CC completing individual projects in less time with higher reliability is certainly attractive. So is the ability of MPCC to complete more projects in a given interval.

MPCC is undoubtedly applicable to a program of related services projects performed for a single client, because the client and service provider can prioritize those projects. On the other hand, the inability of clients to specify start or finish dates is a huge handicap when trying to apply MPCC to a portfolio of unrelated services projects for multiple clients. It means that MPCC as discussed earlier can only support a portfolio of services as available, not services on demand.

What's more, MPCC is predicated on having a stable internal resource constraint. Yet it's sometimes impossible to prevent services constraints from floating. For instance, project scope changes can easily alter critical chains, with a ripple effect on resources, and changes in net consumption can easily shift resource constraints. When the internal resource constraint shifts, the MPCC method requires the entire portfolio to be rescheduled around the new constraint, which is why floating constraints are strenuously avoided. Besides, rescheduling an entire portfolio would not be tolerated by services clients.

It's also not unusual for an enterprise delivering services on demand to have more than one resource constraint simultaneously—at least for a short while. For example, the internal resource constraint on business consulting projects might be the executive consultant, on research projects it could be the lead researcher, on information technology projects it could be the IT architect, and on combined projects it could be any of these resources. When multiple resource constraints intersect, there may be no way to stagger projects without creating contention or gaps.

On some projects, constrained resources belong to the client, where the service provider has even less control. For example, the client's acceptance testing team may be available during only specific periods. If a project is initially delayed by lack of resources, it may later miss the acceptance testing window, and another window may not open until months after the due date.

Therefore, for CC to handle multiple services projects on demand for multiple clients, it cannot be based on an internal resource constraint or the presumption that only one resource constraint exists. PSTS enterprises, however, are accustomed to matching capacity to demand, as discussed in the previous chapter. In such enterprises, the constraint is more often external, in the services market. That is, service providers can generally find a way to staff whatever projects clients will buy, if given enough lead time or a big enough bench. Unfortunately, lead times vary widely across skill groups, and they may be quite long for scarce resources, while big benches are expensive.

The solution to this dilemma is an alternative multi-project method that uses resource management for leverage on project management. In a nutshell, to the degree that Replenishment for Services (R_S) can provide resources on demand, CC is better able to deliver projects on demand. R_S thus eliminates much of the need to stagger projects and strenuously avoid multiple constraints. Moreover, floating constraints no longer require the entire portfolio to be rescheduled.

When using R_S with CC, enough projects must be drawing resources from a common set of skill groups for the aggregation effect in R_S to get traction. The fewer projects that are being managed with CC, the more nervous R_S becomes, to the point that it's a lot like staffing each project separately.

Because the original form of multi-project CC was invented for industry and relies on internal constraints, it will hereafter be referred to as *CC for Goods* (CC_G) or *CC with Internal Constraints* (CC_I). Likewise, because the alternative form was invented for services and handles external constraints, it will be referred to as *CC for Services* (CC_S) or *CC with External Constraints* (CC_E). Finally, because single-project CC is the foundation of both multi-project forms, it will be abbreviated as just CC.

Leveraging Project Management with Resource Management

Replenishment for Services (R_S), as seen in the previous chapter, is a resource manager's method. As such, it manages skill groups for the benefit of all projects without specifying how individual project plans should take R_S into account. Ideally, however, the project manager's method should be aligned with the resource manager's method to optimize a services enterprise.

Therefore, CC_S interlocks with R_S as follows:

- Buffer concepts between R_S and CC_S are reconciled.

- Resource constraints and replenishment times are incorporated into CC_S project plans.

- Resource needs are communicated from project management to resource management.

- Resource status is communicated from resource management to project management.

- Resources not managed via R_S, if any, are handled another way.

- Resource constraints are resolved by exploiting leverage points whenever possible.

As originally envisioned, CC plans contain resource buffers, and CC_G plans contain strategic resource buffers. But those elements serve entirely different purposes than the resource buffers in R_S. Hence, these buffer concepts must be reconciled.

In CC, resource buffers are just reminders sent in advance by the project manager to each assigned resource before their first tasks on the project are scheduled to start. These reminders do buffer the project from inattentiveness, but to avoid confusion with resource buffers as implemented in R_S, the term *reminder* is used here instead.

In CC$_G$, strategic resource buffers are time that is scheduled ahead of the strategic resource's first tasks on each project to ensure that all those tasks' predecessors can be completed before the strategic resource arrives. This is to keep the strategic resource busy because its utilization determines the throughput of all projects. However, CC$_S$ has no strategic resources, so strategic resource buffers are irrelevant.

Instead, resource buffers as implemented in R$_S$ can be incorporated into CC$_S$ plans, as illustrated in the resource view in Figure 5-3. For reference, the precedence view in this figure is the same CC project plan covered in Chapter 3. Recall that Tasks 4, 2, 3, and 6 are the critical chain because they are the shortest path through the project after resource contention is eliminated. Subscripts indicate which resource type is assigned to each task.

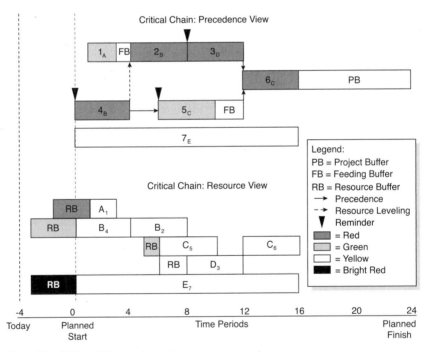

Figure 5-3 Critical chain precedence view versus resource view

A conventional resource view shows when each resource type is scheduled to perform a task. In the figure, subscripts indicate which tasks resources A through E are assigned. If this plan had not been resource-leveled, as required by CC, this view would show overlapping tasks for Resource B.

In this enhanced CC_S resource view, resource buffer (RB) blocks display the connection between the resource manager's world and the project manager's world. That is, RB translates resource availability information into a depiction of constraints and whether they will impact the project.

Length of RB blocks corresponds to the resupply times used to compute the resource buffer size in R_S. If using the rule of thumb, for instance, this would be average time to resupply plus the standard deviation of resupply for each resource type. Thus, rather than being measured in resource units, as in R_S, resource buffers in CC_S are measured in corresponding time periods.

Of course, when resupply time is zero, there is no RB because its length would be zero. Likewise, as soon as a specific resource is assigned, its RB disappears.

RB blocks are marked by color, shading, or labels to indicate whether the buffer level is likely to impose a constraint on the project. Hence, the markings correspond to project manager concerns.

The green RB blocks ahead of Resources B and C indicate that their resource buffer levels are at least in the normal zone, so these resources could be assigned anytime without constraining the project. Nevertheless, the project manager should submit these resource requirements as soon as the project is approved so that they can be incorporated into the resource availability calculations.

Marking of the RB blocks makes no distinction between resource buffer levels in the normal or excess zones, because the difference does not generally affect the project manager's actions. Chapter 8, "Marketing and Sales," however, discusses some implications of excess resources for both current and future projects.

The yellow RB ahead of Resource D indicates that its resource buffer is currently low or depleted, but its RB is short enough and far enough in the future that no action is required now. If that buffer is not replenished by the time the current time approaches the leading edge of this RB, this RB will turn from yellow to red to alert the project manager and resource manager of an impending resource constraint.

On the other hand, if that buffer is replenished, this RB will turn from yellow to green, thereby indicating no resource constraint. As RB levels rise and fall, any of the RB blocks may change length and marking.

The red RB ahead of Resource A indicates that its resource buffer is in the shortage zone but not depleted. Although this resource starts on a noncritical task, it is nevertheless noteworthy because failure to request this resource in advance of the project could have a ripple effect that delays Task 2, which is critical. The feeding buffer after this task protects the project from late task completion, not a late start.

The bright red RB ahead of Resource E indicates that its resource buffer is depleted and RB is currently four periods long. Therefore, the resource manager should receive this resource requirement at least that many periods before the planned project start; otherwise, the project could start late. Ironically, the person who submits such resource requirements is the project manager, who in this case hasn't yet been assigned. This is therefore an example of how a resource assigned to an elastic task can delay an entire project. When resources are chronically in short supply, the buffer management techniques covered in the following section may be required.

For a given resource type, there will be an RB block in the resource view every time another instance of that resource type is required. And if individuals are temporarily released from a project, they will have new RB blocks when rejoining that project later.

All the RB blocks in the figure are marked consistently over their entire duration, which is typical of short replenishment times. Yet, it's possible for some periods within an RB block to be marked differently. For instance, the leading edge might be red while the trailing edge is green, because a large project is ending and resources will become plentiful during the time span covered by RB.

Reminders in the precedence view are typically of fixed duration and are therefore unrelated to the availability of resources. In contrast, RB blocks in the resource view as implemented in CC_S have variable duration directly related to the availability of resources. Furthermore, through its marking, any RB may represent a potential or actual resource constraint on the project.

Buffer Management

All the usual buffer management activities defined by CC apply to CC_S. That is, the project manager must issue reminders to assigned resources regarding upcoming tasks and monitor penetration on all feeder and project buffers. In addition, under CC_S the project manager must issue resource requisitions, monitor the corresponding resource buffers, and interact with resource managers as required to alleviate constraints due to resource shortages.

If a resource type is not managed via R_S, which is much like having a resource buffer level perpetually at zero, its RB is marked red in the resource view of the project plan, and its length is based on an estimate unless a specific availability date is known. Having resources not managed via R_S occurs most often when they are provided by the client or subcontractors rather than the service provider. Although it is possible to insert a time buffer (such as a feeding buffer) following the tasks assigned to a nonreplenishable resource, this could lengthen the project schedule unnecessarily, so it is not a preferred approach.

Whenever a resource arriving late could delay the project start or otherwise delay the critical chain, the resource manager and project manager have many leverage points to consider. Thus, a potential resource constraint will not necessarily become an actual constraint on the project.

Here are just a few ways the resource manager can alleviate a resource constraint:

- Assign a resource already in the pipeline who can arrive sooner than the end of the RB.
- Expedite a resource from a source with shorter-than-average resupply time.
- Redeploy a resource currently assigned to another project on noncritical tasks.
- Substitute an available resource from another skill group with compatible skills.
- Assign a fractional resource who has less than a full-time assignment elsewhere.

Likewise, the project manager can

- Suspend or truncate a noncritical task and reassign its resource to a critical task suffering the resource constraint.

- Split the constrained task and assign each part to a different resource so that they can be completed concurrently when resources become available.

- Authorize overtime to make up a delay.

- Shift responsibility from the client to the service provider or vice versa, depending on who has available resources.

- Do nothing, because a feeding buffer or the project buffer can absorb the delay.

- Do nothing, because the client is changing project scope or due date, thereby necessitating a more significant change in the plan.

Resource managers and project managers also have to deal appropriately with early arrivals. Resources can arrive early when newly hired or when returning from other projects. Indeed, as CC_S pulls more projects to on-time or early completion, resources will return earlier than from comparable CP projects.

If a resource arrives for a project before preceding tasks assigned to other resources are complete, the resource manager assigns the early arrival to a sensible investment, such as training or mentoring, or to another project where the additional resource could alleviate significant buffer penetration. After all, in this case, the early resource can't start work without the work products from preceding tasks; otherwise, there would be no reason for the precedence relation. However, the resource manager takes the same action when a resource arrives early for a task at the start of a feeding chain, because this prevents excess work-in-process. In other words, starting the feeding chain early probably wouldn't make the project finish early because the feeding chain is already buffered.

On the other hand, when a resource arrives earlier than expected and all preceding tasks are complete, that resource starts immediately because this minimizes buffer penetration on the assigned project, and the result is not considered excess work-in-process. In other words, this early resource arrival enables an early task start that may compensate for a late task finish elsewhere in the chain.

Finally, if a resource arrives early for the start of the critical chain and the client has requested completion of the project as soon as possible, the resource and project managers assess whether the entire project can be pulled earlier. If not, even the critical chain waits for its scheduled start because CC projects are executed like a relay race—and a relay won't work if some runners are missing.

Thus, actions by resource managers and project managers can involve cross-project decisions, but projects overall are much more loosely coupled under CC_S than CC_G. This and other differences are discussed in the following section.

Impact of Critical Chain for Services

Operations within services enterprises can be extremely complex, so having an enterprise constraint in the market does not mean there are never internal constraints. It just means they aren't universal or continuous. If a service provider offers a diverse service line, the resource constraint on one class of projects may be entirely different from the resource constraint on other project classes. The resource constraint in one geography may be entirely different from another geography. And the resource constraint next quarter may be entirely different from this quarter. Such is the nature of services on demand.

If the enterprise constraint is external, however, it's reasonable to wonder why a services enterprise can't just use the resources it already has and hire additional resources as needed, thereby making CC_S unnecessary. The answer mostly comes down to timing and affordability. If time to resupply is longer than clients will wait for their projects, those clients perceive the service provider as being unresponsive—and therefore not delivering services on demand. If unreliability of resupply is high, service delivery is similarly unreliable. Finally, because net consumption of resources in services does go negative at times, a services enterprise has to be wary of unaffordable bench levels. CC_S addresses all these issues.

Some differences between CC_G and CC_S can be seen by comparing Figure 5-2 to Figure 5-4. Recall that CC_G staggers projects according to strategic tasks and therefore usually cannot accommodate clients' desire for specific start and finish dates. Thus, the strategic resource is the constraint for both individual projects and the portfolio overall.

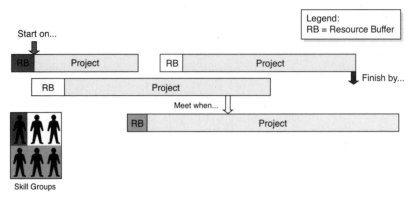

Figure 5-4 Multi-project Critical Chain with Replenishment

In contrast, CC_S schedules projects according to clients' requested start and finish dates, if such requests are feasible. And when resources are insufficient, they are replenished as needed. Nevertheless, if projects need to be linked due to dependencies on resources or deliverables, CC_S can handle it. Any skill group can be a project constraint in the short term, but in practice, commodity skills are rarely a constraint. And beyond the short term, the market is the constraint on the portfolio.

Table 5-3 compares CC_G and CC_S.

Table 5-3 Multi-Project Critical Chain for Goods Versus Services

Multi-Project Critical Chain For ...	Goods (CC_G)	Services (CC_S)
Scheduling is done as ...	Staggered projects	Independent projects
Linkage between projects is ...	Strategic tasks	Deliverables (optional)
Project schedules determined by ...	Resource availability	Client due dates
Project schedules protected by ...	Strategic resource buffers	Resource buffers
Resource managers perform ...	Hiring	Replenishment for Services (R_S)
Rescheduling affects ...	All downstream projects	Only linked projects
Work rules allow ...	No bad multitasking	No bad multitasking
Delays affect ...	One project	One project
Sponsors/clients can specify ...	Project priority	Planned start/finish dates
Enterprise constraint is ...	Internal resource	External market

Under CC_G, capacity is fixed unless a change in strategy dictates a change in resources. Under CC_S, capacity is variable with market demand. Moreover, scope, schedule, and resource changes can be highly disruptive under CC_G, but they are much less so under CC_S.

Several CC_S outcomes are noteworthy:

- Whereas CP pushes work through projects, CC_S pulls work through projects, just as CC_G does. In addition, CC_S also pulls resources as needed, and CC_S pulls market demand by being responsive.

- CC_S creates the flexibility in project planning and execution that's essential when delivering services on demand.

- CC_S is scalable. Indeed, the more projects, the better, because aggregation smoothes resource requirements.

- CC_G and CC_S are compatible. A service provider might use both forms concurrently for different service lines or for different clients being served within one service line. And enterprises that offer a mix of goods and services can use both forms as appropriate.

As shown in Table 5-4, CC_S isn't a panacea. It addresses many but not all of the special needs of services projects outlined earlier in this chapter. Risk-reward sharing and intellectual capital, for instance, are covered in Chapter 7. Certification of professional project managers in CC and CC_G is already available, so certification in CC_S may one day be available, too.

One position on making the cultural transition is that CC makes sense when an enterprise's project management is in such disarray that there is little or no culture to transform. An opposing position is that CC makes sense when an enterprise's project management is so mature that it can take a leap of faith with a new method. But both these positions ignore the vast middle ground where most enterprises lie.

Table 5-4   Special Needs Met by Critical Chain for Services

Special Need of Services Projects	How CC_S Meets the Need
Wide variety of services project types and resource types	Replenishment for Services (R_S)
Ambiguity in tasks and deliverables	Replan projects as needed
Estimates made before resources assigned	Standard estimating method
Measurements more flexible than milestones	Buffer penetration measures
Scope and due dates subject to change	Decouple except on deliverables
Communicate resource constraints between provider, client, and subcontractors	Resource buffer levels
Shift selected responsibilities between provider, client, and subcontractors	Match resource skill codes
Quality assurance that's effective but not burdensome	Focus on critical chain
Risk management in larger business context	Better on-time delivery
Risk-reward sharing	
Intellectual capital	
Professional project managers	

Implementation is the topic of Chapter 10, "Implementation and Technology," but it's worth noting here that in many cases where CC has been successfully adopted, it was accomplished through leadership. Someone just decided to make this happen. Of course, there's much more than that to completing the journey, but without that first step, the journey will never be undertaken.

CC_S is different from CC_G because services projects are different from industrial projects. R_S is a prerequisite to CC_S, so on that basis alone, CC_S can be harder to implement than CC_G. Yet for an enterprise striving to deliver services on demand, CC_S can bring out the best in both project management and resource management.

Summary

Critical Chain for Services (CC_S) is the TOC_S application for project management in services. It is based on the original single-project Critical Chain (CC) application in TOC_G, which takes both task precedence and resource constraints into account. Thus, in a given project plan, the critical chain often is different from the critical path unless resource leveling is done on the critical path. Even then, however, there often are differences because CC uses markedly different estimating guidelines and work rules. Furthermore, the critical chain tends to be more stable than the critical path, so replanning projects is less common. Because projects tend to be shorter and more predictable under CC, it is well suited to delivering projects on demand.

Though CC_S adopts the same Critical Chain method used by CC_G for single projects, it adapts how CC is applied to multiple projects. In CC_G, the schedules for multiple projects are staggered around an internal resource constraint. In CC_S, however, Replenishment for Services (R_S) enables multiple projects to be scheduled around client due dates. Thus, project managers and resource managers each manage their respective buffers, but they coordinate with each other to ensure that resources are available to projects when needed.

Among project management methods, Critical Path (CP) is still the perennial favorite, but Critical Chain (CC) is an up-and-comer. Although CC is ultimately simpler than CP, the cultural transition can be formidable. Nonetheless, there are sufficient cases to demonstrate that it can be done.

Endnotes

1. Robert C. Newbold, *Project Management in the Fast Lane*, St. Lucie Press, 1998.

2. Lawrence P. Leach, *Critical Chain Project Management*, Artech House, 2000.

3. Claude Besner and Brian Hobbs, "An Empirical Investigation of Project Management Practice: A Summary of the Survey Results," University of Quebec at Montreal, 2004.

4. Robert L. Glass, "IT Failure Rates—70 percent or 10–15 percent?," *IEEE Software*, May/June 2005, pp. 110–113.

5. Matt Gelbwaks, "Segway and an Agile Critical Chain," *Cutter IT Journal*, March 2003, pp. 24–28.

6. Willy Herroelen and Roel Leus, "On the Merits and Pitfalls of Critical Chain Scheduling," *Journal of Operations Management*, 19, October 2001, pp. 559–577.

7. Tzvi Raz, Robert Barnes, and Dov Dvir, "A Critical Look at Critical Chain Project Management," *Project Management Journal*, December 2003, pp. 24–32.

8. "Frequently Asked Questions," The TOC Center, www.tocc.com/FAQ.html.

9. Capers Jones, *Applied Software Measurement*, McGraw-Hill, 1991.

10. Peter Johnson, "LeTourneau Technologies—Offshore Products Group," *Constraints Management User Conference*, Chicago, Illinois, 2007.

11. Frederick Brooks, *The Mythical Man-Month*, Addison-Wesley, 1975.

12. Richard E. Zultner, "Getting Projects Out of Your System: A Critical Chain Primer," *Cutter IT Journal*, March 2003, pp. 10–18.

13. Mandyam M. Srinivasan and William D. Best, "Back on the Runway," *APICS Magazine*, 16:3, March 2006, pp. 20–4.

6

Process Management

Operations management for services can sometimes be enough like operations management for manufacturing that Drum-Buffer-Rope (DBR), the Theory of Constraints (TOC) application for operations, can be applied directly. For example, a pharmacy is an inventory-based services operation, auto care is a technology-based service operation, and lawn care is a low-tech services operation. Yet all these *service operations* can be managed with DBR, largely as described in Chapter 3, "Theory of Constraints."

A pharmacy can fill more prescriptions and provide more advice when licensed pharmacists, a resource constraint, delegate as many tasks as possible to pharmacy clerks, technicians, and robots. Likewise, an auto care business can serve more customers with a wider range of services if major repairs, a technology constraint, are separated from routine maintenance, such as oil changes. And a lawn care business can serve more customers in a timely manner if mowing, a task constraint, is decoupled from fertilizing, weeding, trimming, and pest control.

In each case, the enterprise gets leverage simply by identifying its internal constraint ("drum"), using it to the fullest extent, and ensuring that nonconstraints do whatever necessary to support the constraint. Of course, if the enterprises actively manage their work-in-process ("buffer") via information systems ("rope"), they can get even more leverage.

Nevertheless, neither pharmacies nor auto care nor lawn care deliver services on demand because their capacity is relatively static, and customers usually must accept the service provider's schedule. Sometimes customers can request a general time frame for service, but there's seldom much direct consequence to the service provider for missing a commitment because its constraint was overloaded.

Contrast that with a limousine service, where customers expect reliable service on demand because airlines won't hold flights for late passengers. The consequences to the service provider of missed pickups and late drop-offs are severe: irate passengers, demoralized drivers, and no repeat business. Furthermore, a limousine service is subject to considerable uncertainty because half its airport business involves pickups that are susceptible to late flight arrivals, and all its business is susceptible to traffic delays. Hence, this is an example of a service that is sufficiently different from manufacturing to make the direct application of DBR impractical because the provider cannot compete if it schedules service only around its internal operations constraint.

This is just one of several characteristics that make the original DBR application hard to apply universally to services. In addition, when services are delivered business-to-business rather than business-to-consumer, the provider-client relationship is more often formalized in legal contracts that create another class of constraints. And when services are continuous rather than independent transactions, the client-provider relationship may include performance-improvement objectives that tend to create floating constraints.

Therefore, the original DBR application, hereafter referred to as *DBR for Goods* (DBR_G), can be readily applied to transactional, business-to-consumer services as available. But continuous, business-to-business services on demand are more likely to require an adapted application that will be called *DBR for Services* (DBR_S). This chapter covers how and why DBR_S is different from DBR_G.

Services Domains

On-demand service operations, such as limousine dispatching, are not the only services domain that may be unable to use DBR_G. A *business process* is a set of activities performed in support of a business on a continuous or frequently recurring schedule with no termination date, such as procuring supplies and materials, providing product maintenance or technical support, conducting consumer surveys or clinical trials, creating advertising or contracts, and processing payroll or tax returns. When business processes like these are performed by a service provider, rather than internally, they are coming from the Professional, Scientific, and Technical Services (PSTS) sector.

Business processes are used in every enterprise, regardless of whether it produces goods or services. Yet some business processes can be performed better by external service providers. Payroll, for instance, is increasingly complex, but it's not a core business process. That is, it's not directly involved in production of the enterprise's goods or services, so it's often better to have a service provider do it.

Like service operations, business processes can be analogous to manufacturing processes. Of course, this isn't a perfect analogy because neither service operations nor business process produce inventories of finished services. Nonetheless, business processes on demand are another domain where DBR_S may apply.

A given service provider may do projects, service operations, business processes, or a combination thereof. For example, when a service provider agrees to perform service operations or business processes on behalf of a client, that service provider may also conduct information technology (IT) implementation projects that enable better performance.

Table 6-1 compares projects, service operations, and business processes. Projects were covered in Chapter 5, "Project Management," but are included here to show how they differ from services where DBR applies. The primary differences stem from repeatability: Projects are far less repeatable than service operations or business processes, which may be customized once and then performed millions of times. Projects have finite duration, while operations and processes are ongoing. Projects are measured against their individual schedule and budget, while operations and processes are measured against service levels, which cover activities during an interval of time.

Table 6-1   Projects Versus Service Operations Versus Business Processes

	Projects	Service Operations	Business Processes
Purpose is …	Create deliverables	Serve customers	Support the business
Examples include …	IT implementation	Pharmacy or limousine	Payroll or procurement
Repeatability is …	Low	High	Moderate to high
Overall duration is …	Finite	Ongoing	Ongoing
Task duration is …	Moderate (hours)	Variable (minutes to months)	Variable (minutes to months)
Resource assignments are …	Short-term	Variable	Long-term
Workload is driven by …	Project plan	Service requests	Transactions and case files
Activities are …	Manual	Manual, semi-, fully automated	Manual, semi-, fully automated
Performance is measured on …	Schedule and budget	Service levels	Service levels
TOC application is …	Critical Chain (CC)	Drum-Buffer-Rope (DBR)	Drum-Buffer-Rope (DBR)

For purposes of understanding how DBR applies, however, service operations and business processes are more similar than different. They can be entirely manual, semiautomated, or fully automated. They can be performed in a front office with direct customer contact or in a back office without direct customer contact. They can be core or noncore. And they can deliver services as available via DBR_G or services on demand via DBR_S.

Service operations and business processes can differ in workload drivers. Service operations are driven primarily by service requests from customers, such as calls for limousines. On the other hand, business processes can be driven primarily by transactions, such as payments, or by case files, which include bundles of related services delivered in a coordinated manner over an extended period. Differences in drivers thus can cause service operations and business processes to differ in task durations and length of resource assignments.

Overall, however, service operations and business processes are sufficiently similar that they will hereafter be referred to as simply *processes* unless a distinction is meaningful. Indeed, when a service provider performs a business process for one client, the service operation and business process may be one and the same from the service provider's viewpoint. On the other hand, when a service provider performs multiple business processes for multiple clients, service operations take on new dimensions if the processes are customized for each client or if service level agreements differ across clients. Multi-process, multi-client service operations are addressed later in this chapter.

Process Topologies

Processes can take many configurations, but most are variations on a few basic patterns. Figure 6-1 illustrates a serial process. In this pattern, most services are delivered by performing activities on the main path, but there can be inbound and outbound branches for unusual situations. For example, if the process is payroll, new employees get special handling, and employees on leave are exceptions. The constraint, Activity 1.3, has a work-in-process buffer ahead of it.

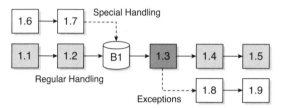

Figure 6-1 Serial process

Processing licenses at a motor vehicles office while customers are present is an example of a serial front-office process. Processing of insurance claims submitted through the mail or an agent's office is an example of a serial back-office process.

Figure 6-2 illustrates a parallel process. In this pattern, multiple servers each perform the same process concurrently for different service requesters, and one or more queues are ahead of the servers. For example, a bank with multiple tellers fits this pattern. So does a contact center in which agents receive calls via an automatic call distributor that monitors the queues.

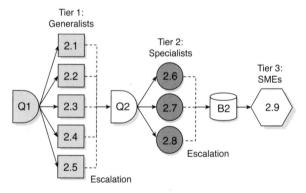

Figure 6-2 Parallel process

The figure, however, illustrates a variation on the basic parallel process pattern in which agents have peers. In the figure, issues that cannot be resolved by generalists are escalated to an appropriate specialist. Likewise, specialists can escalate issues to subject matter experts (SMEs). In some implementations, skills-based routing can send some calls directly to specialists.

Although all tiers have queues, specialists are the constraint in this example because their queue tends to be the longest, and therefore the most prone to abandoned calls. There will be times, however, when the constraint lies elsewhere. For instance, early in the day, the generalist queue may exceed the specialist queue because few issues have yet been escalated or routed to specialists. Likewise, after a major legislative or regulatory event, SMEs may be the constraint.

Figure 6-3 illustrates a hybrid process. This pattern is part parallel, part serial. For example, order-taking may be parallel, and then order fulfillment and billing/collections may be serial, thus comprising an order-to-cash process. In the figure, customers can use self-service to enter their orders, interactive voice response (IVR) to check order status, and the phone to raise issues. Having spoken to an agent, customers can be directed to the web or IVR for self-service. Orders proceed through fulfillment and billing, which may be semi- and fully automated, respectively.

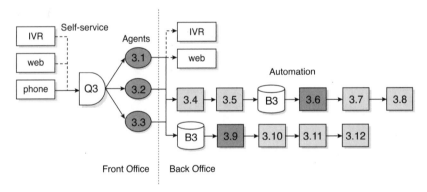

Figure 6-3 Hybrid process

Employee relocation services are another example of a hybrid process. When an employee is relocated, many front-office and back-office activities may be required to arrange documentation, moving and storage, transportation, housing, health care, schooling, and more. Those activities may be handled as separate transactions or as a case file comprising coordinated services for the entire duration.

The figure shows potential constraints in the front office as well as both paths in the back office. Therefore, the service provider might cross-train some resources so that they can alleviate more than one constraint, if necessary.

Actual process topologies are considerably more complex than these simple examples, of course. Nevertheless, the basic patterns are sufficient to illustrate why processes are prone to multiple floating constraints. A service provider performing processes on demand can attempt to define a single stable internal constraint, but even that constraint has to be flexible enough to keep up with fluctuating demand.

Services On Demand

Services on demand means that the service provider adapts to various needs and external conditions. There are, of course, several ways to adapt:

- **Real-time**—Clients or service recipients need immediate service.
- **Schedule-based**—They need it by or on a specific date and time.
- **Price-based**—They need it within their budget.
- **Result-driven**—They need it a particular way.

Timeliness, price, or results can be the dominant need. And it may or may not be possible to meet all needs simultaneously. Nonetheless, on-demand service providers strive to engineer their processes to meet more than one need when necessary:

- **Standardization**—The provider uses consistent skills, methods, software, hardware, and so on.
- **Customization**—The client needs special service.
- **Personalization**—The service recipients need special service.

Though it might seem that standardization would conflict with customization and personalization, standardization can actually support them. For example, the majority of functions built into software applications are often usable across multiple clients even though some clients or recipients have different needs. Duplicating common functions would increase the maintenance load unnecessarily. With standardization, the application for a specific client can be configured with a small number of functions unique to that client plus parameters that govern the availability and behavior of standard functions. When it's time to deliver the service, attributes of individual recipients can further determine the availability and behavior of any function.

The provider then has a maintainable application it can leverage across multiple clients. Each client gets a customized process, if necessary. And service recipients can get personalized service if that's what the client ordered. Thus, migrating clients to a standard application can improve timeliness, price, and results simultaneously. And the same can be true for manual tasks.

Services Constraints

In addition to external and internal constraints, as discussed in previous chapters, providers of services may also confront *interface constraints*, as illustrated with the dashed lines in Figure 6-4. Recall that *external constraints* are said to be in the market when clients will not buy all that the service provider could deliver. Conversely, *internal constraints* occur when the provider does not have enough capacity to deliver all the services clients would buy.

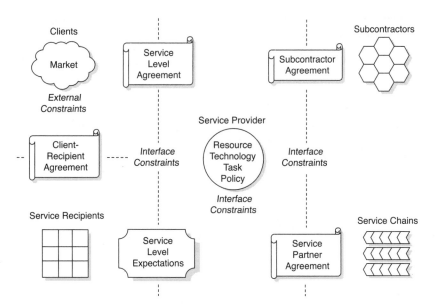

Figure 6-4 Service constraints

Interface constraints are, however, neither external nor internal. They exist literally at the interfaces between the service provider and its clients, its subcontractors, its service partners, and its recipients if they are separate from clients. If the client is a business, the recipients may be its customers, suppliers, employees, retirees, or shareholders. Or if the client is a university, the recipients may be its students, faculty, or staff. And if the client is a government, the recipients may be its citizens, aliens, or visitors.

An interface constraint applies when something at an interface prevents the provider from delivering more service, and thereby prevents the client or recipients from consuming more service than they otherwise would. For instance, if a restaurant management company (provider) has 20 waiters (subcontractors) available, and many patrons (recipients) are waiting at the restaurant (client), but the service level agreement (SLA) only allows up to 15 waiters, that's an interface constraint.

This may appear to be an external constraint that begs to be broken, but other aspects of the SLA probably explain it, such as bar revenue or kitchen safety or quality control or ambiance. Therefore, this is an interface constraint because both the client and provider have agreed to service levels that maintain a reasonable balance across multiple performance measures, each of which has to be maintained at or above some minimal level in order for the client to achieve its goal.

The service provider faces complications if the SLA with the client differs from the recipients' service level expectations, because they may be dissatisfied even if the provider meets all other terms of the SLA. The service provider likewise faces complications if the SLA is incompatible with its subcontractor or service partner agreements, because those parties may be unable or unwilling to help the provider meet the SLA. Hence, the service provider must strive to eliminate conflicts. Otherwise, it becomes impossible to satisfy all constraints simultaneously, and the provider will likely oscillate from one side to the other of the conflicts.

Service provision constraints lie on the boundary between the middle and right segments of Figure 6-4. For example, a subcontractor agreement may require additional lead time whenever the provider increases or decreases its resource requisition by more than a specified amount.

Service level constraints lie on the boundary between the left and middle segments of the figure, and they can be implicit or explicit. Business-to-consumer services typically have implicit service level expectations. For example, most restaurant patrons have informal standards for acceptable queue and service times for a given restaurant, date, and time. On the other hand, business-to-business services often have explicit SLAs. For example, a payroll service typically must deliver paychecks by a specified time each payday—no excuses.

Regardless of whether they are implicit or explicit, service level constraints govern how, when, and where services are delivered. They are, therefore, *policy constraints*—but a different kind of policy constraint from those that TOC_G typically addresses. In DBR_G, policy constraints are often internal because they include non-physical limits that manufacturers impose on themselves. For example, a no-overtime decision is a policy constraint. Service providers obviously can have internal policy constraints, too. And any enterprise can have external policy constraints, because they include laws and regulations.

Service level constraints define acceptable ranges for speed, cost, quality, and volume. For example, when the number of incoming calls to a contact center run by a service provider falls within a given range, the SLA typically specifies acceptable values for average speed of answer and average handle time. If performance on those measures becomes unacceptable, the service provider takes corrective action; otherwise, the client may be contractually entitled to a discount for that period. Note, however, that some service level constraints intentionally work in opposition. For example, the provider cannot arbitrarily cut calls short, thereby reducing average handle time, without endangering first-call resolution, an effectiveness measure, and caller satisfaction, a quality measure.

Service levels may also define the degree and pace of change. For instance, when a client engages a service provider to run a contact center, the client expects benefits beyond the business results it could attain by itself. The SLA may be negotiated to include different ranges for speed, price, volume, and quality for various periods in the contract. To make improvements attainable, the service provider may agree to introduce new technology and a streamlined process, while the client agrees to pay for these transformations. If the service provider can use its expertise, technology, and scale to offer the client better performance at a lower price overall, both the client and provider benefit.

SLAs also stipulate client responsibilities, such as forecasting inputs to the process because the client's business decisions may be the key driver. The service provider then schedules its capacity according to the forecast and adjusts capacity as required to meet deviations within a specified band. Inability to meet extraordinary demand outside the specified band does not count against the provider's performance measures. To the degree that services are provided on demand, however, the provider provides additional value to the client by reducing the impact of deviations from the forecast.

In contrast to manufacturing, where a producer tends to have either an external or internal constraint for extended periods, service providers more often have unstable constraints. Indeed, a given provider may experience external, internal, and interface constraints on the same day, if not at the same time. For example, a restaurant can have an internal constraint during lunch, an external constraint during mid-afternoon, and an interface constraint during dinner. Or an accounting firm can simultaneously be oversold in its auditing practice, undersold in its consulting practice, and limited by SLAs in its tax practice. And within a single business process, different activities may constrain *cycle time*, price, and quality.

State of the Art

Just as it was helpful in previous chapters to know the problems those other TOC_S applications solve, it will be helpful in this chapter to know the issues that DBR_S addresses. For that we need a quick review of the state of the art.

Process management methods typically boil down to steps like these:

1. Establish an SLA.
2. Forecast demand for services, covering both trend and seasonality.
3. Optimize planned capacity across all activities needed to meet the SLA.
4. Staff to maximize utilization of all resources.
5. Schedule resources within the limits of planned capacity.
6. Perform the process.
7. Execute a recovery plan after unusual events, such as demand surges or service outages.

8. Monitor service levels relative to the SLA.
9. Repeat the preceding steps as necessary to correct deviations.

Analytical queuing models are widely used to manage parallel processes. For example, Erlang models are applied in contact centers.[1] Once a demand forecast is available, such models can optimize capacity. When the assumptions become too complicated for precise solutions— blocking, abandonment, redials, self-service, multiple tiers, and virtual centers—simulation models may provide approximate solutions. In either case, *Workforce Management* (WFM) tools then are used to schedule within planned capacity.

Business Process Management (BPM) tools are increasingly used to manage serial processes, such as those performed at service centers.[2] At a minimum, BPM tools support graphical models of processes. They may also have analytical and simulation capabilities. They may operate in conjunction with middleware that automates workflows. And they may incorporate business rules that automate some activities and allow workforce management for the rest.

Of these two process patterns, the one most like manufacturing is, of course, the serial process. A serial business process is in some ways like make-to-order discrete manufacturing: A service center is analogous to a factory, and a service is analogous to a product, but there are no service inventories. Thus, this is a logical place to look for issues that DBR_S can address.

Comparing the process management steps just listed to the characteristics of traditional manufacturing described in Chapter 3, the following points of similarity emerge. Service capacity varies with the demand forecast. Service optimization therefore depends on predictability. Service capacity is balanced throughout the process. Resource utilization is maximized everywhere. Service constraints can occur anywhere. Finally, work-in-process can accumulate anywhere.

Of course, if a service provider has only an external constraint, it can readily deliver services on demand with the traditional approach, though resource utilization may suffer. In contrast, if that provider has internal or interface constraints, as most do at one time or another, delivering services on demand becomes problematic.

Consider what happens when TOC principles are applied to process management, however. Service capacity varies with actual demand rather than just a forecast. Service optimization depends on adaptability more than predictability. Service flow, not capacity, is balanced. Resource utilization is maximized at constraints, but not necessarily everywhere else. Service constraints are strategically located rather than allowed to form anywhere. Finally, work-in-process accumulates mainly ahead of the constraint, not just anywhere.

The traditional and TOC approaches to process management are summarized in Table 6-2. Details of DBR_S, the TOC approach, are covered in the following section.

Table 6-2   Process Management with Traditional Versus TOC Approach

Process Management By ...	Traditional Approach	TOC Approach
Capacity varies with ...	Demand forecast	Actual demand
Optimization depends on ...	Predictability	Adaptability
Balance is sought for ...	Capacity	Flow
Utilization is maximized ...	Everywhere	At constraints
Constraints occur ...	Anywhere	At strategic activities/resources
Work-in-process accumulates ...	Everywhere	Ahead of constraints

DBR for Services

Recall from Chapter 3 that DBR_G maximizes production by unbalancing capacity so that nonconstraints have enough sprint capacity to keep the constraint fully utilized. DBR_G does this because every hour of production lost on the constraint is an hour lost by the entire manufacturing process. DBR_G therefore schedules work on the constraint and releases only as much work into production as needed to keep the constraint fully utilized. Because process capacity is essentially fixed at any given moment, when the constraint is overloaded, active orders may finish later than their due dates, customers may cancel existing orders, or the manufacturer may decline new orders. Hence, the manufacturer controls the inputs directly and the outputs indirectly, but any change in the location of the constraint or its capacity requires production to be rescheduled.

Contrast that with a business process that must be performed on demand. The service provider may know from experience or a forecast what the general demand pattern is likely to be, but the provider may have no control over when or how many items actually enter the process. It's not practical to schedule work on the constraint if the volume of items is massive, the amount of work required for each item is impossible to determine in advance, or service must start so soon after each item is received that the schedule might never stabilize. Moreover, SLAs generally do not permit the service provider unlimited flexibility to complete items later than their due dates or to decline items. Hence, when the provider can control neither the inputs nor outputs of a process, managing process capacity—flow through the constraint—is the only viable option.

DBR_G and DBR_S are illustrated in Figure 6-5. For reference, the DBR_G section includes the same diagram used in the overview of traditional TOC in Chapter 3. In that section, RM stands for raw materials, WIP for work-in-process, and FG for finished goods, which are all forms of inventory. Solid lines represent product flow, and dashed lines represent information flow.

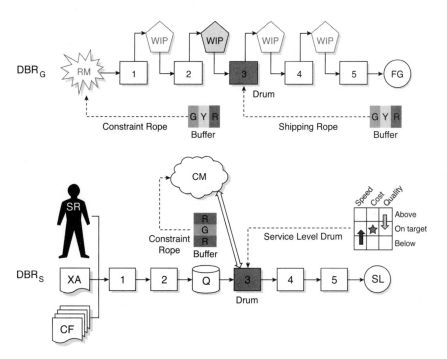

Figure 6-5 DBR for Goods versus DBR for Services

In the DBR$_S$ section, dashed lines still represent information flow, but solid lines represent service flow, which can be composed of paper or digital records rather than physical inventory. Other symbols are as follows:

- Service requests (SR) include contacts in person, as well as phone calls, faxes, and text messages.

- Transactions (XA) include paper documents and digital records received from customers, suppliers, employees, retirees, and regulators.

- Case files (CF) include bundles of related services delivered in a coordinated manner over an extended period, such as litigation, advertising, or drug trials.

- A queue (Q) can form ahead of any activity, but ahead of the drum is the most likely place.

- Capacity management (CM) is procedures, information systems, models, and rules of thumb for adjusting capacity to meet an SLA.

- Service levels (SL) can be measured in many ways, including speed (number of service requests finished within the target completion time), cost (dollars spent per case), and quality (number of transactions processed per period without error).

Of course, DBR$_G$ and DBR$_S$ each have a drum (constraint), buffer (WIP/queue), and ropes (information systems). However, their composition, arrangement, and behavior are different.

In DBR$_G$, the buffer contains the schedule of work ahead of the constraint. That buffer is unidirectional: The red zone triggers expediting to keep the constraint busy. The constraint rope governs release of work into process. The shipping rope governs work on the constraint. The buffer and both ropes are measured in units of time.

In DBR$_S$, the buffer contains the total amount of work ahead of the constraint, which is more than just the work queued immediately ahead of the constraint. That buffer is bidirectional: Either red zone may trigger a change in capacity. The constraint rope governs changes in capacity at the constraint. The service level rope governs work on the constraint. The buffer is often measured in items, the constraint rope is measured in items per period (flow rate), and the service level rope is measured according to the SLA.

DBR$_S$ can thus be implemented as follows:

- The buffer can be monitored by counting incoming SR, XA, and CF and then subtracting items closed on or before the constraint, as well as items diverted around the constraint.

- Changes in the flow rate needed to achieve service levels are translated into resource levels during capacity management. For example, if 100 agents are handling 1,000 items per hour, if the SLA requires consistent cycle time, and if the buffer level rises to 1,100 items, capacity must rise to 110 agents to maintain a consistent flow rate.

- Work on the constraint is not necessarily done first come, first served (FCFS). Priorities and due dates stipulated by the SLA may affect the order in which items are completed.

DBR$_G$ and DBR$_S$ are compared in Table 6-3. Many of the differences should be familiar at this point, because they are inherent in goods versus services. However, some differences are notable because they affect how DBR$_S$ is implemented. In DBR$_G$, the process constraint can be internal or external, but it's the same as the enterprise constraint. In DBR$_S$, the enterprise constraint is usually external, yet the dynamics of services on demand means that the process can be subject to internal or interface constraints. In DBR$_G$, capacity is relatively rigid, while in DBR$_S$, capacity is more elastic. Thus, DBR$_G$ controls a manufacturing process via buffer management, while DBR$_S$ controls a business process via capacity management.

The central principle behind DBR$_S$ is if inputs aren't controllable and an SLA imposes interface constraints, capacity has to be elastic. When buffer sizing and buffer zones drive buffer management, as in Replenishment for Services (R$_S$), covering those topics in order makes sense. But when buffer sizing and buffer zones drive capacity management, as in DBR$_S$, it's better to understand capacity management first.

Table 6-3   DBR for Goods Versus DBR for Services

	DBR_G	DBR_S
Process types are ...	Manufacturing process	Business process on demand
	Service operations as available	Service operations on demand
Primary resources are ...	Physical capital	Intellectual capital
	Labor	Skills
Process customization is ...	Unusual	Common
Process repeatability is ...	High	Moderate to high
Automation is ...	High	Variable
Work-in-process inventory is ...	Tangible	Intangible
Finished-goods inventory is ...	Common	Impossible
Connection to customers is ...	Transportation	Direct or transmission
Production is determined by ...	Customer due dates	Demand level
	Constraint availability	Service level agreement
Work discipline is ...	First come, first served (FCFS)	Priorities and due dates
Buffer is ...	Time (unidirectional)	Items (bidirectional)
Constraint rope is ...	Time	Items per period (flow rate)
Shipping rope is ...	Time	Service levels
Enterprise constraint is ...	Internal or external	External
Process constraint is ...	Same as enterprise constraint	Internal or interface
Capacity is relatively ...	Fixed	Elastic
Process is controlled with ...	Buffer management	Capacity management

Elastic Capacity

Adjusting the flow rate through the constraint is the essence of capacity management in DBR_S. Unless capacity on the constraint significantly exceeds average demand, random variability in demand and service times will naturally generate a queue ahead of the constraint, and possibly elsewhere. Queues are not necessarily harmful, however, even when services must be delivered on demand.

The significance of queues depends on how *queue times* and *service times* relate to the SLA. Figure 6-6 illustrates how excessive queue time (white arrows) can turn on-time performance into late completion even when service times (grey arrows) are consistent. As the queue ahead of the constraint grows, so does queue time. And if additional queues form ahead of activities before or after the constraint, their queue times add to overall cycle time, perhaps pushing it beyond the SLA if those additional queues are not transient.

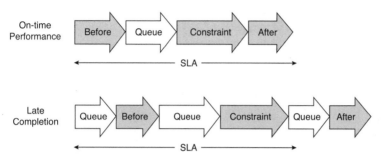

Figure 6-6   Service time, queue time, and service level

To illustrate some dynamics of capacity management, Figure 6-7 compares rigid capacity to elastic capacity for a given process. In all scenarios, service time is constant, and demand follows the same simple sine wave pattern: It starts at 100 items per period, rises to 110, falls to 90, and then rises back to 100. *Backlog* is the amount of work going through the process at a given moment, so it includes items being processed or sitting in queues.

Capacity management is different in each scenario. Consequently, the backlog and utilization lines display dramatically different patterns. Of course, no business process behaves quite so smoothly, but even these simple scenarios are sufficient to illustrate some key points. More-realistic assumptions are illustrated in Appendix B, "Process Simulation."

In the top scenario, capacity is fixed at average demand: 100 items per period. As demand rises above capacity, the backlog grows. Once demand falls below capacity in Period 25, the backlog shrinks. Utilization, plotted against the right axis, is consistently 99 percent or higher. Thus, when capacity is stable, the backlog is dynamic. (The denominator of the utilization ratio in this example excludes all non-billable time, including vacations, holidays, and training.)

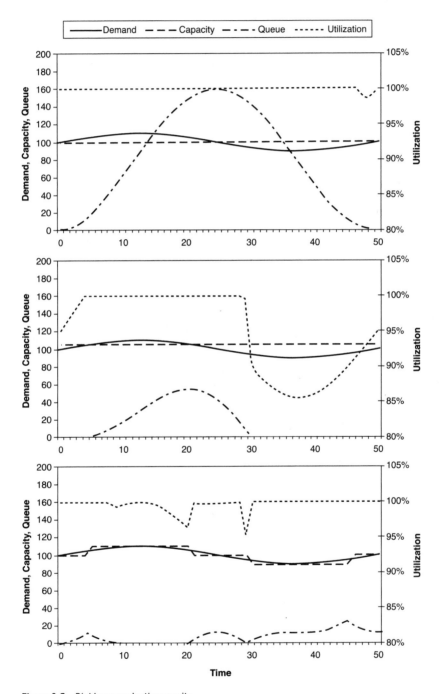

Figure 6-7 Rigid versus elastic capacity

In the middle scenario, capacity is fixed at 5 percent above average demand, or 105 items per period. Until demand rises above capacity in Period 5, there is no backlog, and utilization is less than 100 percent. Eventually, the backlog grows, but its peak is much lower than in the previous scenario. Once demand falls below capacity in Period 20, the backlog begins to shrink rapidly to zero. And without a backlog of work, the excess capacity in later periods leads to substantially lower utilization. Thus, when capacity is stable, there's a trade-off between reduced backlog and consistently high utilization.

In the bottom scenario, capacity is elastic: It moves in fairly coarse steps of 10 units, or about 10 percent of average capacity. The backlog rises and falls with disparities between demand and capacity, but the peaks are even lower than in the previous scenario. When the backlog falls to zero, utilization declines, but only momentarily. Thus, with elastic capacity there is no trade-off between reduced backlog and consistently high utilization: It's possible to have both at once without compromise.

Note that the middle scenario uses 5 percent more capacity than the top scenario. On the other hand, the bottom scenario uses exactly the same overall capacity as the top scenario. The bottom scenario just manages it more effectively over time.

Also note that queue times differ substantially across scenarios. In the top scenario, average queue time is 0.78 periods, and variance is high. In the middle scenario, it falls to 0.15 periods, and variance is moderate. But in the bottom scenario, it falls further to 0.08 periods, and variance is small. Moreover, maximum queue time in the top scenario (1.59 periods) is more than five times as long as in the bottom scenario (0.28 periods).

Thus, depending on the SLA, some scenarios might not produce cycle times short enough for services on demand. Moreover, when the constraint shifts between internal and external, elastic capacity outperforms rigid capacity on every measure.

Capacity Management

If each time period in the scenarios just discussed represents one week, Replenishment for Services (R_S) can yield elastic capacity like the bottom scenario. On the other hand, if each time period represents one hour, R_S cannot adjust capacity fast enough. Hence, R_S is quite applicable to DBR_S for capacity management requiring a change in the number of resources, but alternative methods must be used during time frames too short for resource changes.

Scheduling covers normal working hours, overtime hours, days off, and on-call hours for existing resources. It thus handles predictable short-term demand patterns. For example, resources can be rescheduled from projects to processes during peak season, and then back to projects during the off-peak season.

Scheduling also covers key events in the business process itself. For example, because service center contacts often spike shortly after bills are issued, spreading billing dates throughout the month, and away from peak days of the week, helps smooth demand.

Adjustment covers demand outside the normal range by adding or cutting time worked by some resources as needed to respond to exploding or vanishing backlogs. It thus handles unpredictable short-term demand patterns. Adjustments can be handled via flextime, which gives workers some control over timing. And telecommuting may reduce the delay in implementing adjustments.

Adjustment also covers information technology handling fully and semi-automated processes. For example, bringing up additional web servers as needed can keep response time within the thresholds defined by an SLA. And with virtual web servers, this adjustment can be quite rapid.

Deflection covers extraordinary demand that even adjustments cannot handle:

- *Channel shifting* provides service through different means, such as using a kiosk or IVR system instead of a live agent to give or get routine information.

- *Space shifting* provides service from an alternative location, such as a remote service center with available capacity instead of a local center that's overloaded.

- *Time shifting* provides service at another time, such as callbacks that convert current inbound calls into later outbound calls.

Deflection is thus an alternative to queuing. Moreover, if service recipient expectations are managed well, it can be seen as a better alternative than waiting in line or on hold.

These capacity management methods make service capacity elastic over quite different time scales ranging from months to seconds. Yet not all capacity changes come through management actions. If individual or team performance evaluations are tied to meeting an SLA, workers themselves can adjust their personal and team productivity by working smarter during peak periods and emergencies.

Buffer Sizing

Buffer sizing for DBR_G typically starts with a rule of thumb, and then the buffer size is increased if holes appear in the schedule and is decreased if excess work-in-process accumulates. The DBR_G section in Figure 6-8 illustrates two rules of thumb that yield approximately the same result. One rule of thumb is to initialize the buffer at half the original lead time ahead of the constraint because most of it is queue time that will disappear under DBR_G. An alternative rule of thumb is to initialize the buffer at three times the service time of activities preceding the constraint. In either case, the resulting buffer size is the length of the constraint rope that governs release of work into production.

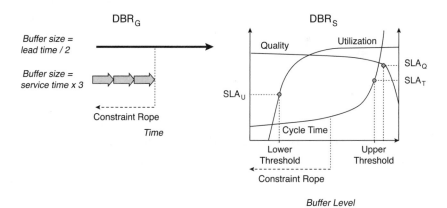

Figure 6-8   Buffer sizing

Alas, there are no rules of thumb for buffer sizing in DBR_S. There are, however, guidelines. The DBR_S section in Figure 6-8 illustrates how buffer levels are related to cycle time, utilization, and quality. These relationships are used to size the buffer, which includes all items upstream from the constraint. The length of the constraint rope is the buffer level, which capacity management uses to determine an appropriate flow rate at the constraint. Unlike DBR_G, where the length of the constraint rope is constant, the length of the constraint rope in DBR_S is variable within limits.

When items have consistent service time and are too numerous to track separately, the buffer can be sized in terms of the number of items. Alternatively, when items vary widely in service time and are few enough to track separately, the buffer can be sized in terms of the work expected. The first alternative works as follows:

- The first step is to understand how increases in the buffer level affect cycle time. At low buffer levels, cycle time is at its minimum because it includes only service time. As the buffer level grows, cycle time rises gradually due to increasing queue time. However, once the average number of incoming items exceeds the flow rate through the constraint, queues and cycle time rise rapidly.

- The second step is to understand the effect on utilization. At low buffer levels, utilization is low because there's not enough work-in-process to keep resources busy. As the buffer level grows, utilization rises steadily due to reduced idle time. However, once incoming items approach the maximum flow rate through the constraint, thereby keeping resources continuously busy, utilization levels off at its maximum, which may exceed 100 percent.

- The third step is to understand the effect on quality. At low buffer levels, quality is high because there's plenty of time to work carefully. As the buffer grows, quality may decline slightly. However, once incoming items approach the maximum flow rate through the constraint, quality may decline markedly due to haste.

The middle range of these curves—where they are all approximately horizontal—represents *dynamic equilibrium*. Within that range, incoming and outgoing items are roughly equal because demand fluctuations either average out on their own or are handled by capacity management. If the buffer level drops below that range, however, the process is starved for work. And if it rises above, the process is swamped with work. Thus, suitable places for buffer thresholds are somewhere around the knees of the curves.

- The fourth step in buffer sizing is to identify where the service level agreement for cycle time (SLA_T) meets the cycle time curve, because that often determines the upper threshold on the buffer. When cycle time rises above SLA_T for a specified duration or for a specified percentage of items, the service provider is no longer meeting the SLA.

- The fifth step is to identify where the service level agreement for utilization (SLA_U) meets the utilization curve, because that determines the lower threshold on the buffer. When utilization drops below SLA_U, the service provider is not meeting the SLA. In many contracts, the SLA actually quantifies this relationship in terms of the provider's price rather than utilization. But the service provider can translate utilization into price, so the relationship is essentially the same, even though it is indirect.

- The sixth and final step is to identify where the service level agreement for quality (SLA_Q) meets the quality curve, because that determines the upper threshold if quality dominates cycle time. When quality drops below SLA_Q, the service provider is no longer meeting the SLA. For instance, SLA_Q may tolerate only a certain number of errors per thousand items processed.

These upper and lower thresholds thus define a target buffer range rather than a single buffer size. Note, however, that where the cycle time, utilization, and quality curves cross one another is arbitrary, and therefore meaningless, because they are plotted against independent vertical axes. The curves could have been plotted on separate charts, but instead they were combined into a single chart to illustrate how various terms of the same SLA translate into one pair of buffer thresholds.

The location and shape of each curve can change over time. Indeed, resource, process, and technical transformations are intended to do precisely that. For example, as skills improve, as the process is simplified, or as activities are automated, the thresholds may move apart. This topic is explored further in Chapter 10, "Implementation and Technology."

Clients generally want service providers to drive down cycle time, drive up utilization, and drive up quality, thereby pushing each threshold toward the middle. Conversely, service providers must be careful not to agree to SLAs so tight that capacity management is forever in danger of letting the buffer level slip past a threshold. A well-designed process requires adjustment occasionally, not continuously. If unpredictable demand fluctuations are wider than the thresholds that would result from the SLA under negotiation, both the service provider and client should be wary.

Finally, recognize that these buffer sizing guidelines are based on a conceptual model that may be impossible to quantify precisely in practice. Some processes receive input batches or must produce output batches rather than continuous flows, so their buffer levels rise and fall naturally over a wide range. Though service times are often relatively consistent for the majority of items flowing through business processes, some items may have much higher service times. And contracts containing SLAs for complex services can be hundreds of pages long. Nonetheless, service providers know at least approximately where the knees of the curves are, and they can use that as a reference for locating buffer thresholds even if they can't quantify the curves.

Buffer Zones

As seen in previous TOC applications, *buffer zones* are decision aids. In the unidirectional buffer of DBR$_G$, the green zone means no action is required, the yellow zone means prepare for action, and the red zone means take action to keep the constraint busy. The bidirectional buffer of DBR$_S$, however, has two red zones: The low one triggers a decrease in capacity, while the high one triggers an increase.

Using buffer thresholds from the preceding section to set DBR$_S$ buffer zones directly would not be appropriate because the process would already be missing the SLA by the time the buffer level strayed into a red zone. Instead, buffer zones should be set where they will allow sufficient lead time for capacity changes to be enacted before the buffer level passes either threshold.

One way to do that is to inset the red zone boundaries relative to the thresholds by the net change in the buffer level expected during time to change capacity. Figure 6-9, a subset of the previous figure, shows the zone boundaries being inset from the thresholds by the mean plus standard deviation of net change.

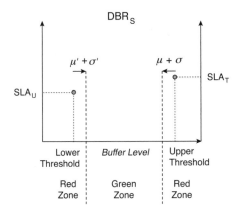

Figure 6-9 Buffer zones

The less time required to change capacity, the smaller the inset can be, and the closer the zone boundaries can be to the thresholds. For example, if it takes two hours to call more resources in to work, the inset would have to be much wider than if it takes only a few minutes to begin deflecting excess incoming items to an IVR. Likewise, if it takes 20 minutes to activate another physical web server but only a minute or two to activate another virtual web server, virtual servers allow a smaller inset, and therefore a wider green zone.

The insets do not have to be symmetric. For instance, if it takes two hours to call in more resources, but they're then each contractually guaranteed four hours of paid overtime, the time to increase the on-call capacity is shorter than the time to decrease it.

In a manner similar to R_S, when the buffer level crosses into a red zone, the process manager has to decide whether to adjust capacity. For instance, if a spike in inputs occurs shortly before the time when inputs typically decline, adjusting capacity would be inappropriate, because the situation will likely correct itself after a brief decline in performance.

Rather than increasing capacity every time the buffer level strays into the upper red zone, different delay tolerances by some service recipients may be used to deflect selected inputs. For instance, some recipients with nonurgent needs will opt for self-service—or try again later—when told that their estimated queue time is more than a few minutes. Self-service is a powerful alternative because it can handle the majority of items in some processes at a fraction of the cost of live agents.

It may also be possible to increase the delay tolerance of some service recipients. Bars in restaurants, mirrors in elevator lobbies, and exhibits near valet parking are all subtle methods of making people less aware of or anxious about delays. In a business process, one way to accomplish this is to provide feedback via automatic e-mail or text messages as each step of the process is completed. Another way is to allow service recipients to check on the progress of their service request or transaction by visiting a web portal whenever they want.

Capacity Constrained Resources

In manufacturing, nonconstraints have spare capacity by definition. However, some nonconstraints may have relatively little spare capacity. When a nonconstraint has the potential to become the *bottleneck* in a manufacturing process because it cannot always sprint fast enough to keep the constraint busy and complete orders on time, it's called a *capacity constrained resource* (CCR). Whenever the constraint gains capacity, through capital investment or additional shifts, CCRs usually need additional capacity as well. Otherwise, a CCR may become the new constraint.

Of course, services enterprises have CCRs, too. Therefore, whenever a red zone triggers capacity management, the capacity of CCRs must be adjusted along with the constraint. How and when CCR capacity is managed depends, however, on the specific process being managed. The development of quantitative models for such situations is called *applied analytics*.

If overall process cycle time is short, and the constraint and CCRs are not used in constant ratios, the changes have to be calculated to provide adequate sprint capacity. Moreover, if the process is lengthy, CCRs ahead of the constraint may need their capacity changed well before the workload reaches the constraint, while CCRs behind the constraint may need their capacity changes delayed until the workload changes have passed the constraint. Thus, the buffer level ahead of the constraint triggers capacity management, but capacity management applies to the entire process, not just the constraint.

Cross-trained resources can alleviate some shortages, but facilities and technology can impose limits. For example, if there's not enough workspace or network capacity, it may not matter whether there are enough cross-trained workers. Likewise, there may not be enough computer processing or storage capacity for extraordinary demands, such as when an unplanned surge in demand coincides with a regular processing cycle.

Figure 6-10 shows capacity for tasks comprising a process. The tops of the solid floating bars represent the maximum flow rate that can be scheduled with resources currently available. The bottoms represent the minimum flow rate that achieves the utilization or cost assumptions in the SLA.

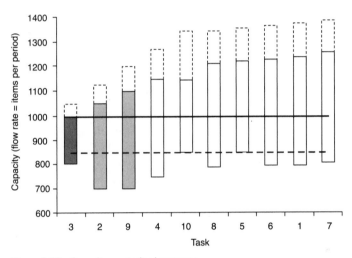

Figure 6-10 Capacity constrained resources

A flow rate higher than the top of any solid bar will require sprinting. Sprint capacity is shown as dashed bars atop the floating bars.

Task 3 is the internal constraint because it has the lowest maximum, as indicated by the solid horizontal line. However, Task 2 has only 5 percent spare capacity, so it's clearly a CCR. Likewise, Task 9 has only 10 percent to spare, so it's probably a CCR, too.

The dashed horizontal line marks the highest minimum, which helps in identifying tasks that would have excess capacity if the flow rate fell below that amount. That is, if the rate dropped below this line, Tasks 5 and 10 would be the first ones with low utilization.

Unlike manufacturing, where standard paths through the process are predefined for each product, the paths some items take through a business process may not be predefined. Key decisions may be made at many points, thereby making it impossible to predict all paths, even for work already in process. This dynamic behavior can make it economically infeasible to unbalance capacity to the extent that CCRs never become bottlenecks. Nevertheless, DBR$_S$ relies on unbalanced capacity to optimize the process.

Unbalanced Capacity

In DBR$_G$, *unbalanced capacity* means the constraint governs the process, most nonconstraints never are a bottleneck, and even CCRs are only transient bottlenecks. In contrast, unbalanced capacity means something different in DBR$_S$ because the capacity of every resource, including the constraint, is usually adjustable within limits.

Although the limits may be tightest around the constraint, business processes and the resources who perform them can be quite adaptable:

- **Generalist/specialist model**—If resources can shift between nonconstrained and constrained tasks, even the constraint can sprint. For instance, if the constraint in a business process is a task requiring general skills, specialists can augment generalists working on the constraint when necessary.

- **Expert/assistant model**—If nonexperts can perform some tasks, experts can concentrate on tasks that do require expertise. For instance, as demand for legal expertise increases, increasing paralegal capacity can enable attorneys to focus more of their time on the constrained task.

- **Master/apprentice model**—If resources with lower skills can be substituted for resources with higher skills, more items can be handled. For instance, junior staff accountants can handle simple accounts with minimal supervision, and by assisting senior staff accountants with complex accounts, the junior staff grow their skills.

- **Near/remote model**—If resources with critical skills are available remotely, and portions of the process can be performed remotely, that can relieve a constraint at the nearest service center. For instance, a remote service center can access records from afar and transmit results back to the near center—or directly to service recipients.

■ **Primary/secondary model**—If an interface constraint supersedes an internal constraint, the spare resources are available to be used elsewhere. For instance, they can assist with marketing, sales, training, intellectual capital, and research into new services.

Even though capacity management under DBR_S applies to all resources, there are several reasons to engineer a process with unbalanced capacity. They all aim to simplify process management.

First, balanced capacity is particularly elusive when services must be delivered on demand because the volume and mix of services is less predictable. Trying to balance capacity overall or tie capacity management to anything other than the true constraint will likely just bump into its limits anyway.

Second, the constraint may provide flood control for downstream tasks, thereby dampening their volatility. Engineering a particular activity or resource type as the constraint can place the main work queues at specific locations in the process. Management attention can then change to balancing work flow rather than capacity.

Finally, if you don't pick a strategic constraint, a nonstrategic constraint may pick you. A nonstrategic constraint may encourage undifferentiated services, motivate price reductions, and maximize utilization. In contrast, a strategic constraint can create competitive advantage, serve targeted market segments, and maximize profit.

Locating Constraints

DBR_G has several methods for finding the current constraint. They can be used separately or together.

First, insider knowledge relies on past engineering and current experience to focus on the likely constraint. For instance, if production is all too often stalled by repairs on a complex machine that was supposed to be more productive than the old machines it replaced, that new machine may be the active constraint. Even insiders can be wrong, however. The belief that constraints are everywhere is a symptom that insiders are still focused on utilization and balanced capacity.

Second, direct observation uncovers the constraint by noting which activity or resource type is often working feverishly while others don't have enough work to keep every resource busy. Direct observation can be done by outsiders with no preconceived notions or by insiders if they truly observe the process.

Finally, picking an activity or resource and implementing DBR_G around it will reveal the true constraint, even if the initial choice is wrong, because the real constraint will stand out as DBR_G draws off the excess work-in-process. It's like draining a pond: No matter where you start, the tallest rock or stump—the constraint—will stick out farthest.

These methods for finding the active constraint work for DBR_S, too. However, because services on demand are dynamic, the methods may have to be applied over a wider range of operating conditions to locate all the constraints and CCRs. Though there can be more than one constraint, the number is typically small. Thus, even for a complex process, just a handful of distinct capacity management scenarios can be sufficient for all but extraordinary circumstances.

The location of current constraints and CCRs can be accidental. Furthermore, precedent and competitive positioning may conspire to put them where they impede rather than support an enterprise's strategy. For example, if a particular services market has been dominated by niche strategies, it can be hard to make the jump to a full-service strategy. Likewise, a national services strategy may not scale internationally. Nevertheless, such strategic transformations may be necessary to grow and optimize the enterprise.

Strategic Constraints

Having a *strategic constraint* means its location is intentional, not accidental. This matter is explored more in Chapter 9, "Strategy and Change," but it's worth noting a few key aspects here because the most effective implementations of DBR rely on strategic constraints.

In DBR_G, a strategic constraint maximizes net profit in both the short and long term. If the constraint is external, this means choosing an assortment of products that appeal to customers. If the constraint is internal, it means refusing some orders, and perhaps dropping some products, because others are more profitable. An underlying assumption, therefore, is that such decisions won't hurt future business.

Similar decisions and the same assumption apply when services are delivered as available, but not necessarily when services are delivered on demand. When DBR_S is subject to interface constraints, refusing some requests or dropping some services may not possible. Then again, directly maximizing the provider's net profit isn't the only criterion for locating a strategic constraint. Here are some others:

- Put the strategic constraint where adjustment time is shortest because this fosters adaptability and shorter cycle time leads to higher service recipient satisfaction.

- Locate the strategic constraint where it creates the widest buffer range associated with dynamic stability because this minimizes capacity changes—and their cost.

- Set the strategic constraint where the process yields highest quality because that's the client's overriding concern.

- Leave the strategic constraint where additional resources are not generally available, but make sure all nonstrategic resources fully support those strategic resources by off-loading all nonessential work.

These alternative criteria for locating a strategic constraint in DBR_S are intended to achieve the same goal as DBR_G: Maximize the service provider's net profit in both the short and long term. However, they do this by maximizing client value because it ultimately drives net profit, a topic that is explored further in later chapters.

Process Improvement

There are other approaches to *process improvement* besides TOC, of course.[3] Advocates of each approach cite legitimate success stories.

A common pitfall in practice, however, is to attempt to improve anything and everything that can be improved. That's disruptive and expensive, so a more targeted approach may prevail. Specifically, what to change and how to change it are key questions. Contrary to conventional wisdom, harvesting "low-hanging fruit" is another potential pitfall. Both pitfalls are based on the assumption that local optimizations add up to global optimization, which simply isn't true.

One distinctive aspect of TOC is its focus on constraints.[4] When considering what to improve and how to improve it, DBR_S steers process improvements to constraints. Indeed, nonconstraints that could be improved often should not be improved, because the investment would not lift overall performance.

Nevertheless, SLAs generally include multiple objectives, which means they can be subject to multiple constraints. For instance, decreasing processing time on the constraint decreases overall cycle time. Although automating or eliminating a nonconstraint may not decrease cycle time as much as it decreases overall cost, cost may be the dominant constraint, especially during extreme swings in demand. Likewise, increasing processing time on the most error-prone activity may have a minor effect on cycle time, but a major effect on quality, which can be considerably more subjective in services than in manufacturing. Precisely the same service, delivered to different recipients, can yield vastly different perceptions of quality.

A dilemma for service providers is that the amount of change that can be accomplished in the short term is always far less than what can be accomplished in the long term, yet clients generally want as much change as possible during the early years of a services contract in order to maximize value. Improving the constraint not only creates the most leverage, it also helps front-load the improvements.

Shared Service Centers

When a service provider performs multiple processes for multiple clients, service operations take on new dimensions, particularly if those processes are customized for each client or if SLAs differ across clients. A *shared service center* (SSC) is composed of the people, information, equipment, technology, and physical facilities needed to perform such processes.

SSCs enable service providers to generate economies of scale from multiple clients and economies of scope from multiple processes. Furthermore, a network of well-placed SSCs gives a service provider broader geographic coverage or "reach." When SSCs back up each other, this creates greater protection against natural and man-made risks.

Then again, even the benefits of scale, scope, and reach are not limitless. Beyond the optimal size, SSC unit costs grow rather than shrink. So self-service and automation are necessary adjuncts.

SSCs can be actual or virtual. That is, elements of an SSC often are, but do not have to be, located at one physical site. For example, some people may work on-site, while others have remote offices, and still others are mobile, which means they connect to the service provider's network and work from various locations as needed. Distinct SSCs exist when they have separate management, perform different processes, serve different geographic areas or time zones, or handle different languages or cultures.

SSCs are relevant to DBR$_S$ because they create added leverage. First, aggregation of service requests from multiple clients dampens random variability. Second, acquiring clients with counter-cyclical demand dampens systematic variability. Third, sharing facilities and resources increases flexibility during capacity management. Unfortunately, some benefits of SSCs cannot be fully realized if a client insists on having its service separated, so service providers must factor that into their SLAs, pricing decisions, and service center configurations.

Impact of DBR for Services

Table 6-4 compares process management via the balance capacity approach to DBR$_S$. In a process managed toward balanced capacity, there can be a trade-off between predictability and performance: The less predictable demand is, the more erratic overall cycle time is because the process is engineered to meet a forecast that's less accurate. The primary impact of DBR$_S$ is to make a process more adaptable to unpredictable demand while at the same time reducing its overall cycle time, thereby resolving the conflict.

Table 6-4 Balanced Capacity Versus DBR for Services

Process Management By ...	Balanced Capacity	DBR$_S$
Capacity adjustments are driven by ...	Forecast	Buffer level
Adjustments are done ...	Periodically	As needed
Optimization depends on ...	Predictability	Adaptability
Prevailing constraint is often ...	Internal	Interface or external
Internal constraints are ...	Floating	Stable
Queues build ...	Anywhere	Ahead of constraint
Primary goal is ...	High utilization everywhere	Short cycle time
Secondary goal is ...	Short cycle time	High utilization of constraint
Balance is sought for ...	Capacity	Flow
Service is delivered ...	As available	On demand

DBR_S can do this because considerable cycle time in a serial process with balanced capacity is composed of queue time, not service time. Under DBR_S, the longest queue time often occurs when items reach the constraint. As queue time decreases elsewhere, so can excess resources because they're no longer needed to protect cycle time. In other words, there's less running hard everywhere to catch up, and more running hard only when it's necessary to keep up.

Close tolerances in the balanced capacity approach also generate floating constraints, which can appear to be ubiquitous constraints. When a process is short on capacity everywhere, capacity has to be added everywhere. In contrast, when DBR_S is short on capacity at the constraint, capacity has to be added at the constraint, and perhaps at the CCRs, but not necessarily elsewhere.

Several DBR_S outcomes are noteworthy:

- Whereas the balanced capacity approach pushes items through processes for utilization, DBR_S pulls items through processes to achieve SLAs. In addition, DBR_S pulls resources as needed via R_S. And DBR_S pulls projects via CC_S as needed to implement process and technology improvements.

- DBR_S is accommodating, which is essential for delivering services on demand.

- DBR_S is scalable. Indeed, the more clients and processes the better, because aggregation smoothes demand and shared resources create flexibility.

- DBR_S and DBR_G are compatible. A single enterprise can use them simultaneously if it does both manufacturing and service. And pure service providers can use DBR_G for services as available while at the same time using DBR_S for services on demand.

Compared to other TOC_S applications seen so far, DBR_S is more complicated than either R_S or CC_S because SLAs usually contain multiple performance measures, and capacity adjustments have to occur on demand, if not in real time. In contrast, neither R_S nor CC_S has to occur on demand to support services on demand. Furthermore, over the life of a services contract, the client and service provider will typically modify the SLAs more than once because the client's needs change or the service provider's capabilities change.

Information technology (IT) plays vital roles in DBR$_S$. It's used for self-service and automation, for applied analytics and capacity management, and to transmit data to and receive results from SSCs. Without IT, communication delays are often second only to queue time in contribution to overall cycle time. With IT, cost to perform a business process is typically a fraction of what it would be without IT.

As noted earlier, to maximize its benefits, the constraint that drives an implementation of DBR$_S$ should be strategic. But locating a constraint strategically requires an understanding of finance and accounting as they apply to services on demand. These are topics of the next chapter.

Summary

Queuing Theory is a mainstay of stable processes. Services on demand are, however, characterized by demand and supply that are unstable at times, which makes Queuing Theory harder to apply.

When processing capacity is rigid, Drum-Buffer-Rope for Goods (DBR$_G$) can be used to maximize net profit. On the other hand, when services must be delivered on demand, rigid capacity cannot meet SLAs. Hence, DBR for Services (DBR$_S$) uses buffer levels and zones at the constraint to manage elastic capacity. The management challenge is then to maximize client value because it ultimately drives the service provider's net profit.

Setting the buffer size and zones is more complicated in DBR$_S$ than DBR$_G$ because SLAs typically contain separate objectives for cycle time, cost, and quality. Optimizing any one without regard for the others has serious consequences, so DBR$_S$ implementation must consider all relevant objectives.

DBR$_S$ is directly applicable to serial processes because it balances flow. However, when a parallel process is tiered so items can flow between tiers, DBR$_S$ may apply.

Compared to DBR$_G$ in manufacturing, the constraint in DBR$_S$ can flip from external to internal and back much more rapidly. Furthermore, DBR$_S$ is often subject to interface constraints, which are not recognized in DBR$_G$.

In contrast to the conventional balanced-capacity approach to services management, DBR$_S$ turns the push for high utilization everywhere into the pull of service levels. Moreover, DBR_S simplifies capacity management because queues build in fewer places and it isn't always necessary to adjust capacity at every point in the process simultaneously.

Hence, DBR_S enables a service provider to deliver services on demand, even when demand is unpredictable. Ways to amplify the benefits of DBR_S include locating constraints strategically, applying process improvements to constraints, and using shared service centers.

Endnotes

1. Ger Koole, *Call Center Mathematics*, www.math.vu.nl/obp/callcenters, 2005.

2. J. Sinur, "Business Process Management Suites Will Be the Next Big Thing," *Gartner Analyst InSight*, RAS Core Research Note G00125461, February 2005.

3. Dave Nave, "How to Compare Six Sigma, Lean and the Theory of Constraints," *Quality Progress*, March 2002, pp. 73–78.

4. Domenico Lepore and Oded Cohen, *Deming and Goldratt*, North River Press, 1999.

7

Finance and Accounting

As covered in previous chapters, various applications of Theory of Constraints for Services (TOC$_S$) can be used to manage resources, projects, and processes. These are the basic building blocks for services on demand. However, effective constraints management requires different information than many services enterprises have used before. And none of the TOC$_S$ applications covered previously deal with investment decisions or performance measurement at the business unit or enterprise levels. These are among the topics covered in this chapter.

Recall from Chapter 3, "Theory of Constraints," that the original Throughput Accounting (TA) application is a radical alternative to the dominant management accounting method, Cost Accounting (CA). TA is radical because it discards some vestiges from an earlier era while reversing typical management priorities. As the product mix decision example showed, TA is notable because it can find profitable alternatives that CA overlooks.

Thus, like the TOC applications already seen, TA runs counter to conventional wisdom:

- CA leads a quest for universally high utilization, on the assumption that local optimizations add up to global optimization. TA, on the other hand, drives global optimization directly, even if that means some parts of the enterprise cannot have high utilization.

- TA differs markedly from CA in its treatment of inventory. Whereas CA creates incentives to build inventory, sometimes to excess, TA creates strong incentives to minimize inventory.

- While CA relies heavily on product costs to drive decision-making, TA makes no use of product costs whatsoever. There simply is no product cost construct in TA.

Whether TA applies to services enterprises, such as those found in the Professional, Scientific, and Technical Services (PSTS) sector, has so far been an unanswered question. After all, such enterprises often have little or no physical products and inventory, so the absence of product costs and the incentive to minimize inventory would seem to have little relevance. On the other hand, utilization measures are such a pillar of labor-based services management that their replacement would have to be an extremely convincing alternative.

Given its heritage, the original TA application will be referred to as *TA for Goods* (TA_G). A version previously adapted for software, and summarized in Appendix C, "Throughput Accounting for Software," will be referred to as *TA for Software Engineering* (TA_E) and *TA for Software Business* (TA_B). The version adapted here for services will be referred to as *TA for Services* (TA_S). This chapter covers how and why TA_S is different from TA_G, but it also contrasts TA_S with CA, which is still the dominant management accounting method in services, too.

Decision-Making in Services

Executives, managers, and practitioners in every services enterprise wrestle with conflicts. Each of the TOC_S applications seen in previous chapters is designed to resolve specific conflicts without compromise because that eliminates the all-too-common oscillation from side to side of those conflicts. TA_S does likewise.

Although all other TOC_S applications do rely on measures, none of them incorporates a complete and consistent set of measurements outside their specific domain: resources, projects, or processes. This chapter therefore covers measures that can resolve conflicts throughout a services enterprise.

Capacity versus utilization is a classic services conflict. Service providers need adequate capacity to grow, but they also need high utilization to maintain profitability. As seen earlier, prevailing practice is often to adjust capacity by hiring to plan or hiring to deal. Alternatively, capacity can be adjusted on demand using Replenishment for Services (R_S). Because R_S is typically used by resource managers, however, it doesn't necessarily affect the decisions of project and process managers or the behavior of individual practitioners.

Local versus global optimization is a conflict that many enterprises, including service providers, don't even realize they have. As seen in previous chapters, most enterprises generally just try to optimize individual resources, projects, and processes because conventional wisdom says this is the best route to optimizing the enterprise. However, it's possible for individual resources, projects, or processes to do well while the enterprise does poorly if it has excess capacity or it fails to invest sufficiently in systems, skills, intellectual capital, and assets that will sustain it in the future. Critical Chain for Services (CC_S) optimizes projects and

Drum-Buffer-Rope for Services (DBR$_S$) optimizes processes, but these applications provide no guidance on the right level of investment.

Cost versus revenue is another classic services conflict. Service providers in the PSTS sector have traditionally based their prices on billable hours because their services are labor-intensive. As cost goes up, price goes up and demand goes down. As cost goes down, price goes down and demand goes up. Of course, none of this has much to do with the value that clients see. So as client needs become more strategic and as service providers develop reusable assets, value pricing becomes more attractive for both parties. Likewise, as funding requirements rise and client risks increase, risk-reward sharing becomes more attractive to both parties. There are, however, other issues. For instance, speed itself has value because a project completed early starts the client's benefits sooner. Although CC$_S$ enables speedier projects and DBR$_S$ enables shorter cycle time for processes with variable demand, they do not apply at the enterprise level, nor do they address the impact that speed has on either the client or the provider. Furthermore, interactions between cost, revenue, value, risk, and speed can be hard to quantify.

Investment versus delivery is a conflict often seen in PSTS because the same resources may produce intellectual capital and assets as well as deliver services based on them. Service providers must deliver services to generate revenue and profit, of course, but they must also invest in skills, intellectual capital, and assets to maintain their expertise, which is the foundation for sales in the PSTS sector. Investments are rarely billable activities because their connection to sales and delivery is seldom direct. Thus, finding the right level of investment is often more art than science, and natural forces tend to push against investments. For instance, when demand is low and resources are available for training and development of intellectual capital and assets, pressure to contain costs is high. Conversely, when demand is high and resources have little time for training and development projects, more investment funds are available.

Asset-based versus labor-based services is a relatively recent conflict to emerge in the PSTS sector. Because sales are made on expertise and reputations are kept by delivering on expertise, labor-based services still dominate the sector. Furthermore, the extensive customization that characterizes PSTS makes construction and utilization of reusable assets difficult. Nevertheless, technology now enables assets to substitute for some labor on a widening array of tasks. For instance, design tools now enable architects and engineers to eliminate entire steps because they can be confident that parts and subassemblies will fit precisely after fabrication. Likewise, search tools now enable junior resources to locate legal, scientific, or engineering knowledge that used to require senior resources and a lot more time. Whenever services are customized from a standard template or are repeatable after customization, they may be amenable to leverage via assets. The conflict for service providers comes in investing in assets that could create competitive advantage when there may be nothing to show for it in the short run.

Troubled projects versus risk-taking is a perennial services conflict. Service providers strive to avoid troubled projects and rapidly turn around those that cannot be avoided because troubled projects erode profits and are likely to create client dissatisfaction. Yet service providers must take risks to win business, and those risks create the possibility that some projects will become troubled. Because it can take several profitable projects to recoup the loss on just one troubled project, managing risk is a critical success factor. An obvious conflict for service providers occurs when they become too risk-averse and thereby erode their competitive advantage or become too risk-prone in their quest to attain competitive advantage. A hidden conflict for service providers occurs when they have resources available to turn around troubled projects, but their own measurement system prevents that.

Role conflicts are yet another classic conflict. Everyone in a services enterprise is typically measured on multiple criteria covering matters such as quality and timeliness of deliverables, attainment of service level agreements, and client satisfaction. Yet the dominant measure for each specific role can put it at odds with other roles. For example, if partners are measured on revenue, project managers are measured on profit, resource managers are measured on skills, and practitioners are measured on utilization, an assortment of conflicts arise. Partners can sell risky projects to attain revenue. Project managers can limit hours and travel to protect profit. Resource managers can maintain a sizable bench to ensure that skills are available. And practitioners can work as many billable hours as possible to attain individual utilization credit. However, even if everyone reaches their primary targets, the enterprise as a whole may not perform as well as it could if their measurements were aligned.

Finally, services as available versus services on demand is an emerging services conflict. Being able to offer a particular service on demand does not necessarily mean it's advisable to do so. By the same token, sticking with services as available in a market segment coming to be dominated by services on demand may not be a viable strategy, either. Consumer lifestyles, workplace trends, business models, and technology are all leading the PSTS sector toward offering more services on demand. Thus, service providers are increasingly making strategic decisions about which services and which market segments to offer services as available (subject to an internal constraint) and which to offer services on demand (subject to an external constraint), all the while taking interface constraints into account. These strategic decisions have implications for resources, assets, profitability, segmentation, client selection, and SLAs. Hence, the default decision to stick with services as available can be the right decision; but if it's wrong, the consequences can touch most aspects of the service provider's enterprise.

Although every services enterprise relies on some form of measurement, prevailing ones not only fail to resolve the conflicts mentioned previously, but they may actually be the source of those conflicts. In contrast, TA_S is specifically designed to eliminate those conflicts without requiring compromise. Because previous versions of TA do that in the sectors for which they were designed, it's reasonable to ask why those versions can't simply be applied in the PSTS sector. That question is answered next.

Previous Throughput Accounting

As explained in Chapter 2, "Services On Demand," the Manufacturing sector, Information sector, and PSTS sector each have distinguishing features. Although all TA implementations share fundamental principles, the distinguishing features of each sector explain why adaptations are required. Those features are summarized in Table 7-1. Note that even though the sectors are distinct, most TA measures are similar, if not the same.

Table 7-1   Throughput Accounting for Goods, Software, and Services

Throughput Accounting For...	Goods	Software	Services
Inputs are predominantly ...	Capital	Varies	Labor
Outputs are most often ...	Nonreusable	Reusable	Customized
Throughput comes from ...	Products	Licenses	Deliverables and service levels
Investment is largely ...	Machines and materials	Requirements and tools	Skills and intellectual capital
Optimization centers on ...	Constraint	Constraint	Constraint
Financial measures include ...	T, I, OE	T, I, OE	T, I, OE
Performance measures include ...	NP, ROI	NP, ROI	NP, ROI
Resource measures include ...	T/CU	T/CU	T/CU
Control measures include ...	TDD, IDD		PDD, RDD

Throughput (T)—akin to revenue—is generated differently in each sector. In manufacturing, T is generated mainly by the sale of goods, which generally occurs once per item for a given enterprise even though each item may be resold by multiple enterprises. In software, T is generated mainly by the license of intangible assets, which generally occurs many times—sometimes millions of times—per product. And in services, T is generated mainly by contracts to perform projects or processes, which generally occur many times for each type of contract even though each individual contract is unique. Despite these differing methods of generating T, more is usually better, regardless of sector. (An exception to "more is better" occurs if an enterprise unjustifiably sacrifices future T for current T, or vice versa.)

Investments (I) are also different across each sector. In manufacturing, the biggest I is often plants, machinery, and inventory, which are tangible. In contrast, software assets are largely intangible, and so are services assets. Moreover, manufacturing inventory is seldom reusable, so the value of remaining inventory is decreased by each sale. Software vendors, on the other hand, deliberately develop reusable assets, the value of which typically increases with each instance of reuse via a license to another customer. Service providers, however, often have no physical inventory and may develop few if any assets as readily reusable as software if their services must be highly customized for each client. Thus, the minimization of I that's so important in manufacturing doesn't make as much sense in software and may make no sense in services. Making sense of this in software and services requires a closer look at what really constitutes good investments.

Finally, Operating Expense (OE) is arguably the most consistent aspect of TA across manufacturing, software, and services. It's money spent turning I into T. Though manufacturing, software, and services differ in the specifics, they all have direct labor as well as selling, general, and administrative expenses. Where they differ the most is in the means by which they can minimize their respective OEs. This topic is explored later in this chapter for services and in Appendix C, "Throughput Accounting for Software."

State of the Art

Just as it was helpful in previous chapters to know the problems those other TOC_S applications solve, it will be helpful in this chapter to know the issues that TA_S addresses. For that, we need a quick review of the state of the art.

Despite the significant differences between manufacturing and services enterprises outlined in Chapter 2, CA methods for a services business are highly similar to those for a manufacturing business.[1] Both use cost allocation to derive standard costs, which then drive accounting for sales and delivery.

Figure 7-1 illustrates selected elements of CA for services. Decision support is on the left; actual results are on the right. It may be instructive to compare this figure to Figure 3-7 in Chapter 3 illustrating CA for manufacturing. (The figures are highly similar.)

CA accumulates revenues and costs by department, and then rolls them into cost and profit centers. Profit centers deal directly with clients, so they have both revenues and costs, and thereby produce profits or losses. In contrast, cost centers provide services to other departments, so they have only costs, which they recover from the profit centers.

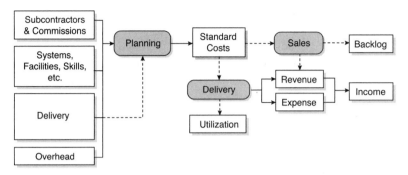

Figure 7-1 Cost Accounting for services

In addition, revenues and costs are usually accumulated in the services equivalent of manufacturing's Job Order Cost Accounting. That is, revenues and costs are accumulated by the types of service being provided, such as a consulting contract, engineering project, research study, or technical services contract. Because resources performing the work may come from multiple profit and cost centers, this accumulation provides a cross-center view composed of the work done for each specific client. Costs directly attributable to a job are billed directly to clients. The remaining costs are absorbed by the enterprise, which recovers them indirectly by allocating them to centers.

Where manufacturing costs were once entirely allocated to products based on direct labor, those costs are today much more often allocated on the basis of activities because technology has driven down direct labor to a small part of total cost. Under *Activity-Based Costing* (ABC), a recent variant of CA, products requiring more and longer activities get allocated more cost. In similar fashion, CA allocates costs in a services enterprise based on the result of activities, such as legal documents filed, architectural plans approved, scientific experiments run, business transactions processed, or service requests completed. Alternatively, ABC allocates costs in a services enterprise based on inputs to activities, such as hours worked by each resource. Services requiring more and longer activities thus get allocated more cost.

Operating and flexible budgets are also prepared for services enterprises in much the same way as for manufacturing. The operating budget is based on the expected activity level for the budget period and includes the revenues and costs generated at that level. If the actual activity level deviates significantly from the expected level, a flexible budget contains adjusted values and indicates whether costs are being controlled relative to the actual activity level. Flexible budgets can be created for the enterprise, centers, departments, and even for contracts. Such a budget might, for instance, be used to decide whether a prospective deal would be profitable at a particular price.

Finally, just as in manufacturing, standard costs can be developed for services. To begin, costs are classified as fixed or variable. *Fixed costs*, such as rent, do not vary with activity level. On the other hand, *variable costs*, such as direct labor, are assumed to vary with activity level. Fixed and variable costs are estimated for the expected level of activity, and then budgeted cost divided by activity units equals standard cost. For direct labor, anticipated utilization often quantifies activity level. Subsequently, *standard costs* are used to identify unfavorable variance, which triggers cost controls. Likewise, standard costs can be used to price services: Standard cost times activity units per service, plus margin and contingency, equals price per service.

Like CA for manufacturing, CA for services thus relies heavily on cost allocation and standard costs. Of course, if the allocation is incorrect, decisions based on standard costs will be incorrect as well. Furthermore, unfavorable variance, as indicated by resource utilization, makes cost control a top priority. Yet in services, just as in manufacturing, there are limits to how low costs can be driven and still have a viable, if not thriving, enterprise. Severe restrictions on investment, for instance, trade future revenue for current cost savings, even though increasing revenue is the only way to grow most enterprises. Hence, many of the decision-making conflicts outlined earlier are impossible to resolve with CA.

Throughput Accounting for Services

In a nutshell, the purpose of TA_S is to support good decision making throughout an organization. Good decisions take an organization toward its goal, which in for-profit enterprises is to make money now and in the future. Alternatively, in not-for-profit and governmental organizations, the goal can be expressed in appropriate "goal units," such as students taught, patients treated, or citizens served. Market share, service levels, client satisfaction, employee relations, public service, and charitable contributions may be necessary conditions, but they are not the goal.

Consistency across all levels and between all departments is an objective of TA$_S$. If measures are not consistent, productivity and utilization at the micro level may indicate that good decisions have been made even as net profit and return on investment (ROI) indicate at the macro level that bad decisions have been made. Furthermore, decisions made by practitioners, resource managers, project managers, process managers, partners, and executives should not conflict with each other.

Like previous forms, TA$_S$ reverses typical management priorities. T, which is composed mainly of cash generated by services, has highest priority because it enables growth. Next comes I because it's what the enterprise turns into T. Last comes OE, which is what the enterprise expends turning I into T.

Expense control is still important, yet not the top priority, because an enterprise dominated by expense control cannot grow as fast or as far as one pursuing T. Here's why. OE is lower-bounded at zero, but enterprises lose their growth momentum well before they approach that boundary. I is ultimately limited by the difference between T and OE, but enterprises dominated by expense controls tend to narrow that difference because they aren't focused on T or I. T, however, is limited only by the marketplace and the value a service provider has to offer its clients. If an enterprise can manage its OE with respect to its T, it can simultaneously grow its profit and investment.

Like previous forms, TA$_S$ is in no way a substitute for financial reporting according to generally accepted accounting principles (GAAP). It is, however, an alternative to CA and ABC for management decision-making. Contrary to CA/ABC, TA$_S$ does not allocate costs because direct labor costs seldom vary with services rendered. That is, service providers in the PSTS sector don't change their workforce every time they start or finish contracts, and few if any of their practitioners are paid by the hour.

Like previous forms, TA$_S$ centers around the constraint. For example, a service mix decision depends on the constraint: Change the constraint, and the service mix must change as well to maximize T. The possibility of multiple, floating constraints in services makes such decisions much harder, but constraints remain at the heart of service enterprise optimization.

TA$_S$ provides information needed to do the following:

- Identify constraints
- Improve performance
- Ensure that nonconstraints keep internal constraints working at full capacity
- Avoid under- and overinvestment
- Set priorities for constraints
- Make service mix decisions
- Make other decisions that improve the bottom line

Figure 7-2 illustrates selected elements of TA$_S$. Decision support is on the left; actual results are on the right. It may be instructive to compare this figure to Figure 3-8 in Chapter 3 illustrating TA$_G$. (The figures are nearly identical.)

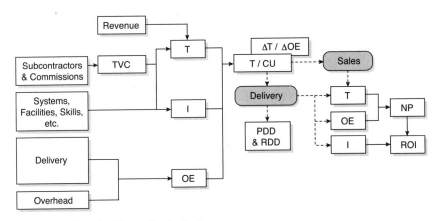

Figure 7-2   Throughput Accounting for Services

Measures comprising TA$_S$ are presented in several categories. First, financial measures provide more precise definitions of T, I, and OE for services. Second, performance measures provide a view of net profit, ROI, and productivity based on T, I, and OE. Third, resource measures provide a view of T and OE relative to constrained and nonconstrained resources. Fourth, decision-support measures show how strategic decisions may affect the enterprise. Finally, control measures show whether resources, projects, and process are deviating from desired results.

Financial Measures

TA's *financial measures* answer the following questions, regardless of whether an enterprise provides goods, software, or services:[2]

- How much money is generated by the enterprise?
- How much money is spent to operate it?
- How much money is captured by it?

Although the questions are the same, how they are answered by TA for Services (TA_S) differs from TA for Goods (TA_G), covered in Chapter 3, and TA for Software, covered in Appendix C.

In PSTS, *Throughput* (T) is cash generated through deliverables and service levels. It is computed as sales prices minus totally variable costs (TVC), such as sales commissions, performance bonuses, and subcontractor fees.

- **Deliverables** include documents, computer hardware, custom software, data, and so on.
- **Service levels** are related to transactions processed, calls handled, problems resolved, and so on.

Investment (I) is all money spent on service production systems, facilities, skills, intellectual capital, and assets—plus money spent responding to requests for information, preparing bids and proposals, and negotiating contracts.

- **Service production systems** support resource management, project management, process management, and service delivery activities, such as transaction processing, call handling, issue management, collaboration, and so on.

- **Facilities** are places from which services are delivered, such as professional offices, contact centers, data centers, network operations centers, and research laboratories.

- **Skills** are human capital acquired through education, training, mentoring, and experience—and lost through retirement, attrition, lack of use, and obsolescence.

- **Intellectual capital** (IC) includes intangibles that enable labor-based revenue generation, such as methodologies, benchmarks, templates, best practices, and architectures.

- **Assets** are non-labor-based revenue generators, such as software components, patents, and IC that can be licensed apart from labor, such as methodologies and benchmarks.

- **Requests for information** (RFI) cause service providers to document their capabilities so that clients can choose which providers, if any, will receive requests for proposals (RFP).

- **Bids and proposals** (B&P) document service requirements, client and service provider responsibilities, schedules, prices, and anticipated client benefits.

- **Contracts and negotiations** (C&N) include due diligence as well as specification of terms and conditions in a legal agreement.

Operating Expense (OE) is all money spent to produce deliverables and service levels from investments. It is primarily direct labor of practitioners, managers, and partners, but it also includes selling, general, and administrative (SG&A) costs.

- **Delivery** is billable labor, plus nonbillable labor attributable to a particular project or process (for instance, labor needed to recover a troubled project).

- **Overhead** is everything else—and is nonbillable (for instance, sales calls, headquarters functions, and billable resources without a current assignment).

The same principles behind TA_G are behind TA_S. For example, TA in general is conservative in terms of revenue recognition. So long as goods can be returned, their revenue is not recognized as T by TA_G. So long as services are subject to refunds or penalties, their revenue is not recognized as T by TA_S.

Though TVCs are no longer dominant today, they still do occur in TA_S, just as they still occur in TA_G. For example, if a service provider uses subcontractors who bill by the hour, such as computer programmers, that's TVC. If a provider uses subcontractors who are paid by the transaction, such as some business partners, that's TVC. And if a provider uses employees who are paid by the hour, such as part-time contact center agents, that's TVC, too.

Investment is the area where TA_G and TA_S differ the most. In TA_G, I is composed largely of capital investment and tangible inventory. In contrast, I in TA_S is composed of service production systems, skills, intellectual capital, and intangible assets. Unlike capital investments and manufactured inventory, most PSTS investments are perishable: They can be rapidly eroded by attrition, obsolescence, and competition. They therefore must be continually renewed. Fortunately, I in TA_S is easier to sustain once it reaches critical mass. That is, it's easier to maintain PSTS investments when they are generating robust T than to build such investments from scratch because few can be acquired off the shelf.

In TA_S, I also includes discretionary investments, such as RFI responses, B&P, and C&N. This I occurs before a contract is signed and T starts to flow. While RFIs can be highly reusable because they describe the provider's capabilities, B&P and C&N investments are far less reusable because they are customized for each client's needs. RFIs, B&P, and C&N are treated as I rather than OE in TA_S because they define scope, select solutions, plan delivery of complex services, and define SLAs. Treating them as I that may or may not be recoverable in T enables ROI analysis that's useful for marketing and sales decisions, as explained in Chapter 8, "Marketing and Sales."

If the client-provider relationship is strong or the potential T is small, there may be no RFI, and the B&P and C&N investment are often vastly reduced. On the other hand, for the largest and most complex contracts, this B&P and C&N can occur over a year or more and can involve dozens of resources. However, the majority of people working on RFI, B&P, and C&N are in service delivery or support rather than sales roles, so only a small portion of the overall effort goes directly into OE via SG&A.

Whereas development and enhancement of service production systems are included in I, operation and maintenance of those same systems are treated as OE because OE turns I into T. Similar logic applies to skills. Training on billable skills—hot or not—is included in I because those skills can be used to generate T. On the other hand, training on nonbillable topics, such as business ethics and regulatory compliance, is treated as OE because it doesn't generate T. This is not meant to diminish the importance of such training, but just point out that it serves a different purpose, which must be reflected in TA_S.

The question of what belongs in I versus OE can be answered with this rule of thumb for TA_S:

- If an expenditure is for an RFI, B&P, or C&N—or it contributes to T more than once—treat it as I.

- Otherwise, treat it as OE, which includes expenditures that yield no T or yield T just once.

For example, RFIs, B&P, C&N are investments necessary to win contracts, while hot skills training is an investment that can be used to deliver services on multiple contracts. On the other hand, compliance training is a general cost that yields no T, and each hour of service delivery labor yields T just once, so they are examples of OE.

To the degree that a manufacturer has few TVCs, its OE is largely fixed. However, even if a service provider has little TVC, its OE can still vary significantly. First, R_S can adjust the workforce on demand, so the service provider's OE is not entirely fixed. Second, services labor costs flow into OE and I in varying proportions, depending on the relative emphasis over time on sales, delivery, and investment.

Unlike manufacturing inventory, which moves from I to OE as goods are sold or scrapped, some services investments are reusable. They move from I to OE over the useful lifetime of the investment, no matter how many times they are reused. For instance, the lifetime of basic skills can be many years, though high employee turnover means those skills are lost by the enterprise sooner. On the other hand, the lifetime of hot skills can be just a few years. And the lifetime of software assets can be a year or less, depending on the release schedules.

One of the problems solved by TA_G, arbitrary cost allocation to products, is not a problem to be solved by TA_S, inasmuch as PSTS has no tangible products. Then again, PSTS does have project and process costs. Fortunately, direct labor, often the majority of those costs, is directly attributable to specific projects and processes. Nevertheless, there are other problems that TA_S must address, such as performance measurement, which is covered next.

Performance Measures

Several conflicts outlined earlier in this chapter are at least aggravated, if not caused, by incompatibilities between local and global measures. In TA_S, local measures apply to a project, process, asset, or resource. In this context, however, "global" is not synonymous with "worldwide." Rather, global measures apply to any business unit that owns projects, processes, assets, or resources.

Thus, a business unit may be a line of business, division, geographic region, or the entire enterprise. For TA_S purposes, however, a professional practice is not a business unit if it shares resources or investment with other practices because their performance is not distinct. On the other hand, if one business unit uses resources from another within the same enterprise, such as a profit center using a cost center's resources, those resources are treated for TA_S purposes as though they're internal subcontractors.

Performance measures quantify progress toward an organization's goal, of course. The following TA_S performance measures are based on the financial measures covered previously:

- Net Profit of project or process: $NP_p = T_p - OE_p$
- Net Profit of asset: $NP_a = T_a - OE_a$
- Net Profit of business unit: $NP_{BU} = T_{BU} - OE_{BU}$
- Return on Investment of project or process: $ROI_p = NP_p / I_p$
- Return on Investment of asset: $ROI_a = NP_a / I_a$
- Return on Investment of business unit: $ROI_{BU} = NP_{BU} / I_{BU}$
- Productivity of project or process: $P_p = T_p / OE_p$
- Productivity of asset: $P_a = T_a / OE_a$
- Productivity of business unit: $P_{BU} = T_{BU} / OE_{BU}$

The names and equations for TA_S performance measures may appear conventional, but the underlying financial measures are different, so the resulting performance measures are different, too. For instance, T is not revenue, and I is not just tangible assets. Hence, quantities calculated by TA_S for NP, ROI, and P will always be different from similarly named measures under CA. Moreover, neither TA_G nor TA_S computes gross profit. In CA, revenue minus cost of goods sold (COGS) equals gross profit, from which OEs are subtracted to compute net profit. TA does not separate COGS from OE, however.

At a minimum, OE_p includes direct labor, equipment, licenses, travel, and other expenses attributable to specific projects or processes. OE_a does the same for an asset, though it may contain different proportions of sales and delivery expenses. Since overhead is not allocated, OE_{BU} is more than the sum of the business unit's projects, processes, and assets. Of course, if managers of individual projects, processes, and assets can't control business unit overhead (or interest and taxes for that matter), there's little decision-making benefit to mixing it with things they can control.

When investments are used by multiple projects and processes over time, allocating I could be arbitrary. RFIs, B&P, and C&N, however, are attributable to particular projects and processes, so they may be the most sensible basis for ROI_p. Even though this doesn't account for all of I_{BU}, this method is sufficient to guide decision-making toward the goal. When based on just RFIs, B&P, and C&N, ROI_p can still be useful for deciding which prospective projects and processes warrant these investments, and for later evaluating how effective those decisions were. When bids are lost, ROI_p is zero, but ROI_{BU} is depressed. When bids are won, ROI_p can be positive, negative, or zero, with corresponding effects on ROI_{BU}.

TA_S performance measures are consistent at the local and global levels in the sense that decisions that improve local performance generally improve global performance, too. This does not mean, however, that a business unit is simply the sum of its projects, processes, and assets. If it has unutilized resources, they weigh on the business unit. For reasons explained in previous chapters, achieving high utilization everywhere is not an objective of TOC_S. Nevertheless, so long as it does not interfere with an internal constraint, higher utilization usually generates more T. Therefore, resource measures are needed in addition to performance measures.

Resource Measures

PSTS enterprises can have various structures, but hierarchies and matrixes are common. In a *hierarchy*, partners are responsible for selling and delivering work, but they leverage themselves by delegating to managers and practitioners primarily within their own practice.[3] In a *matrix*, partners are still responsible for sales and delivery, but practitioners are managed by resource managers and organized into skill groups readily available to more than one practice. Practitioners then work under the direction of project or process managers while on assignment. Hence, responsibilities are more diffused in a matrix, but skill specialization and assignment flexibility are greater, which enables larger, longer, and more complex services. Moreover, for projects and processes that reach across many countries, a matrix may be the only practical structure.

Resource measures are essential, no matter what structure applies. Nevertheless, how resource measures are reported and acted upon will differ according to structure. Various resource measures apply under TA_S:

- Totally Variable Cost: TVC = subcontractor fees, commissions, travel and living expenses, and so on.
- Throughput per Constraint Unit: T/CU = (Revenue − TVC) / Constrained resources
- Utilization: U = Time a resource spends producing / Time available to produce

T/CU is the measure used in TA_G to prioritize use of the constraint by selecting the product mix that maximizes T. An example of this was presented in Chapter 2. Likewise, if there is a stable internal constraint, T/CU can be used in TA_S to prioritize use of that constraint by selecting the service mix that maximizes T.

In addition to the basic resource measures discussed previously, these additional measures can be helpful:

- Throughput per hour: T/h = (Revenue − TVC) / Productive hours
- Operating Expense per hour: OE/h = (Direct labor + SG&A) / Available hours

T/h is a more general measure than T/CU. That is, T/h can be computed for any resource, not just the constraint. At first glance, T/h may appear to be equivalent to a standard billing rate, but it is not. For one thing, billing rates are planned, while T/h is observed from the contract price and work effort, but the differences go much deeper. Billing rates derived from standard cost rates are based on cost allocation, while T/h is purely Throughput per hour.

The traditional approach to PSTS under CA uses billing rates to price contracts, and billing rates are based on cost rates. Once a year or so, cost rates are set for each skill level via a complicated procedure that boils down to summing the expected costs of the enterprise and dividing by the number of expected billable hours. Then standard billing rates are set for each skill level by adding a target profit margin. Problems with this approach include the following:

- Actual costs and revenues often deviate from expected costs and revenues.

- Embedding TVC in cost rates applies it universally instead of selectively.

- Prices based on billing rates are driven by costs rather than the business value clients receive.

Consequently, standard rates can make contracts appear more profitable than they really are, or vice versa. And standard rates can cause the enterprise to forego contracts that could actually contribute to the bottom line. Of course, neither situation optimizes the enterprise.

In contrast to standard rates, which can remain fixed for extended periods regardless of where the market is going, T/h automatically varies across contracts and over time. And just as T/h is not a billing rate, OE/h is not a cost rate. A contract that uses a mix of resources at higher salary bands has higher OE/h, so OE/h also varies across contracts and over time.

Utilization (U) is the percentage of time a resource is billable or contributing to investment. For example, here are some typical rules. Training others counts in U, but being trained does not. Likewise, administrative time does not count toward U, but billable overtime does, even if that overtime is unpaid. Holidays, vacation, and sick days are counted in available time, but are not billable, so resources typically have utilization less than 100 percent, unless they work billable over-time.

Utilization plays a primary role in CA but a secondary role in TA_S because U is a local efficiency measure. That is, CA strives to maximize U everywhere on the assumption that this optimizes the enterprise. In contrast, TA_S maximizes U on the internal constraint, if any, while driving U of nonconstraints only as high as the constraint will allow. TA_S further cautions that Utilization without commensurate client value will fail to achieve the enterprise's goal of maximizing T in the future.

Given the central role that resources play in PSTS enterprises, resource measures are an essential complement to the financial and performance measures seen earlier. Nevertheless, major decisions require additional support, which is the next topic.

Decision-Support Measures

In PSTS, major decisions include whether to start a promising new practice, enter a foreign services market, fund an innovative line of scientific research, or embrace an emerging technology. They also include whether to discontinue a weak practice, leave a declining market segment, and so forth. The defining characteristics of major decisions are that they have the potential to shift the constraint or require the enterprise to forfeit some T on existing services to gain more T on new services.

For major decisions, T/CU is an inadequate measure for optimizing the enterprise because it assumes a stable constraint and defined service types. Therefore, the following *decision-support measures* apply to TA_S as well as TA_G:

- Change in Net Profit: $\Delta NP = \Delta T - \Delta OE$
- Payback: $PB = \Delta NP / \Delta I$

As you saw in Chapter 3, the delta symbol (Δ) comes from mathematics and stands for "difference." It thus represents a comparison between alternatives. For example, if a business unit currently generates $20 million of T per year and has $19 million of OE, its NP is $1 million. Suppose, however, that it could enter another market segment for an incremental investment of $2 million, and that would generate an additional $3 million of T per year with $2 million of OE. As a result, ΔNP would be an incremental $1 million, and PB would be two years.

Of course, no major decision would be based on so little information, but for purposes of illustration, this investment opportunity appears to move the enterprise toward its goal. Unless another alternative offered more ΔNP or shorter PB, this one would likely be analyzed further for financial risk, technical feasibility, strategic fit, and other critical success factors.

Because most major decisions in PSTS affect T, I, and OE simultaneously, the power of these decision-support measures comes from bringing together all these TA_S financial measures. For instance, a proposed cost-cutting initiative that slashes OE and requires no ΔI will look a lot less appealing if it also jeopardizes T to the point that ΔNP is insignificant or erratic. Conversely, an investment proposal with only modest ΔNP can look quite appealing if its ΔI is trivial and resources are readily available.

In addition to making major decisions, every enterprise also needs measures that enable it to implement those decisions. Control measures, covered next, are the final class of measures comprising TA_S.

Control Measures

Control measures show whether projects, processes, and resources are deviating from desired results. The following control measures apply in TA_S:

■ Project or Process Dollars per Day: $PDD = NP_p / Days$
■ Resource Dollars per Day: $RDD = Excess\ resources \times OE / Day$

PDD and RDD are both rates. PDD is the rate at which a project or process produces NP_p. RDD is the rate at which excess resources erode NP_{BU} by generating OE_{BU} that cannot be recovered by T_{BU} or redirected into I_{BU}. If an enterprise uses a different currency, these measures can be recast as Project or Process Value per Day (PVD) and Resource Value per Day (RVD).

PDD in TA_S corresponds to Throughput Dollar Days (TDD) in TA_G in the sense that both encourage on-time delivery, but "on-time" has a somewhat different meaning in PSTS. In manufacturing, the production start date is relevant to other members of the supply chain, but customers usually care only about the finish date unless they're somehow involved in the manufacturing process, which is rare. In PSTS, however, both the project start date and finish date are generally relevant to clients. One reason is financial: Billing for services is often bounded by those dates. A second reason is logistical: The PSTS firm may need space and equipment at the client site. Another reason is managerial: Clients have their own responsibilities, such as providing resources and oversight. Yet another reason is tactical: Business benefits can begin to flow at any point after a project starts, not just when it finishes.

In light of such dependencies, a PSTS firm cannot unilaterally change start or finish dates: Date changes must be negotiated with the client, and sometimes vendors or third parties, too. Such negotiations are quite common because changes to scope and duration occur often while PSTS projects are underway. Therefore, PDD measures on-time delivery against the currently negotiated duration rather than the original planned finish date. When a project is late, the numerator decreases (because T_p is constant while OE_p rises) and the denominator increases (because duration lengthens), both of which shrink PDD. Moreover, because PDD is a rate, it can be predicted before a project starts and tracked well before project completion, not just after it has become late.

In general, the higher the value of PDD, the better. Yet PDD can be negative if a project is unprofitable. PDD is based on NP_p rather than T_p to encourage delivery within budget as well as on time. Client satisfaction is usually measured too, so gains in PDD will not be achieved by sacrificing quality.

PDD is, of course, compatible with Critical Chain for Services (CC$_S$), as covered in Chapter 5, "Project Management." If T generated by a project is based on its business value to the client rather than the hours worked, the less project buffer penetration there is, the higher PDD is.

PDD is defined for both projects and processes, so their measures can be combined or compared at the business unit level. However, there is a subtle difference in how PDD is computed for processes because projects always have a defined duration, while processes are ongoing for the life of the contract.

- Project Dollars per Day goes up when T increases, OE decreases, or project duration decreases.
- Process Dollars per Day goes up when T increases, OE decreases, or process cycle time decreases.

Because business processes are ongoing, on-time completion of process iterations is measured according to the SLA. Chronically completing process iterations later than the required cycle time decreases T (because fewer service requests are completed by a constant number of resources) or increases OE (because more resources must be assigned to complete a constant volume of service requests), both of which affect the numerator rather than denominator of PDD. That is, unlike the denominator of PDD for projects, which varies with project duration, the denominator of PDD for processes is always some number of workdays rather than cycle time, while the numerator contains NP_p for those particular workdays.

PDD has these features in common across projects and processes:

- PDD can measure an individual contract or a set of contracts. For example, it can cover the current contract for a given client, no matter when it is delivered, or it can cover all contracts within a particular business unit, no matter to whom they are delivered.

- PDD can measure contracts over their entire duration or just a specific interval of time. For example, average PDD can be computed for all contracts of a specific type, even if they have different durations, or it can be computed for just a particular past period.

- PDD can measure completed, active, and planned contracts so long as the numerator and denominator are consistent. For example, for active contracts, the numerator is NP to date and the denominator is elapsed days to date. For planned contracts, PDD could cover just a particular future period.

Whereas manufacturing is in control when TDD is zero, PSTS is in control when PDD is within or rising above its normal range. In a seasonal business, PDD is lower during some quarters, but these predictable variations do not mean PDD is out of control unless year-to-year comparisons show deviations. A baseline (initial value) and benchmark (target value) can be helpful in judging progress on PDD.

Figure 7-3 plots PDD for a portfolio of projects and processes over time in a Box-and-Whiskers chart. Six statistics are plotted for each period:

- Top of whisker—100th percentile or maximum
- Top of box—75th percentile or top quartile
- Line within the box—50th percentile or median
- Diamond within the box—arithmetic average or mean
- Bottom of box—25th percentile or bottom quartile
- Bottom of whisker—0th percentile or minimum

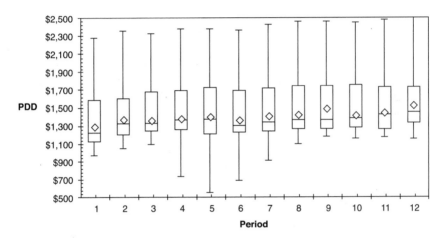

Figure 7-3 PDD over time

In general, the trend is positive with PDD for most projects and processes rising over time. During Periods 4 through 7, however, minimum PDD declines significantly. And over all periods, the range of PDD is rather wide, indicating that some contracts are considerably more profitable than others.

In addition to serving as a control measure, PDD also can be used for comparisons. For instance, when comparing projects that yield the same NP_p over different durations, the projects with shorter durations deliver more NP_p per period, so they have higher PDD. Hence, if the business unit does more projects with high PDD, its NP_{BU} will be higher, too.

Turning next to controlling resources, Resource Dollars per Day (RDD) in TA_S corresponds to Inventory Dollar Days (IDD) in TA_G in the sense that both discourage unnecessary investment in whatever is being sold. RDD quantifies the OE of excess nonbillable resources. It thus goes down when excess resources or OE per day decrease, though the former is far more controllable in the short term than the latter. Ideally, RDD should be zero, so the definition of "excess resources" is crucial.

For a given skill group, excess resources are measured in relation to the target resource buffer as determined by Replenishment for Services (R_S). As you saw in Chapter 4, the size of the target resource buffer increases with net consumption of resources, average time to resupply, and higher unreliability of resupply. Zones are set around the target buffer level, however, so normal variation will not trigger hiring or lay-offs. That is, it's common for resources to be on the bench briefly between assignments or for the bench to be depleted briefly while resources are returning from assignments, so the normal (green) zone cautions resource managers against taking action when capacity will likely stabilize naturally. Excess resources occur only when the actual buffer level rises beyond the upper threshold of the normal zone into the excess (red) zone. Even then, the resource manager would take action only if there's reason to believe the actual buffer level will stay in the excess zone.

Suppose the target resource buffer for a given skill group is three resources, and the threshold that marks the top of the normal zone is five. Further suppose that OE per resource per day for this skill group is $300. If there were just four resources on the bench, RDD would be zero because none of them are excess resources, no matter how long they're on the bench. They're there to protect T from uncertainties in net consumption and resupply. That is, over the long term, T would be significantly lower without this resource buffer. On the other hand, if there were seven resources on the bench, RDD would be two excess resources times $300 a day, or $600. If they're on the bench for a week, RDD times five days equals $3,000, which is the amount of NP_{BU} eroded during that period.

Among all measures comprising TA_G, TDD and IDD are arguably the least used because their quantities are not dollars and not days, but the product of dollars times days. The quantities thus grow rapidly with increments in either dollars or days in order to stimulate an urgent response, but the results can become so big so fast that they lose credibility with managers and practitioners.[4] In contrast, the corresponding measures in TA_S, PDD and RDD produce quantities that are just dollars. They grow more slowly with increments in either dollars or the number of days over which they are accumulated, yet managers and practitioners often have an intuitive understanding of and reasonable comfort level with what these TA_S measures say about progress toward the goal.

Service Mix Decisions

Just as TA_G is used to decide what product mix to offer, TA_S can be used to decide what service mix to offer.[5] And just as CA and TA_G reach different conclusions about the relative profitability of products, so do CA and TA_S about services. Figure 7-4 contains sample service type data that will be used to illustrate a services mix decision.

Typical Contract

Service type	Status	Duration (months)	FTE	C	CCR	NC	SUB	yr/E	Client price	Engage-ments
A	current	4	8	20%	60%	20%	0%	0.33	$537,600	100
B	current	6	10	10%	50%	30%	10%	0.50	$888,000	150
C	current	9	12	5%	20%	65%	10%	0.75	$1,404,000	125
D	current	9	15	5%	20%	50%	25%	0.75	$1,674,000	60
E	future	12	18	8%	12%	20%	60%	1.00	$2,384,640	50
F	future	84	50	3%	12%	5%	80%	7.00	$40,488,000	1
G	future	60	120	1%	7%	10%	82%	5.00	$65,664,000	2

	C	CCR	NC	SUB	Total
Billing rate	$150.00	$100.00	$75.00	$50.00	
Cost rate	$105.00	$75.00	$60.00	$42.50	
Target margin	30%	25%	20%	15%	
TVC	$0.00	$0.00	$0.00	$42.50	
OE/h	$105.00	$75.00	$60.00	$0.00	
Total FTEs	294	1,026	1,554	1,133	4,007
Current FTEs	218	895	1,347	356	2,817
Future FTEs	76	131	207	777	1,190

Resource types:
C=resource constraint (expert skills, always short unless the constraint is external)
CCR=capacity constrained resource (specialist skills, occasionnally a constraint)
NC=non-constraint (generalist skills, never a constraint)
SUB=subcontractor (commodity skills, never a constraint)

160 hours per FTE per month

Figure 7-4 Service types

Among the service types described, some are currently offered, while others could be offered in the future by redeploying resources, expanding capacity, or reducing current service types. Because some service types are composed of projects lasting a year or less while others represent business processes spanning many years, the service types span a wide range of durations, total full-time equivalent resource (FTE) requirements, mix of resource types, prices clients are willing to pay, and potential number of contracts. To simplify the illustration, each service type is independent: No contract from one service type requires a matching sale of a contract from another type, nor does one sale change the probability of another.

Every FTE is assumed to bill 160 hours per month even though individual resources may in fact work less than that if they have less than 100 percent utilization or more than that if they work overtime. Fractional FTEs represent part-time or overtime work. Thus, FTEs are not necessarily equivalent to resource head count.

Some service types require a higher percentage of certain resource types. The internal resource constraint (C) cannot easily be increased, but it can be redeployed across service types. The capacity constrained resource (CCR) has some spare capacity, but not enough to protect the constraint under abnormal conditions. The nonconstraint (NC) is readily available internally. Subcontractors (SUB) are available as needed from outside sources.

Under CA, the service provider sets its billing rates by adding its target profit margins to its cost rates, and it assigns a higher margin to scarce resources with higher skills. Under TA_S, TVC applies only to subcontractors, while OE/h applies to all internal resources, but they are the same as the corresponding cost rates under CA to simplify this illustration.

The service provider has about 2,800 FTEs for its current service types. It would need an additional 1,200 for its future service types if it continues to offer all its current ones, but the internal constraint may make it impossible to offer every possible service type. This FTE increase may seem massive, but it represents only a 7 percent annual growth rate over five years.

Figure 7-5 shows the results for CA and TA_S as calculated for each service type using the previous assumptions and the methods covered earlier in this chapter. Some service types have much larger scope and therefore much higher prices per contract. On the other hand, there are fewer opportunities to perform large contracts.

Cost Accounting
Contract View

Service type	Status	Blended billing	Blended cost	Revenue	Cost	NP	Margin	Rank
A	current	$105.00	$78.00	$537,600	$399,360	$138,240	26%	1
B	current	$92.50	$70.25	$888,000	$674,400	$213,600	24%	2
C	current	$81.25	$63.50	$1,404,000	$1,097,280	$306,720	22%	3
D	current	$77.50	$60.88	$1,674,000	$1,314,900	$359,100	21%	4
E	future	$69.00	$54.90	$2,384,640	$1,897,344	$487,296	20%	5
F	future	$60.25	$49.15	$40,488,000	$33,028,800	$7,459,200	18%	6
G	future	$57.00	$47.15	$65,664,000	$54,316,800	$11,347,200	17%	7

Throughput Accounting
Contract View

Service type	Status	T/h	OE/h	TVC	T	OE	NP	FTE_C	T/FTE_C	Rank
A	current	$105.00	$78.00	$0	$537,600	$399,360	$138,240	1.60	$1,008,000	7
B	current	$88.25	$66.00	$40,800	$847,200	$633,600	$213,600	1.00	$1,694,400	4
C	current	$77.00	$59.25	$73,440	$1,330,560	$1,023,840	$306,720	0.60	$2,956,800	2
D	current	$66.88	$50.25	$229,500	$1,444,500	$1,085,400	$359,100	0.75	$2,568,000	3
E	future	$43.50	$29.40	$881,280	$1,503,360	$1,016,064	$487,296	1.44	$1,044,000	6
F	future	$26.25	$15.15	$22,848,000	$17,640,000	$10,180,800	$7,459,200	1.50	$1,680,000	5
G	future	$22.15	$12.30	$40,147,200	$25,516,800	$14,169,600	$11,347,200	1.20	$4,252,800	1

Figure 7-5 Service scenarios

Note that NP, net operating profit before interest and taxes, is the same for each service type under CA and TA_S in this example. As you will see, these methods nonetheless lead to different service mix decisions.

Under CA, blended billing and cost rates for each service type are calculated according to its resource mix. CA leads to the conclusion that all prospective service types have lower profit margins than the current service types. Indeed, if the provider has a minimum margin it's willing to accept, it might reject some service types on that basis alone.

Under TA_S, T/h is computed from the price, so the same T/h applies to all resource types. T/h under TA_S, however, is different from the blended billing rate under CA in most scenarios. T/CU is quantified as annualized Throughput per Full-Time Equivalents of the Constrained Resource (T/FTE_C). Ranking based on this TA_S measure is quite different from the CA ranking because the service types vary widely in their use of the constrained resource. That is, some service types get much more leverage from the constraint than others. TA_S is sensitive to this, but CA is not.

In TA_G, products that require none of the constraint are called *free products*. They can be produced up to the point that they create additional CCRs and thereby endanger production of constrained products. The services equivalent is a "free service." Note that in this example, however, all service types require some amount of the constrained resource, so there are no free services.

Figure 7-6 shows how CA and TA_S can lead to different service mix decisions. This illustration assumes the internal constraint will remain stable and there will not be excess resources to confound comparisons. Recall that an *external constraint* means the market will not buy everything the enterprise could produce. An *internal constraint* means the enterprise cannot produce everything the market would buy.

If the constraint is external, should any of the prospective service types be added, assuming capacity can be expanded as necessary to meet additional market demand?

- CA says all, some, or none of the prospective service types should be added, depending on the minimum acceptable margin.
- TA_S says E, F, and G would all contribute positive NP, so they should be added.

If the constraint is external, should any service types be dropped?

- CA is equivocal because A has high margin but low NP.
- TA_S says all service lines should be kept because they contribute positive NP.

If the constraint is internal, should any service types be added, assuming the constrained resource can be redeployed but not increased?

- CA says E and G should be added because their NP is highly ranked.
- TA_S says E, F, and G would all contribute additional NP.

If the constraint is internal, should any service types be dropped?

- CA says A should be dropped and D reduced because they have the smallest NP.
- TA_S says A should be dropped and E reduced because they have the smallest T/FTE_C.

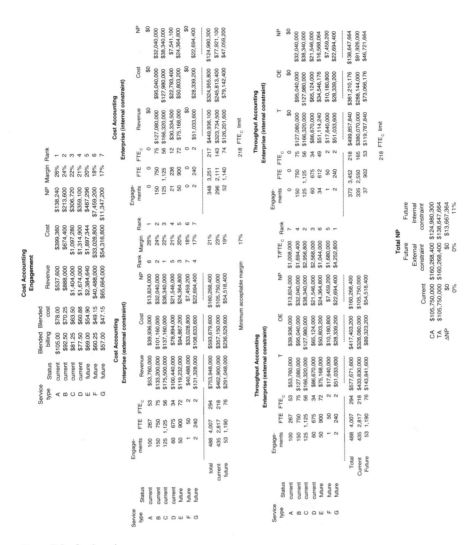

Figure 7-6 Service mix

Under the internal constraint scenario, both CA and TA$_S$ would require more total FTEs than the enterprise currently has, even though the number of constrained resources (FTE$_C$) is unchanged. This raises the possibility that CCR would become a constraint, at least temporarily. If so, increasing the capacity of CCR would be a priority. Otherwise, the service mix decision will have to be reconsidered, treating the resources that had been CCR as the new constraint.

Even when CA and TA$_S$ face the same demand and use the same resources, they may not select the same service mix. If the constraint is external, CA and TA$_S$ can yield virtually the same NP, because they both choose the service mix that the market will buy. However, CA and TA$_S$ encourage different marketing and sales approaches, so what the market will buy from them is not necessarily identical. This topic is explored in Chapter 8.

Moreover, when the constraint is internal, CA and TA$_S$ will almost always select substantially different service mixes. In the prior example, for instance, TA$_S$ produces ΔNP of well past $13 million (11 percent more) because it allocates its constrained resources in the manner that maximizes T/FTE$_C$, a measure that's unknown in CA.

The service mix found by TA$_S$ using T/FTE$_C$ is mathematically optimal, yet it is found without solving an optimization model. Conversely, the service mix found with CA is not optimal because neither service line NP nor margin truly indicates which service types contribute most to total NP when the constraint is internal.

Impact of Throughput Accounting for Services

TA emphasizes consistent measurement for one simple reason: When measures are inconsistent, no one can reliably predict what people will do. They may do what seems best for their clients, their business units, their contracts, or themselves. Or they may search in vain for a perfect compromise because they're trapped in a conflict.

TA$_S$ eliminates many conflicts that afflict services enterprises by establishing a consistent set of measures at the macro and micro levels. Under TA$_S$, good decisions for contracts and resources are also good decisions for business units, which is not always the case under CA. Furthermore, TA$_S$ is simpler than CA because it does not require data and procedures for cost allocation. These and other differences are summarized in Table 7-2.

Table 7-2 CA Versus TA$_S$

	CA	TA$_S$
First priority is ...	Operating Expense	Throughput
Second priority is ...	Revenue	Investment
Third priority is ...	Investment	Operating Expense
Revenue recognition is ...	Liberal	Conservative
Measures depend on ...	Cost allocation	Separation of TVC from OE
Maximum utilization is a target for ...	Every resource	Constraints
Service mix decisions are based on ...	Standard costs	T/FTE$_C$
Control measures are ...	Cost variance	PDD, RDD
Global optimization comes from ...	Local optimization	Constraint optimization
Macro and micro measures lead to ...	Conflicting decisions	Consistent decisions

In contrast to CA, which calls for maximum utilization of all resources, TA$_S$ calls for maximum utilization of constraints, but modulated utilization of nonconstraints. Constraint utilization is maximized, of course, because it governs Throughput of the entire enterprise. On the other hand, nonconstraint utilization is subordinate to the constraint: If higher nonconstraint utilization interferes with the constraint or doesn't generate additional T, it isn't moving the enterprise toward its goal.

Like TA$_G$, TA$_S$ reverses management priorities. T drives decisions. I and OE are managed in light of their effects on T.

TA$_S$ supports aggregation and comparison across very different entities within a services enterprise. For instance, projects and processes have different resources, organizations, methods, and time frames. Small-, medium-, and large-scale contracts each pose different management challenges. Resources can be managed via hierarchies or matrixes. And within a given period, contracts can change status from planned to active to completed. Yet TA$_S$ accommodates all these variations in a common measurement framework.

TA$_S$ is not an alternative to financial reporting according to GAAP, but it is an alternative to full-absorption CA and ABC for purposes of management decision-making. As illustrated earlier, TA$_S$ leads to optimal decisions where CA/ABC cannot. It remains to be seen, however, whether TA$_S$ will someday transition into an emerging body of knowledge known as *Constraints Accounting*, which so far covers mainly manufacturing enterprises.[6]

TA$_S$ works with other applications of TOC for Services. For example, RDD in TA$_S$ works with R$_S$ to minimize excess resources. Rapid project completion under Critical Chain for Services (CC$_S$) is reflected in higher PDD in TA$_S$. Better service-level performance under Drum-Buffer-Rope for Services (DBR$_S$) is likewise reflected in higher PDD in TA$_S$.

Several TA$_S$ outcomes are noteworthy:

- TA$_S$ accommodates both services as available, which are subject to internal constraints, and services on demand, which are subject to external and interface constraints.

- TA$_G$ and TA$_S$ are compatible. A single enterprise can use them both if it does manufacturing and services. For that matter, an enterprise can also use TA for Software.

- TA$_S$ shapes investment strategies by guiding major decisions that would shift the constraint or forfeit some Throughput on existing services to gain more Throughput on new services. TA$_S$ also tracks investment performance without distortions from cost allocation.

- TA$_S$ helps select the optimal service mix and tune innovative service types.

Whereas TOC$_S$ applications covered in previous chapters turn push into pull, TA$_S$ tells the enterprise what to pull. That is, TA$_S$ provides the information needed to make resource, project, process, and investment decisions that pull the entire enterprise toward its goal.

Armed with such information, a services enterprise is positioned to examine its marketing and sales. Is it possible, for instance, to generate more Throughput by changing marketing and sales from push to pull? This question is explored in the next chapter.

Summary

An old aphorism says "What gets measured gets done ... so be careful how you measure." Despite this warning, however, many service providers use measurement methods that say resources, projects, and processes are performing well individually even when the enterprise is performing poorly overall. Hence, local optimizations do not necessarily add up to global optimization.

Throughput Accounting for Services (TA$_S$) therefore strives to eliminate conflicts between macro and micro measures. That way, good decisions by resource managers, project managers, process managers, executives, partners, and practitioners are also good for the enterprise.

TA$_S$ follows the same basic principles as TA for Goods (TA$_G$). It reverses typical management priorities so that Throughput comes first, then Investment, then Operating Expense. It achieves global optimization by maximizing utilization of the constraint rather than every resource. It does not use standard costs. It supports strategic decisions as well as operational decisions. It provides control measures consistent with other TOC$_S$ applications.

Nevertheless, TA$_S$ handles features of services enterprises in the Professional, Scientific, and Technical Services (PSTS) sector. Throughput is generated by deliverables and service levels rather than goods. Investments are frequently intangible. And Operating Expense stems mainly from the labor of experts. TA$_S$ is thus faithful to the fundamental principles of TA$_G$ while adapting it for the services sector most different from manufacturing.

Endnotes

1. Horace R. Brock and Linda A. Herrington, "Cost Accounting for Services Businesses," *Cost Accounting: Principles and Applications*, McGraw-Hill, 6th edition, 1999, Chapter 26, pp. 673–82.

2. Eliyahu Goldratt, *The Haystack Syndrome: Sifting Information Out of the Data Ocean*, North River Press, 1990.

3. David H. Maister, *Managing the Professional Service Firm*, Free Press, 1993.

4. Eric Noreen, Debra Smith, and James T. Mackey, *The Theory of Constraints and Its Implications for Management Accounting*, North River Press, 1995, pp. 20–23.

5. Yoram Eden and Boaz Ronen, "Service Organization Costing: A Synchronized Manufacturing Approach," *Industrial Management*, Sept–Oct. 1990, pp. 24–26.

6. John A. Caspari and Pamela Caspari, *Management Dynamics: Merging Constraints Accounting to Drive Implementation*, John Wiley, 2004.

8

Marketing and Sales

It's common knowledge that marketing leads customers to want certain products or services, and then sales close the deals. Of course, the more compelling the offers created by marketing, the stronger sales can be. As you might expect by now, however, Theory of Constraints (TOC) brings a different perspective on what constitutes attractive offers and what impedes sales.

Despite the apparent emphasis that TOC places on managing internal constraints, at least two out of three companies actually have an external constraint at the enterprise level: The market simply will not buy everything they have the capacity to produce.[1] And for those with an internal constraint, when the standard TOC applications are implemented, the enterprise constraint eventually moves from internal to external—sometimes quite rapidly. Hence, every TOC implementation sooner or later must address marketing and sales.

Standard applications in TOC for Goods (TOC_G) were summarized in Chapter 3, "Theory of Constraints." The guiding principles and basic designs of those applications are consistent across enterprises even when specific implementation details differ. In contrast, there are no standard TOC applications for marketing and sales because every TOC-based marketing program is unique, and sales depend on those marketing programs.

Chapters 4 through 7 showed how TOC for Services (TOC_S) extends the standard applications for managing resources, projects, processes, and finances in services enterprises. Like the originals, those TOC_S applications can be standard across services enterprises—at least in the Professional, Scientific, and Technical Services (PSTS) sector. As in TOC_G, however, there are no standard TOC_S applications for marketing and sales.

Nevertheless, guiding principles of TOC apply broadly, even when there are no standard applications. This chapter therefore explores how TOC affects marketing and sales of services in the PSTS sector.

One guiding principle that unites marketing and sales with the standard TOC_S applications seen earlier is that enterprises are optimized by turning push into pull. Replenishment (R_S), Critical Chain (CC_S), and Drum-Buffer-Rope (DBR_S) turn push into pull for internal constraints on resources, projects, and processes. Then Throughput Accounting (TA_S) indicates which services mix pulls the most net profit.

Marketing and Sales for Services ($M\&S_S$) follows this principle by turning push into pull for external constraints. That is, rather than pushing services that may not truly maximize the business value each client receives, M&S$_S$ devises marketing offers that pull services with the highest value to clients. Of course, maximizing clients' business value is already seen by most partners and managers in PSTS as the best way to maximize their own enterprise's net profit. What TOC contributes is an alternative view of clients' business value that can be considerably larger than that typically generated by non-TOC methods.

Another guiding principle that unites M&S$_S$ with standard TOC$_S$ applications is that most constraints are actually policy constraints or interface constraints, not physical constraints. That is, the policies that service providers impose on themselves and their clients are more likely to limit what they can sell than any physical barrier. Pricing services from standard costs, as described in the previous chapter, is the preeminent example of a provider-imposed policy constraint. Likewise, the policies that clients impose on themselves and their service providers are more likely to limit the business value that clients receive than any physical barrier. Selecting a provider based on competitive bidding rather than net business value is the preeminent example of a client-imposed policy constraint. Finally, if subcontractors can't or won't align their resources and services with the primary service provider, that may limit what can be delivered, and therefore should limit what can be sold.

M&S$_S$ considers both service providers' and clients' constraints and the conventional wisdom behind them. If these constraints can be broken, however, opportunities for mutually beneficial engagements become much larger.

State of the Art

Just as it was helpful in previous chapters to know the problems those TOC$_S$ applications solve, it will be helpful in this chapter to know the issues that M&S$_S$ addresses. For that we need a quick review of the state of the art.

Most customers were satisfied with standard products a generation ago, but today most are not.[2] Although services are rarely as standardized as manufactured products, the same trend has affected services—and PSTS more than most. Increasing heterogeneity and sophistication mean clients frequently have unusual combinations of requirements, if not unique requirements. Hence, clients increasingly choose services on demand over services as available. Though it is still common for providers to design standard service offerings, they cater to the most price-sensitive clients with the least differentiated requirements. Results-oriented clients rightly insist on at least some nonstandard services, and they aren't surprised when the price is higher. Providers therefore have to match their service offerings to their preferred market segments and then tailor them as needed for specific clients.

Most customers were profitable a generation ago, but today most are not. The same heterogeneity and sophistication that have moved customers away from standard products and services have also tended to increase manufacturers' and service providers' costs. And some customers cost far more than others. Yet when adjusted for inflation, some products and services—especially those based on information technology and other innovations—are priced lower today than a generation ago. Proliferation of products and services reflects burgeoning market segmentation. As more segments emerge and each segment includes fewer customers, economic lifetimes of products and services get shorter. Consequently, if an enterprise pursues every available customer, the top third of its customers may generate all its profit, while the bottom third just erodes that profit. Careful customer selection has thus replaced universal customer retention as a critical success factor.

Standard pricing divides any market into three parts: customers who won't buy, those who will buy, and those who would pay more than the standard price. Changing the price shifts customers among these groups, but there's a trade-off: Getting more customers to buy gives up revenue from those who would pay more, while capturing more revenue from those willing to pay more gives up some customers who then won't buy. Pricing optimization models can find the price that maximizes current revenue, but they have a harder time considering the effect that today's price has on customer expectations, which can make it difficult for an enterprise to reach its goal in the future. Of course, many prices are negotiable, but the starting point and underlying assumptions exert a powerful influence on the direction, extent, and tone of those negotiations.

Sole-source deals occur in PSTS when a service provider has a strong relationship with the client, when the provider has an outstanding reputation with others the client trusts, or when the scope of work is small enough that it poses minimal risk. The provider's cost of sales and the client's cost of procurement are generally lowest when a provider and client negotiate one-on-one. On the other hand, when a prospective service provider has a weak relationship, the client seeks an unfamiliar service, or the client's business is in distress, a sole-source deal may require the client or provider to accept more risk.

Competitive bidding thus is common in some PSTS markets as clients strive to reduce their risk. The premise, of course, is that the client will get a better deal if there is more than one offer to choose from. Yet competitive bidding creates difficulties for clients as well as providers. Providers often have a hard time resolving ambiguities in the client's request for proposal (RFP). So the larger, more complex, and less certain the requirements, the harder it is for clients to discern where providers' bids differ—let alone *why* they differ—because there are so many ways to produce a deliverable or achieve a service level. Thus, if competitive bidding leads to a better deal on price, the client cannot always be sure that the low-price service is really comparable to the others. For a marginally lower price, the client may be giving up far better service and not even know it.

Service providers have the converse problem: They may be offering much better service for a lower price and not even know it. Though providers often know who their competitors are on a deal, they seldom have solid information about the proposed deliverables and service levels behind the other bids. Moreover, even after conducting due diligence, providers often have less information than they'd like about the client's base case and future requirements. In some cases, that's because even the client doesn't know. For instance, getting a comprehensive and accurate inventory of the client's computing hardware, software, and network can be a time-consuming and expensive undertaking. And if the client wants the provider to improve a service level relative to a baseline, verifying that the client has ever actually attained the purported baseline—let alone sustained it—can be surprisingly difficult.

For services with long sales cycles, service providers manage a pipeline of opportunities. The more competitive the market, the more that pipeline is funnel-shaped. That is, many opportunities may enter, but only a few emerge as signed deals. Getting opportunities into the pipeline is marketing; getting them out is sales. Hence, the sales process is as much about identifying the best opportunities and moving them through the pipeline as rapidly as possible as it is about closing deals.

Finally, the terms and conditions of PSTS contracts vary widely, with some based on the provider's cost and others on the client's business value:

- **Fixed fee** charges a predetermined price based on standard cost for a given scope of work.

- **Time-and-materials** adds a profit margin to the hourly cost rate when project scope varies.

- **Utility pricing** charges according to unit prices when business process volumes vary.

- **Value pricing** is based on the value the client is expected to receive.

- **Risk-reward sharing** is based on the value the client actually receives and the risk the provider carries.

Regardless of type, PSTS contracts allow for change requests, which are inevitable unless the contract is small and the client's requirements are stable.

Notice that nowhere in this brief review of the state of the art has there been any mention of the constraint that keeps the client's enterprise from reaching its goal, which is presumably to make money—or produce "goal units"—now and in the future. As you will see, however, the client's constraint is a key ingredient in what makes the TOC approach to marketing and sales different.

TOC Approach to Marketing and Sales for Services

Marketing and Sales require providers to identify and address client needs. TOC doesn't change that. What TOC does do, however, is give providers different tools for determining whether specific opportunities are good ones, and if they are, ways to close the sale. Thus, TOC is not a substitute for marketing and sales skills, but it generally leads to different decisions. That is, some opportunities that look undesirable with a conventional approach look desirable with a TOC approach, and vice versa.

The constraint that limits what a service provider sells can take many forms. As mentioned earlier, competitive bidding is a client policy constraint that restricts service providers to bidding on a specific scope of work, though providers can and do offer value-added activities where they see additional business value. Unfortunately, the client-stipulated scope of work may have little or nothing to do with the client's enterprise constraint, thereby limiting the business value of that service. Furthermore, the provider's pricing method can be its own policy constraint and lead to overbidding on some deals and underbidding on others, while the provider's sales management may lead it to pursue clients and deals with low odds of winning or high odds of profit erosion.

The following sections explain how TOC-based $M\&S_S$ can address those issues in PSTS. First, service pricing based on Throughput Accounting (TA) information links the provider's pricing to its own enterprise goal during competitive bidding. Second, focusing the proposed services on one or more of the client's core problems ties those services to opportunities to add large amounts of client business value. Third, compelling offers not only produce a bigger-than-expected leap in the client's business value, but they also tie the service provider's return to the magnitude of that leap. Fourth, market segmentation recognizes that a given service does not necessarily generate the same business value for every client and therefore deserves to be marketed and delivered differently in each segment—yet treating every client as its own microsegment may not be optimal either. Finally, effective sales management winnows out the undesirable opportunities and prioritizes the sales effort on the rest.

Service Pricing

A service provider is usually caught in a conflict when a client solicits competitive bids and the provider's policy is to use its standard price for its bid. Even when the provider has some negotiating latitude, it can easily make a bid that falls in the client-won't-buy or client-would-pay-more categories. The previous chapter laid the groundwork for explaining why this is so. In a nutshell, standard costs are the foundation for standard prices, but standard costs are based on cost allocations that distort the true contribution each service makes to net profit. Furthermore, standard pricing does not bring the operating expense of idle resources directly into the pricing decision.

Figure 8-1 compares information from Cost Accounting (CA) to information from Throughput Accounting for Services (TA$_S$) for a single project under three pricing scenarios. To facilitate comparisons, scope, duration, staffing, billing rates, cost rates, totally variable costs (TVC), and operating expense (OE) are the same across all scenarios. In addition, Operating Expense per hour (OE/h) for employees and TVC for subcontractors under TA are identical to CA's cost rates for those resource types. The allocation of full-time equivalent (FTE) resources between employees and subcontractors is the same in all scenarios.

Scenario #1

		Cost Accounting						Throughput Accounting					
	FTEs	Billing rate	Cost rate	Revenue	Cost	NP	Revenue/h	TVC	T/h	OE/h	T	OE	NP
employees	15	$100	$75	$2,880,000	$2,160,000	$720,000	$68		$68	$75	$1,950,000	$2,160,000	-$210,000
subcontractors	35	$65	$55	$4,368,000	$3,696,000	$672,000	$68	$55	$13		$854,000	$0	$854,000
total	50	$76		$7,248,000	$5,856,000	$1,392,000					$2,804,000	$2,160,000	$644,000

	CA	TA	Δ
client price	$6,500,000	$6,500,000	
bid price	$7,248,000	$6,500,000	
bid result	loss	win	
NP	$0	$644,000	$644,000
margin	19%	10%	

Scenario #2

		Cost Accounting						Throughput Accounting					
	FTEs	Billing rate	Cost rate	Revenue	Cost	NP	Revenue/h	TVC	T/h	OE/h	T	OE	NP
employees	15	$100	$75	$2,880,000	$2,160,000	$720,000	$83		$83	$75	$2,400,000	$2,160,000	$240,000
subcontractors	35	$65	$55	$4,368,000	$3,696,000	$672,000	$83	$55	$28		$1,904,000	$0	$1,904,000
total	50	$76		$7,248,000	$5,856,000	$1,392,000					$4,304,000	$2,160,000	$2,144,000

	CA	TA	Δ
client price	$8,000,000	$8,000,000	
bid price	$7,248,000	$8,000,000	
bid result	win	win	
NP	$1,392,000	$2,144,000	$752,000
margin	19%	27%	

Scenario #3

		Cost Accounting						Throughput Accounting					
	FTEs	Billing rate	Cost rate	Revenue	Cost	NP	Revenue/h	TVC	T/h	OE/h	T	OE	NP
employees	15	$100	$75	$2,880,000	$2,160,000	$720,000	$73		$73	$75	$2,100,000	$2,160,000	-$60,000
subcontractors	35	$65	$55	$4,368,000	$3,696,000	$672,000	$73	$55	$18		$1,204,000	$0	$1,204,000
total	50	$76		$7,248,000	$5,856,000	$1,392,000					$3,304,000	$2,160,000	$1,144,000

	CA	TA	Δ
client price	$8,000,000	$8,000,000	
bid price	$7,248,000	$7,000,000	
bid result	loss	win	
NP	$0	$1,144,000	$1,144,000
margin	19%	16%	

12 months in project duration
600 person months in project scope
160 hours per FTE per month
96,000 hours per project

Figure 8-1   Service pricing

Under CA, the provider sets its billing rates by adding its target profit margins to its cost rates, and it assigns a higher margin to employees (25 percent) than subcontractors (15 percent), but it bills clients at a single blended billing rate even if the resource mix changes while the project is underway. Under TA, Throughput per hour (T/h) is computed from the project price, so the same T/h applies to all resource types, but T/h is different from the blended billing rate under CA in all scenarios.

Based on the business value this project is expected to produce, the client is willing to pay $6.5 million in Scenario #1 and $8 million in Scenarios #2 and #3. How a contract produces business value is the subject of a later section. In this section, we simply take these values as given.

Under CA, the provider's bid price is based on standard billing rates in all scenarios. Under TA, the provider's price is either what the client is willing to pay or something less than what its competitor is willing to bid, whichever is lower.

In Scenario CA #1, bid price exceeds client price, so the bid is lost and net profit (NP) is zero. Since the provider built its target profit margins into its billing rates, getting approval to make its best-and-final offer low enough to win this deal seems highly unlikely. And if the employees who would have worked on this project remain on the bench while the provider pursues other opportunities, that leaves more than $2 million of OE uncovered—with a corresponding loss to the enterprise.

In TA #1, the bid price meets the client price, so the bid is won and NP is $644,000. This represents a 10 percent profit margin, but that's after the $2 million of OE is covered for resources that remain on the bench in CA #1. If the provider has other opportunities with better Throughput (T), it should, of course, pursue them. Even if it doesn't, TA #1 adds $2.6 million more to the bottom line than CA #1—and it does this while accepting negative NP on employee resources.

In CA #2, the bid price is less than the client price, so the bid is won and NP is $1.4 million. This achieves the target profit margin. However, because the bid price is less than the client price, it leaves $752,000 of revenue on the table.

In TA #2, the bid price meets the client price, so the bid is won and NP is $2.1 million. However, because all OE for assigned employees is already covered, the entire $752,000 that CA #2 left on the table goes straight to the bottom line of TA #2. This achieves a much higher profit margin.

Scenarios #1 and #2 thus compare CA and TA pricing alternatives for a single PSTS enterprise when the price the client is willing to pay is either substantially below or above the provider's standard cost. Scenario #3, however, illustrates a competitor using CA to bid against a PSTS provider using TA.

In CA #3, the provider's competitor is happy to bid less than the client is willing to pay because, as in CA #2, this would earn NP of $1.4 million and achieve the competitor's target profit margin. This, of course, then challenges the provider to offer a better bid than TA #2, which is based on what the client is willing to pay rather than the competitor's bid.

In TA #3, the provider makes an offer sufficiently below its competitor's bid in CA #3 to win the deal. This earns a change in net profit (ΔNP) of $1.1 million on a deal that the competitor is resigned to let the provider win because the profit margin appears to be below the competitor's stretch limit. And like CA #1, if the employees who would have worked on this project remain on the bench, CA #3 leaves $2 million of the competitor's OE uncovered—with a corresponding loss to that enterprise.

In summary, TA returns a modest profit in Scenario #1, from which CA generates no project profit at best, or a substantial enterprise loss at worst. In Scenario #2, although CA meets its target profit margin, TA exceeds it. And in Scenario #3, TA earns a decent profit on a deal that a competitor using CA considers insufficient. Moreover, in all scenarios, the client is satisfied with the TA deal because it delivers value commensurate with what the client is willing to pay—or better.

The key to understanding this outcome is to recognize that CA applies standard costs as pricing input, while TA accepts T/h as pricing output. And where CA uses target profit margin to decide whether an individual bid is acceptable, TA uses NP to decide whether the enterprise is being optimized. Thus, CA effectively trims away potential profits both below and above its target, while TA can harvest whatever profits the market currently supports. Because different clients may receive different business value from projects with equivalent scope, what they're willing to pay varies—but TA's ability to harvest the full profits available at any price point means it can generate more NP than CA can in both weak and strong markets.

To implement TOC-based service pricing, the service provider's policy of using standard prices to achieve a target profit margin is a constraint that must be broken because it can defeat the goal it's intended to achieve: to make money now and in the future. As the scenarios just described demonstrate, CA maximizes profits only when opportunities around the target profit margin are plentiful—and it may not even do that if a competitor is using TA to optimize its own enterprise.

Without knowing more about why the client is willing to pay more in Scenarios #2 and #3, it's tempting to conclude that Scenario #1, the lowest bid, is the best deal for the client because the provider's work effort is the same across all scenarios. Nevertheless, the client is willing to pay more in some scenarios because it expects the services to generate more business value. For that reason, TOC-based service pricing is based on the client's business value, not the provider's cost.

Business Value

In the broadest sense, anything that enhances what the client's enterprise is worth to its owners, investors, and lenders produces business value. For instance, advertising can enhance the client's brand, investor relations can enhance the client's market capitalization, and auditing can enhance the client's creditworthiness. The most direct measure of business value, however, is ΔNP because it relates directly to the client's goal: to make money now and in the future.

As explained in the previous chapter, clients who rely on CA tend to focus first on cost-reduction initiatives. Hence, many RFPs require service providers to perform a service cheaper—and perhaps better and faster—than the client could itself. Alternatively, the service provider may be called on to enhance the client's ability to perform business functions itself through better information technology (IT), manufacturing methods, business consulting, research and development, legal advice, tax advice, and so forth. In both cases, the client then can focus more on its core competencies.

Cost reduction opportunities are always lower bounded, so service providers generally look for additional ways to add business value. Service providers who themselves rely on CA tend to dig first for additional cost reductions, while those who have embraced TA look first at the client's Throughput because increasing it can have a much bigger effect on net profit than cost reductions can. Of course, the only way to increase Throughput is to help the client get more from its constraint, so helping the client identify and manage its constraint is essential.

Core problems are pain points related to the client's constraint. For example, excess work-in-process inventory, late order shipment, and stockouts are all core problems related to a manufacturing bottleneck. Core problems are a critical subset of client pain points, which can include any aspect of the enterprise where the client feels improvements are needed. For example, missing a sales quota and losing market share are surely pain points, but they aren't yet core problems if the constraint is internal. That is, selling more orders won't increase Throughput if the factory can't produce enough to fulfill existing customer orders reliably. Indeed, selling more of the wrong products could actually decrease Throughput. Thus, service providers need to be mindful of all pain points during marketing because the core problems change whenever the constraint shifts. Yet service providers need to focus their sales on clients' core problems and not be unduly distracted by pain points with no power to alleviate the client's current constraint.

Figure 8-2 illustrates how a service provider in the PSTS sector can generate various amounts of business value with a client. The baseline is shown first, and then a series of service scenarios are shown.

This client currently sells 1 million units of its product annually in each of three market segments. Production costs for each segment are virtually the same because they differ only slightly in components, manufacturing processes, and inspection methods. Units meeting the minimum quality standard are sold in Segment C, while those exceeding the minimum have better performance and reliability, so they're are sold in Segment B. Those meeting the highest quality standard have the best performance and reliability, so they're sold in Segment A. In addition to performance, the functions, availability, and warranties differ enough that customers in Segment A are willing to pay more than B, who pay more than C. Consequently, the view from CA is that Segment A is profitable, Segment B breaks even, and Segment C generates a loss.

The client has seriously considered abandoning Segment C in order to curtail its losses, but it is concerned that its competitors would capture customers who might later buy additional or replacement units in the higher-priced segments, thereby jeopardizing its ability to make money in the future. However, this would require it to improve its production quality or scrap the units currently sold in Segment C. What's more, after a brief tutorial for the client on TA, the service provider pointed out that Segment C actually contributes $5.5 million of Throughput (T) per year. If the client were to abandon Segment C, its losses would deepen significantly unless it also reduced its OE by at least 25 percent. Previous attempts by the client to reduce its OE failed, however, because it could not reduce its employee head count and other OE enough to stem the losses.

Client's Product / Client's Cost Accounting / Client's Throughput Accounting

	Units	Price	Revenue	Cost	NP	TVC	T	OE	NP
Baseline									
Segment A	1,000,000	$12	$12,000,000	$10,000,000	$2,000,000	$2,500,000	$9,500,000		
Segment B	1,000,000	$10	$10,000,000	$10,000,000	$0	$2,500,000	$7,500,000		
Segment C	1,000,000	$8	$8,000,000	$10,000,000	-$2,000,000	$2,500,000	$5,500,000		
total	3,000,000		$30,000,000	$30,000,000	$0	$7,500,000	$22,500,000	$22,500,000	$0
Scenario #1									
Segment A	1,000,000	$12	$12,000,000	$9,500,000	$2,500,000	$2,500,000	$9,500,000		
Segment B	1,000,000	$10	$10,000,000	$9,500,000	$500,000	$2,500,000	$7,500,000		
Segment C	1,000,000	$8	$8,000,000	$9,500,000	-$1,500,000	$2,500,000	$5,500,000		
total	3,000,000		$30,000,000	$28,500,000	$1,500,000	$7,500,000	$22,500,000	$21,000,000	$1,500,000
Scenario #2									
Segment A	1,200,000	$12	$14,400,000	$10,000,000	$4,400,000	$3,000,000	$11,400,000		
Segment B	1,200,000	$10	$12,000,000	$10,000,000	$2,000,000	$3,000,000	$9,000,000		
Segment C	1,200,000	$8	$9,600,000	$10,000,000	-$400,000	$3,000,000	$6,600,000		
total	3,600,000		$36,000,000	$30,000,000	$6,000,000	$9,000,000	$27,000,000	$21,000,000	$6,000,000
Scenario #3									
Segment A	1,300,000	$12	$15,600,000	$10,250,000	$5,350,000	$3,250,000	$12,350,000		
Segment B	1,300,000	$10	$13,000,000	$10,250,000	$2,750,000	$3,250,000	$9,750,000		
Segment C	1,300,000	$8	$10,400,000	$10,250,000	$150,000	$3,250,000	$7,150,000		
total	3,900,000		$39,000,000	$30,750,000	$8,250,000	$9,750,000	$29,250,000	$21,000,000	$8,250,000
Scenario #4									
Segment A+	500,000	$22	$11,000,000	$8,250,000	$2,750,000	$1,250,000	$9,750,000		
Segment A	1,300,000	$12	$15,600,000	$10,250,000	$5,350,000	$3,250,000	$12,350,000		
Segment B	1,300,000	$10	$13,000,000	$10,250,000	$2,750,000	$3,250,000	$9,750,000		
Segment C	1,200,000	$8	$9,600,000	$10,000,000	-$400,000	$3,000,000	$6,600,000		
Segment C-	2,000,000	$5	$10,000,000	$9,500,000	$500,000	$9,500,000	$500,000		
total	6,300,000		$59,200,000	$48,250,000	$10,950,000	$20,250,000	$38,950,000	$28,000,000	$10,950,000

Service Engagements

		Year 1	Years 1-5
Scenario #1	ΔNP	$1,500,000	$7,500,000
	Price	$1,000,000	$2,000,000
	Investment	$200,000	$1,000,000
	Business Value	$300,000	$4,500,000
	ROI	25%	150%
Scenario #2	ΔNP	$4,500,000	$22,500,000
	Price	$1,250,000	$2,500,000
	Investment	$625,000	$1,250,000
	Business Value	$2,625,000	$18,750,000
	ROI	140%	500%
Scenario #3	ΔNP	$2,250,000	$11,250,000
	Price	$2,000,000	$4,000,000
	Investment	$400,000	$2,000,000
	Business Value	-$150,000	$5,250,000
	ROI	-6%	88%
Scenario #4	ΔNP	$2,700,000	$13,500,000
	Price	$2,500,000	$5,000,000
	Investment	$500,000	$2,500,000
	Business Value	-$300,000	$6,000,000
	ROI	-10%	80%

Figure 8-2 Business value

In Scenario #1, the client issues an RFP for Enterprise Resource Planning (ERP) software and consulting in the hope that they can cut its cost. The client cannot implement these improvements by itself because it lacks the IT and expertise. After verifying that the client's core problems really are symptoms of a production bottleneck, the service provider also proposes value-added services in the form of executive education in the Theory of Constraints (TOC), TA software, software evaluation, and upgrades to the client's aging IT. In addition to paying the service provider's price, the client would have to make its own internal investment. Nevertheless, this scenario improves productivity, and thereby reduces OE enough to pay the provider's price and make the internal investment, plus generate a small profit after the first year. Most importantly, however, it provides the client with the information and skills it needs to manage its production constraint.

In Scenario #2, which builds on the previous scenario, the service provider helps the client implement Drum-Buffer-Rope (DBR), internal Replenishment within its manufacturing facilities, and Critical Chain in engineering. This also requires the provider to deliver TOC education to managers, workers, and staff because their buy-in and active participation are critical to success. By managing its internal constraint, the client uncovers latent capacity without investing in additional equipment or expanding its workforce. The increase in productivity is sufficient to shift the client's constraint outside, into the market. Fortunately, this scenario enables the client to reach its profit objective for the first time in several years.

In Scenario #3, the service provider works with the client to implement external Replenishment in the client's distribution chain, build a better website and extranet, and launch an advertising campaign. Replenishment reduces stockouts and overstocks while reducing inventory throughout the distribution chain. A better website reaches more consumers directly with product information and customer support, while a better extranet enables the client to sell through its distribution chain better by providing the necessary information linkage from manufacturer to wholesaler to retailer and back. The advertising campaign sells more units by changing customer perception of existing products, because market research reveals that many customers are unaware of alternative uses for, and benefits of, the client's products. Hence, by managing its market constraint, the client generates more T in each of its market segments with negligible impact on its OE.

In Scenario #4, the service provider helps the client identify and enter new markets. TOC generally favors entering new markets to increase Throughput rather than capturing an overwhelming share in existing markets. This spreads the risk and minimizes retaliation by competitors, but new markets usually represent unknown territory with their own risks.[3] In this scenario, market research reveals untapped market segments both above and below the prevailing segments. That is, the untapped segments include both customers who won't buy and customers who would pay more. Segment C has traditionally been the entry-level segment, with satisfied customers eventually trading up to products in Segments B and A. Segment C-, however, is an economy segment that would attract customers unlikely to trade up, while at the same time not appealing enough to traditional entry-level customers to draw many from that segment. On the other hand, Segment A+ is a premium segment that would draw few customers from the traditional segments because its members value product appearance and the aura of exclusivity even more than performance.

By making the pie bigger (enlarging the overall market) rather than just making its slice bigger (increasing its share), the client is confident it can use the increased Throughput to enter entirely new markets by the time its competitors respond. Because the products sold in Segment C- actually come from another manufacturer with no brand recognition but are sold under the client's brand, eventually abandoning that segment as competitors chase the economy segment's market price below their TVC is part of the client's strategy. Fortunately for the client, there are few barriers to entry or exit from this economy segment, but the window of opportunity to make a profit is limited, so timing on both ends is crucial.

Scenario #4 also requires reassessment of, and adjustment to, any of the client's TOC applications if the constraint shifts. And it requires an IT refresh because the client would otherwise outgrow its existing platform. The client decides to have the service provider build, host, and operate its new IT platform because it requires skills beyond what the client itself can manage. Nevertheless, the return on investment (ROI) on these scenarios is better than any other investments the client has considered. And after the success of Scenario #1, subsequent services are sole-sourced from the incumbent service provider rather than decided by competitive bidding.

Notice that these scenarios represent the client's view. Nowhere is there any mention of the service provider's cost. The price in every scenario is based on what the client is willing to pay, not what it costs the provider to deliver the services. To get there, however, the client has to get past its policy constraints that say cost reduction is the primary objective and the best deal is the lowest price from competitive bidding. This is where the service provider's marketing and sales efforts come in.

Service Offers

Every TOC-based marketing program is unique because it must solve one or more of the clients' core problems. In the scenarios discussed in the preceding section, client core problems included an internal production constraint, then an external market constraint, and finally a potential IT constraint. Although many clients' constraints fall into one of these categories, the specifics vary widely between clients. For instance, if the client had been in a services sector rather than manufacturing, details of the core problems would have been different and might have included interface constraints.

A compelling service offer produces a substantial leap in the client's business value because it helps the client identify and manage its constraint. The most compelling service offers thus increase the client's T rather than decrease its OE, which is the opposite of what many conventional service offers attempt. Moreover, a compelling service offer ties the service provider's return to the magnitude of the client's increase in business value. Consequently, the service provider following TOC-based marketing and sales in the previous section would not bid a fixed price for any of the scenarios, but would instead make its price contingent on the actual business value the client receives.

For the client, this risk-reward sharing reduces risk because service price is linked to the benefits received. It also aligns the service provider's goal directly with the client's goal. Hence, it relieves pressure for the client to oversee every deliverable and service level. With the provider focused on the client's business value, the client can turn more of its attention from monitoring its service provider to running its own enterprise.

For the service provider, risk-reward sharing increases risk because the amount of business value the client attains depends on a lot more than just the provider's services. The client's market may take an unexpected downturn, new competitors may emerge, an innovation may make some of the client's products obsolete, or the client may have difficulty getting past its policy constraints. If the unexpected happens, however, the provider would react in concert with the client to identify its new constraint and manage it accordingly. In addition, the service provider can manage its risk across multiple clients by undertaking contracts unlikely to run into trouble simultaneously.

Although the provider's price in $M\&S_S$ is based on the client's business value, that price is not the maximum amount the client might be willing to pay. The price is instead a minor slice of the increase in business value, so the client captures the majority of incremental business value. In this way, the client always feels that the value it receives more than justifies the price it pays. This contrasts with conventional service offers, where clients pay the provider's price but grumble about it because the ROI is closer to alternative investments.

Generating business value via ΔNP is the most direct method, but there are other ways to generate business value, including speed, quality, reliability, and innovation. Though they should all show up in ΔNP eventually, the routes they take may be different. Thus, when clients want a service provider to generate business value differently, or when clients have different core problems, the provider has an opportunity to segment the market. Dividing a market into segments allows a provider to charge different prices according to the business value generated. On the other hand, aggregating customers with similar needs into segments enables a service provider to standardize its resources and infrastructure, if not its services. Thus, $M\&S_S$ relies on finding the right market segmentation.

Market Segmentation

In a properly segmented market, the price and quantity of goods or services sold in one segment have no effect on what can be sold in another segment. Thus, clients in different segments can compare the value they receive to the price they pay and conclude that each got a good deal. This does not mean, however, that the goods or services themselves have to be dramatically different. Soft drinks are a classic example. Soft drinks sold in restaurants, fountains, and groceries are fundamentally the same product sold in different packages at considerably different prices. Yet the same consumers participate in all these market segments because they perceive different value across venues.

IT provides additional examples. Computer chips rated for different speeds command different prices even though they may have been fabricated in the same batch. And by disabling features or restricting the amount of data, some software products created for business can also be licensed for personal use.

The TOC *market-segmentation principle* is to segment the market, not resources, in order for the same resources to then serve more than one segment.[4] If demand across segments is uncorrelated, aggregate demand is nevertheless smoother. And if segments are countercyclical, aggregate demand can be much smoother.

Equally important, a segmented market can solve the problem mentioned earlier wherein some customers won't buy and others would pay more than the standard price. For example, an overnight delivery service is priced higher than second-day delivery, which is priced higher than standard delivery, yet packages in all these segments may be transported on the same vehicles, with different service levels achieved by prioritized handling. Likewise, amenities and prices differ substantially, but first-class, business-class, and coach-class airline passengers on a given flight all depart and arrive at the same time.

This market segmentation principle applies in PSTS, but PSTS enterprises may also face the opposite problem: too many segments, to the point of microsegmentation with as few as one client per segment. The more disparate the clients' requirements, the more customized the services must be. And the higher the expertise required, the less interchangeable the provider's resources are. The solution, of course, is to standardize what can be standardized and customize only what remains.

Though PSTS sales are made on expertise, portions of service delivery are often amenable to standardization, sometimes to the extent that tasks are automatable. For example, accessing patents, searching pharmaceutical research, and resetting computer passwords are examples of tasks that have been successfully migrated to self-service. And even if tasks are not automatable, they may be scriptable. That is, with a well-built knowledge base, nonexperts can perform some tasks, such as basic troubleshooting, that otherwise would require experts. The challenge for PSTS enterprises is to leverage their expertise and intellectual capital so that competitors find it prohibitively expensive to enter or remain in the targeted market segments.

For a service provider trying to decide whether to segment a market—or react to a competitor's segmentation strategy—TA provides decision support. First, for a prospective investment in segmentation, a provider can examine its own potential ΔNP and payback. Second, the service mix decision framework illustrated in Chapter 7, "Finance and Accounting," can be extended to handle segmented markets. When a given service is sold at different prices in different geographies, via different channels, or to different customer types, those segments can be represented in the service mix table as though they were separate services. The service mix decision framework then reveals which segments are more profitable.

In a departure from product mix decisions, which use the same resource mix but different prices across segments, service mix decisions may use different resource mixes as well as different prices. Here's why. In manufacturing, TOC strives to serve different segments with the same product, so the resource mixes are generally the same. In services, however, a given service may not be delivered in quite the same way across segments. For example, an IT service that's highly customized for large businesses, such as packaged software implementation, may be delivered to small- and medium-sized businesses with much less customization because their requirements are more modest and the price they can pay is far less. Likewise, in one geographic segment, global resources may be quite acceptable, while in another segment, domestic resources may be required by law, regulation, or work councils.

Sales Management

In the PSTS sector, sales management oversees the pipeline of opportunities generated by marketing. The more competitive the market, the more the pipeline is funnel-shaped, with many opportunities entering the sales process, but few emerging as signed deals. Hence, the purpose of sales management is to identify good opportunities and move them through the pipeline as rapidly and successfully as possible. Salespeople can then focus on closing the deals with the highest odds and highest profit potential.[5]

There is no universal terminology, but service providers generally divide their sales processes into stages, such as these:

- **Identification**—The client has a problem it cannot solve on its own.
- **Validation**—The service provider can solve the client's problem.

- **Qualification**—The services have sufficient value to the client and profit for the provider.
- **Proposal**—The services can be delivered in a manner acceptable to the client.
- **Contracting**—The client and provider agree on responsibilities, terms, and conditions.
- **Delivery**—The provider and client implement the services and exercise change control.

Each stage is further composed of activities. For example, activities address problem definition, solution overview, business case, indicative pricing, service center visit, bid, proposal, due diligence, negotiation, and best-and-final offer. Performing each activity requires additional investment by the service provider or client, so either party may withdraw at any point.

The shape of the pipeline is affected by marketing and sales management, as illustrated in Figure 8-3:

Figure 8-3   Sales pipelines

- A typical sales funnel reduces the number of live opportunities at each stage—but the later each opportunity is eliminated, the larger the accumulated investment that is lost.
- Entering new markets and segments widens the inlet by generating more opportunities.
- Value-based offers widen the outlet by closing more sales.
- Sole-sourcing and follow-on contracts shorten the duration by dropping or accelerating activities.

- Competitive bidding lengthens the duration by adding or decelerating activities.

- Analytic models rapidly narrow the neck by filtering out opportunities where the client has low propensity to buy, the odds of winning are low, client business value is weak, or the solution does not rely on the provider's strengths.

Any activity in the sales process can be a constraint. For instance, having too few salespeople to pursue new opportunities is a common resource constraint, but policy constraints embedded in review-and-approval activities are also quite common.

The same techniques used to locate an internal production constraint can be used to locate the constraint in a sales process. For example, a chronic queue of leads awaiting sales calls, qualified opportunities awaiting demonstrations, or bids awaiting approvals may indicate sales constraints.

Changing the shape of the pipeline affects the provider's investment, but it will not increase sales unless the change addresses the constraint. Fortunately, TOC principles used to manage other internal constraints can also be used to manage sales constraints:

- If the constraint is resources, Replenishment can manage resource buffers of salespeople and other participants in the sales process.

- If the constraint is bad multitasking across opportunities, adopting work rules and time buffers from CC can raise productivity.

- If the constraint is sales capacity, DBR can manage the opportunity buffer.

- If the constraint is funding, TA can direct Bid & Proposal (B&P) investment where it maximizes Throughput.

When supporting sales management, CA and TA may rank sales prospects quite differently, as illustrated in Figure 8-4. To facilitate comparison, all projects in this figure have the same duration, scope, and resource mix. If these factors were different, CA and TA could have opposite rankings, as illustrated in Chapter 7. In this figure, however, the differences are more subtle because clients are willing to pay various prices, presumably because the resulting business value varies accordingly.

Cost Accounting

Project	Duration (months)	Effort (hours)	FTEs	Client Price	FTEs used	Billing rate	Cost rate	Revenue	Cost	NP	Margin	Rank	FTEs used
A	12	23,040	12	$2,800,000	12	$100	$70	$2,304,000	$1,612,800	$691,200	30%	1	12
B	12	23,040	12	$2,600,000	12	$100	$70	$2,304,000	$1,612,800	$691,200	30%	1	12
C	12	23,040	12	$2,400,000	12	$100	$70	$2,304,000	$1,612,800	$691,200	30%	1	12
D	12	23,040	12	$2,200,000	12	$100	$70	$2,200,000	$1,612,800	$587,200	27%	4	12
E	12	23,040	12	$2,000,000	12	$100	$70	$2,000,000	$1,612,800	$387,200	19%	5	12
F	12	23,040	12	$1,800,000	0	$100	$70	$0	$0	$0			12
G	12	23,040	12	$1,600,000	0	$100	$70	$0	$0	$0			12
H	12	23,040	12	$1,400,000	0	$100	$70	$0	$0	$0			0
Project Total			96		60			$11,112,000	$8,064,000	$3,048,000	27%		84
Available FTEs per month					30		$70		$336,000				6

90 FTEs (capacity)   80% price cutoff on bids
160 Hours per FTE per month

Throughput Accounting

Project	T/h	OE/h	T	OE	NP	Rank
A	$121.53	$70	$2,800,000	$1,612,800	$1,187,200	1
B	$112.85	$70	$2,600,000	$1,612,800	$987,200	2
C	$104.17	$70	$2,400,000	$1,612,800	$787,200	3
D	$95.49	$70	$2,200,000	$1,612,800	$587,200	4
E	$86.81	$70	$2,000,000	$1,612,800	$387,200	5
F	$78.13	$70	$1,800,000	$1,612,800	$187,200	6
G	$69.44	$70	$1,600,000	$1,612,800	-$12,800	7
H	$60.76	$70	$0	$0	$0	
Project Total			$15,400,000	$11,289,600	$4,110,400	
Available FTEs per month		$70		$67,200		

ΔNP $1,062,400$

Figure 8-4   Sales management

- Using its standard cost and billing rates, CA ranks Projects A, B, and C as peers based on their margins. On the other hand, TA ranks them 1, 2, 3 based on their various T/h values. TA would therefore recommend different B&P investments, where CA would suggest equal amounts. If there were only enough resources to do just these top projects and TA could charge what each project is worth to the client, TA would generate $888,000 more NP than CA.

- CA also accepts Projects D and E but rejects Projects F, G, and H because their margins are insufficient. This leaves 30 resources on the bench at a cost of $336,000 per month. If kept on the bench for the duration of these projects, that amount would wipe out NP on the accepted projects. So if additional projects were not forthcoming, many of the benched resources might be laid off to eliminate this expense. Of course, the layoffs would generate even more expense and jeopardize the service provider's ability to meet its goal in the future.

- TA accepts Projects A through G, even though the NP on Project G is negative, because its T covers most OE for resources that would otherwise be on the bench. And if the target buffer level is 7 percent, having six available resources is normal.

- As shown, TA generates $1 million more NP than CA with the same resources and same projects from which to choose. However, if competition restricted TA to the same revenue as CA on Projects A through E, TA would still generate $174,000 more NP than CA on projects F and G. Also, TA would save $268,000 on bench resources every month while avoiding layoffs. This would prevent skills attrition and position the TA firm to grow faster than the CA firm during a market upturn.

The *winner's curse* occurs when a low bid wins and the service provider finds the deal unprofitable. *Buyer's remorse* occurs when the winning provider is unable to meet the client's expectations. They often are opposite sides of the same coin.

In the scenarios just described, a provider using CA would not bid on Projects F, G, and H, because they look like the winner's curse. On the other hand, a provider using TA to win Projects F and G would have to be careful not to create buyer's remorse by skimping on those projects simply because their T/h is lower. Even at the lower values, their T/h is sufficient to generate superior NP while maintaining a stable workforce.

Impact of Marketing and Sales for Services

M&S$_S$ is guided by the principle that a service provider's market and sales constraints are best addressed by changing push into pull. Rather than pushing services with expected returns on par with clients' other potential investments, M&S$_S$ relies on compelling offers with high value to pull opportunities past a market constraint. Rather than pushing opportunities through the sales pipeline, M&S$_S$ uses constraint management to pull them through the sales constraint. These and other differences between the conventional and TOC-based approach to marketing and sales are summarized in Table 8-1.

Table 8-1   Marketing and Sales for Services

Marketing and Sales for Services	Conventional	TOC-Based
Guiding principle is ...	Push	Pull
Client needs are indicated by ...	Pain points	Core problems
Typical value proposition is ...	Decrease client's OE	Increase client's T
Pricing is based on ...	Provider's cost	Client's value
Service prices tend toward ...	Standard	Flexible
Segmentation principle is ...	Segment the resources	Segment the market
Common growth strategy is ...	Increase market share	Enter new segments
Sales pipeline is ...	Long, narrow funnel	Short, wide funnel
Sales management focus is ...	Entire pipeline	Sales constraint
Primary information source is ...	CA	TA
Opportunities are ranked by ...	Profit margin	ΔNP

Because the client's constraints limit its Throughput, services with highest value address such constraints. As previous chapters have shown, TOC applications are available to manage constraints, regardless of whether the client is in a goods or services sector. However, a client's pain points typically include many issues unrelated, or only indirectly related, to its constraints. And implementing TOC often requires expertise and technology that clients themselves do not have. The provider's marketing therefore must cover constraint management, while its sales focus on core problems.

Pricing services according to the value the client receives rather than the cost the provider incurs requires the provider to break one of its own policy constraints—that there is only one fair price, which is standard cost plus a reasonable profit margin. Because clients' needs differ, what they are willing to pay for service varies, and there is no single price that all are willing to pay for the same or similar services. A service provider using highly flexible pricing across many segments can capture more profit in both weak and strong markets than a service provider restricted to standard pricing in few segments.

The nature of PSTS is to provide highly customized services based on expertise. In the extreme, each client is a microsegment of one. This does not mean, however, that a service provider must segment its resources accordingly. TOC advises managers to segment the market so that many resources can be shared and supported by a common infrastructure. Nowadays, this increasingly means some innovative IT is required.

When a service provider has a genuine external market constraint, clients won't buy everything that the provider can deliver. Yet even if a provider has no external market constraint, it can still have an internal sales constraint. Focusing sales management on that constraint then becomes critical because the entire sales process depends on it. For instance, careful client selection early in the sales cycle can alleviate downstream constraints on resources, time, and budget.

Most clients were profitable a generation ago, but today many are not, especially when viewed through the lens of CA. Hence, marketing and sales have never been more important. TA agrees that not all customers are profitable, but it frequently disagrees with CA on how many and which ones are profitable.

Several M&S$_S$ outcomes are noteworthy:

- There is no standard TOC application for marketing and sales, because every marketing program is unique, but TOC principles are nevertheless the foundation of M&S$_S$.
- M&S$_S$ bases market offers on client value, not provider cost. If the client is an individual rather than a business, personal value is analogous to business value, and M&S$_S$ still applies.
- M&S$_S$ drives sales via constraint management for the client, which usually requires the service provider to isolate core problems rather than address all the client's pain points at once.
- M&S$_S$ relies on DBR, Replenishment, and CC for compelling market offers—plus TA for sales management.

Closing the deal is the essence of sales, and TOC does include sales techniques. TOC uses the same techniques, however, to get buy-in to the many changes that TOC implementation requires. Thus, this topic is deferred to the next chapter on strategy and change management.

Summary

In some Professional, Scientific, and Technical Services (PSTS) markets, clients strive to reduce their risk by soliciting competitive bids for a specified scope of work. In some PSTS markets, standard prices prevail, but the level of expertise actually delivered varies. And providers always prefer sole-sourcing and follow-on contracts, in part because this dramatically lowers their cost of sales. In every instance, however, clients must assess whether the value they receive justifies the price they pay.

The tipping point in TOC-based Marketing and Sales for Services (M&S$_S$) is reached when the client refocuses on driving up its own business value dramatically rather than driving its service provider's price marginally. Price is meaningful only in the context of value, and the value of services varies enormously.

Increasing a client's Throughput (T) generally yields much more business value than decreasing its Operating Expense (OE). Yet requests for proposals (RFPs) often emphasize OE reduction and expect little, if any, increase in T. Moreover, RFPs seldom make a distinction between pain points and core problems because clients are frequently unaware of the central role that their own constraints play in reaching their goals.

In contrast to conventional marketing and sales, which tend to accept a long and narrow sales funnel as inevitable, TOC-based M&S$_S$ strives for a wider and shorter sales funnel. Selling to diverse market segments spreads the provider's risk, while compelling market offers based on extraordinary business value make a provider's services stand out from its clients' other potential investments.

Endnotes

1. Gerald I. Kendall, *Viable Vision: Transforming Total Sales into Net Profits*, J. Ross Publishing, 2005, p. 43.

2. Adrian J. Slywotzky, David J. Morrison, Ted Moser, Kevin A. Mundt, and James A. Quella, *Profit Patterns: 30 Ways to Anticipate and Profit from Strategic Forces Reshaping Your Business*, Times Business, 1999, pp. 127–135.

3. Eric Noreen, Debra Smith, and James T. Mackey, *The Theory of Constraints and Its Implications for Management Accounting*, North River Press, 1995, p. xxvii.

4. Gerald I. Kendall, *Viable Vision: Transforming Total Sales into Net Profits*, J. Ross Publishing, 2005, p. 49.

5. Richard Klapholz and Alex Klarman, *The Cash Machine: Using the Theory of Constraints for Sales Management*, North River Press, 2004, p. 17.

PART **III**

Implementation

9

Strategy and Change

Strategy is the specific way an enterprise chooses to pursue its goal, and change is the way it realigns its marketing, sales, and production to carry out that strategy. Two-thirds of chief executive officers (CEOs) worldwide say, however, that more than a moderate level of change is needed to implement strategy in their enterprise.[1] Of course, when change is the constraint on strategy, it leads to gaps between vision and reality.

Strategy can be proactive when an opportunity is identified or reactive when a threat looms. Often it's a blend of proactive and reactive elements. No matter whether the forces driving strategy come from inside or outside, however, change can be so difficult that many efforts to bring it about are only partially successful.

Strategic innovations come in several forms:

- **Products/services/markets**—Change in products, services, or marketing.

- **Operational**—Change that improves the effectiveness and efficiency of processes.

- **Business model**—Change in the enterprise's structure and/or financial model.

CEOs say these forms are all important and inseparable, but higher-performing enterprises put twice as much emphasis on business model innovation.[2] When an enterprise's business model significantly underperforms, it's change or die. Yet even when a business model outperforms, change is still necessary because competitive advantage can be fleeting.

Theory of Constraints (TOC) supports all forms of strategic innovation. Critical Chain and Marketing and Sales change products, services, and marketing. Drum-Buffer-Rope and Replenishment improve processes. Throughput Accounting changes the business model.

Furthermore, TOC promotes change by answering these fundamental questions:[3]

1. What to change?
2. What to change to?
3. How to cause the change?

TOC reveals what to change—the current state—and what to change to—the future state—by placing heavy emphasis on understanding cause-and-effect relationships. TOC then teaches how to cause the change using pull instead of push. That is, TOC provides a specific sequence of change management steps that can lead people to embrace change rather than fight it.

As you might expect at this point, some unique characteristics of the Professional, Scientific, and Technical Services (PSTS) sector mean that strategy and change are somewhat different there. First, PSTS enterprises are often a source of strategic advisors and change agents for their clients, so expertise in strategy and change is a core competency for some PSTS enterprises. Second, though PSTS enterprises may be filled with strategic advisors and change agents, when it comes to their own enterprise, they and their colleagues can have blind spots regarding strategy and resist change the same as anybody else.

This chapter covers *Strategy and Change for Services* (S&C$_S$) from the perspective of strategic advisors and change agents working on behalf of clients, as well as executives in a services enterprise grappling with their own strategy and change. As you will see, how S&C$_S$ applies in PSTS is largely an extension of its application in other sectors. To begin, however, we need a brief review of the state of the art.

State of the Art

For many practitioners, strategy and planning are so inseparable that "strategic planning" is a unified concept. Yet considerable effort typically goes into planning, while less effort may go into formulating sound strategy. For instance, strategic plans may take current features as immutable, such as products and organization, even when those features are incompatible with new business models infiltrating a market.

Conversely, strategic plans may take future outcomes as assured, even when the conditions and capabilities needed to produce those outcomes are unproven. For example, the once generally accepted belief that the value of a communications network increases in proportion to the square of the number of users is one of the factors that led to significant over-building. Actual connections used in large networks are typically a tiny subset of all possible connections, so networks are now valued more modestly in part because not all potential connections are equally valuable.[4]

Despite fumbled strategies, best practices in formulating strategy do exist. For instance, the strategy of some enterprises today extends concurrently across three horizons: the current core business, emerging business opportunities, and embryonic opportunities.[5] Such enterprises routinely scan the most distant horizon for breakthroughs and nurture the most promising ones through the nearer horizons until the best ones become a core business, which can take years.

Likewise, more enterprises are considering patterns of strategic moves and countermoves when viewing their competitive landscape. Collapse of the Middle, Technology Shifts the Board, Disintermediation, Product to Solution, and Cornerstoning are a few of the many *strategy patterns* that are as familiar to strategic advisors as chess patterns are to chess masters.[6] Well-timed moves and countermoves affect whether enterprises are ultimately on the winning or losing side of an innovation.[7]

Best practices in change management have also evolved. They include creating a vision and sense of urgency, establishing a supporting coalition, communicating widely and often, and recognizing that organizational culture can be a serious impediment to change.[8] They also include social-networking methods to counter threats or exploit opportunities even before they are detected by strategists.

There are a dozen traditional and contemporary schools of thought on how to formulate strategy, and they all have critics as well as advocates.[9] The alternatives range from top-down to bottom-up, formal to informal, and descriptive to prescriptive. For the purpose of understanding how they relate to TOC, however, it's what they don't do that matters most. None of the other approaches puts nearly as much emphasis on understanding cause-and-effect relationships as TOC does. And no other approach uses constraint management as the foundation for strategy and change.

The PSTS sector is composed of diverse enterprises, so there is no universal approach to strategy and change. There are, however, some common challenges.

First, when reduced to its basic elements, a PSTS enterprise strategy often says: This is our field of expertise, these are our clients, here are the services we provide them, and this is what we charge.[10] All too often, however, the enterprise's competitors have precisely the same strategy, so it provides no competitive differentiation. Nor does it consider the possibility of new entrants with disruptive innovations. Even if an enterprise sets stretch objectives, unless its strategy is based on the value its prospective services could provide to potential clients, it may not be apparent that the firm should head in a different direction altogether, rather than push its current strategy harder.

Second, if strategists are measured on billable utilization, and strategic thinking is nonbillable work, devising strategy conflicts with serving current clients. Likewise, if strategists are measured on sales, as many partners are, devising strategy conflicts with selling current services. Yet simply reassigning strategic thinking to staff without utilization and sales targets isn't viable if they lack the knowledge and credibility needed to bring about major change.

Third, PSTS enterprises are subject to goal conflicts because their practitioners generally have strong allegiance to their fields of expertise via diplomas, licenses, certifications, memberships, and publications. Indeed, allegiance to their field can be as strong as or stronger than allegiance to their employer. A professional's goal is to practice his or her chosen profession. A scientist's goal is to make discoveries. A technician's goal is to create and apply technology.

In a not-for-profit enterprise, these personal goals may be perfectly aligned with the enterprise goal of producing goal units, such as professional cases, scientific discoveries, and high technology. Yet in a profit-making enterprise, personal goals may not align quite as well with the enterprise goal of making money now and in the future. Taken too far, pro bono cases, pure science, and exploratory technologies conflict with the enterprise goal. Not taken far enough, they produce little innovation and leave practitioners yearning to take their expertise elsewhere.

Fourth, PSTS enterprises are finding that innovations increasingly come from collaboration in supply chains with goods producers or in service chains with other service providers. For instance, a biotechnology research laboratory, information technology (IT) provider, and pharmaceutical manufacturer can create innovations collaboratively that none of them could create independently.

Finally, resistance to change is a natural human tendency, even in the PSTS sector. Effective change agents know how to break down resistance to change, but the process is difficult, and change isn't sustainable if resistance is just suppressed until the change agents depart. In contrast, the TOC approach to change uses resistance to make change stronger and more sustainable. By getting buy-in to change by actively addressing issues, TOC accomplishes change via pull instead of push.

The TOC approach to strategy and change requires no adaptation for PSTS, yet it addresses the challenges outlined here and more. The following sections first summarize the TOC approach and then its application to PSTS.

TOC Approach to Strategy

Table 9-1 summarizes the TOC approach to strategy. Central to that approach is the assertion that the following conditions are necessary for a successful enterprise:

1. Owners set the enterprise goal.
2. Employees get secure and satisfying work.
3. Customers/clients receive satisfactory products/services.
4. The enterprise achieves ongoing improvement.

Table 9-1   Conventional Versus TOC-Based Services Strategy

Strategy for Services	Conventional	TOC-Based
Basic elements are …	Expertise, clients, services, charges	Goals, constraints, innovations, investments
Schools of thought are …	Varied	Cause-and-effect
Approaches are …	Varied	Solve core problems related to four necessary conditions
Interface constraints affect …	Cost	Throughput and buffer sizing
Breakthroughs come from …	Expertise, service levels, pricing	Breaking multiple policy constraints
Strategic constraints are …	Unseen/arbitrary	Deliberately positioned
Investment decisions are based on …	Cost Accounting	Throughput Accounting
Guiding principle is …	Global optimization comes from local optimization	Global optimization comes from constraint management

If any of these conditions are not met, the enterprise is probably at some risk—perhaps even high risk. Conversely, if any conditions could be improved over the competition, the enterprise has an opportunity—perhaps even a big opportunity.

Effective strategy thus addresses one or more core problems related to these conditions. For example, employee layoffs and customer dissatisfaction are two common core problems. The TOC applications covered in previous chapters are all intended to maintain a stable workforce in order to meet the condition that employees get secure work. And a pay-for-performance plan that ties executive and employee compensation to Throughput (T), now and in the future, meets the condition that customers and clients receive satisfactory products and services.

Despite the emphasis TOC puts on managing internal constraints, some industries are chronically plagued with excess capacity, which means their constraint is external, in the market. In such industries, executives may feel intense pressure to adopt the strategy of competing on price. The consequences are well-known, however. Competitors match price cuts eventually, if not immediately. Employees may feel their jobs are less secure, which affects their productivity and turnover. Suppliers are squeezed to cut their prices, which may reduce their reliability or quality. Finally, customers recognize that price cuts often require a compromise on quality. Critics thus contend that price-dominated strategies all too often become a race to the bottom—until the strategy crashes against the bottom and the enterprise gropes for another strategy.

Because price cuts are the easiest strategy for competitors to match, even if it erases their net profit, the TOC approach to strategy looks for alternatives that are not so easy to match. Segmenting a market in order to satisfy unmet customer needs is a traditional alternative. So are competing on speed and reliability. A modern alternative is to compete on innovation.[11] A goods producer that leads its supply chain to adopt an innovative product, operation, or business model can change the game in its entire industry. Likewise, a PSTS enterprise that helps its clients adopt such innovations can trigger change in each of their respective industries, too.

In TOC terms, an innovation that matters is a change that alleviates or eliminates a constraint. This is a subtle yet profound distinction because an innovation that improves a nonconstraint just doesn't matter insofar as the goal goes. For instance, using an innovation to increase the efficiency of a manufacturing or business process that is already underutilized contributes little toward the goal because Throughput of the enterprise remains unchanged. In fact, this local optimization would be a net negative contribution if it increased overall Operating Expense (OE) without improving Throughput, as local optimizations are prone to do.

Some innovations that matter address physical constraints, such as machines, materials, workspace, and people. But competitors often just acquire equivalents. For this reason, the TOC approach to strategy frequently hinges on policy constraints. When an enterprise truly breaks a policy constraint, it's often hard for competitors to break their comparable constraint.

For example, Throughput Accounting (TA) is conservative toward revenue recognition: It says no enterprise in a supply chain recognizes Throughput until a customer buys. Adopting this policy eliminates the incentive to ship anything that cannot be sold to consumers, which reduces inventory throughout the supply chain and frees production and distribution capacity for goods that are saleable. Yet adopting this policy is hard for competitors' supply chains because it goes against the conventional wisdom that if each member of a supply chain optimizes its own enterprise by recognizing revenue immediately for everything it ships, the entire supply chain will be optimized automatically.

Though it may be hard for competitors to break a policy constraint, it's usually just a matter of time. Depending on the industry, it may take several years or just a few months for them to catch up. The TOC approach to strategy therefore recommends breaking more than one policy constraint because this is much harder for competitors to match.

Pick any TOC application and imagine using it to break a policy constraint. Now pick a second application and imagine using it to break a different policy constraint. Now pick a third. And so forth. Not only are the logistical barriers to competition higher with each successive policy constraint that's overcome, the psychological barrier can prevent some competitors from even trying something so radical.

As noted earlier, the TOC approach to strategy applies to PSTS enterprises both when they are strategic advisors to their clients and when they are managing their own enterprise toward its goal. Strategic advisors in PSTS firms use the knowledge described in this section to advise their clients. How the TOC approach to strategy applies to PSTS enterprises themselves is covered next.

Strategy for Services

Although the TOC approach to strategy does not require adaptation for the PSTS sector, unique characteristics of this sector affect which strategies are more workable. Foremost, a PSTS enterprise must distinguish its expertise because sales depend on it. Strategic investments thus are needed to create and maintain that expertise, while differentiation can be achieved by breaking policy constraints.

With the exception of some firms in the Financial Services sector, such as venture capitalists, and some organizations in the Education sector, such as research universities, PSTS is the sector most likely to provide strategic advice to other enterprises. Strategic advisors' expertise must encompass not only best practices in strategy and change, but also their application in each client's specific industry, as well as implementation of various enablers of strategy, such as IT. Thus, in addition to experts in corporate strategy, governmental affairs, and change management, PSTS enterprises hire experts in specific industries, scientific fields, business processes, and relevant technologies.

The nature of its constraints also affects a PSTS enterprise's own strategy. As noted in earlier chapters, PSTS enterprises are usually subject to interface constraints, so they are another avenue for strategic innovations. For instance, when clients want to impose highly restrictive interface constraints, the service provider can help them view the impact of those constraints on their own Throughput rather than just their OE. Likewise, when subcontractors or business partners balk at aligning their contracts with the contract between the primary service provider and the client, the service provider must help them understand how lack of alignment creates problems. By requiring more and larger resource, time, and financial buffers, the service provider and its subcontractors or business partners become less competitive than they would be with fully aligned contracts and fewer, smaller buffers.

PSTS enterprises are also subject to unstable constraints. That is, the inherent nature of services on demand means that the active constraint can float over time as demand ebbs and flows and as supply expands and contracts. Even when an enterprise uses TOC to manage its resources, IT architects may be the constraint one month, the next month it's project managers, and the next it's industry consultants. By definition, a PSTS enterprise cannot orchestrate its operations around a single internal constraint when services on demand generate instability. Furthermore, PSTS enterprises in high-technology fields are buffeted by technical innovations. Information technologies, for instance, can alleviate constraints to the point that they shift around.

Globalization occurred earlier in manufacturing than PSTS, but only the smallest PSTS enterprises today may remain unaffected by potential or actual competitors elsewhere in the world. Barriers to global operations continue to diminish, so a PSTS enterprise's most formidable competitors may not be among its traditional competition. Conversely, PSTS enterprises can more readily tap educated labor pools and financial markets worldwide, thereby reaping benefits beyond those available domestically.

Compared to capital-intensive industries, PSTS enterprises may face nimble competitors. That is, it can take far less time and capital to open an office and hire practitioners than to build and equip a factory, warehouse, fleet, store, or school with all the physical assets it requires. And when PSTS resources are mobile, the PSTS enterprise itself may need far less of its own office space. On the other hand, research facilities, service centers, and data centers require significant investments, so physical constraints cannot be ignored entirely.

The PSTS sector is heavily populated with experts who are innovative, quick to respond to others' innovations, and smart about strategic follow-through. So as hard as it can be for PSTS enterprises to break their own policy constraints, none can afford to lapse into complacency because it may not be nearly as hard for competitors to figure out how to break their own policy constraints once they comprehend what an innovator has done. The half-life of a strategic innovation in PSTS may be brief unless the first mover continues to innovate, perhaps by breaking multiple policy constraints. On the other hand, innovations not directed at the enterprise goal are hollow victories. For instance, customizing services for market niches is easy; doing it profitably is hard.

Professionals, scientists, and technicians need each others' services, and some of the most demanding clients for any PSTS enterprise are other PSTS enterprises. If they themselves are delivering services on demand, PSTS enterprises will naturally expect other PSTS enterprises they rely on to do the same. Thus, they can be anxious to understand how Theory of Constraints for Services (TOC$_S$) can be leveraged across PSTS enterprises.

In summary, these questions guide the TOC approach to services strategy:

1. What is our goal?
2. Who are our clients and competitors?
3. What are their goals, constraints, and core problems?
4. Are there threats or opportunities on various horizons we should address?
5. What services will we offer our clients, now and in the future, and how will we distinguish them from our competitors' services?
6. Do we have internal, external, or interface constraints?
7. Where do we want to locate our strategic constraints?
8. In light of our constraints, what's our optimal services mix?
9. In light of our services mix, how will we build and sustain our expertise?
10. What investments do we need to reach our goal and continue to improve thereafter?

Many of these questions were covered in earlier chapters, but two remain. Hence, strategic constraints and investments are discussed next.

Strategic Constraints in Services

Whereas any enterprise can have a constraint imposed on it by the market for its services, enterprises using TOC deliberately position their constraints to maximize Throughput and create flexibility if not stability. The guiding principle is that positioning constraints where they support the strategy leads to higher Throughput than suffering arbitrary constraints.

- **Replenishment for Services** (R$_S$) identifies which resources are constrained by the job market and internal resource development.
- **Critical Chain with Internal Constraints** (CC$_I$) designates strategic resources and schedules multiple projects around their availability.

- **Critical Chain with External Constraints** (CC$_E$) relies on R$_S$ to manage resource buffers, especially for resources assigned to the critical chain.

- **Drum-Buffer-Rope for Services** (DBR$_S$) designates strategic tasks, creates unbalanced process capacity around them, and uses them to modulate work flow.

- **Throughput Accounting for Services** (TA$_S$) takes strategic resources into account when determining optimal service mix.

- **Marketing and Sales for Services** (M&S$_S$) incorporates strategic constraints in its ranking of prospective deals.

A policy constraint is a useful strategic constraint if it keeps the enterprise from overreaching. This might seem to contradict the guiding principle that breaking policy constraints is an effective way to create sustainable competitive advantage, but it actually acknowledges that not all policy constraints deserve to be broken at once. In the PSTS sector, for example, policies may reject contracts outside specified size, complexity, geographic, professional, scientific, or technical realms because the enterprise does not have the requisite capacity or expertise. Even within acceptable realms, policies may reject service level agreements (SLAs) that would depart too far from standard. If such contracts would generate unacceptable risk or lead the enterprise into a strategic cul-de-sac, they may be precisely the kind of contracts the enterprise wants its competitors to win.

Because PSTS enterprises rely on expertise and the job market may impose an external constraint on resources, executives may set a strategic constraint on sales in order to maintain quality and reputation. Rather than rejecting good opportunities outright, however, the sales constraint may accelerate or defer certain tasks until appropriate resources are available. Or it may steer deals to particular methods, technologies, or geographies that mitigate the resource constraint.

When an enterprise's strategy changes, its strategic constraints frequently have to change, too. In R$_S$, for instance, resources would have to be restaffed around the new strategic resource. In CC$_I$, projects would be rescheduled around the new strategic resource. And in DBR$_S$, process capacity would be reconfigured around the new strategic task.

As strategic constraints shift, investments may have to shift as well to accomplish the restaffing, rescheduling, and reconfiguring. Furthermore, whenever investments are made, decision-makers should understand the trade-offs involved, both between and within investment choices. Thus, investment decisions are covered next.

Strategic Investments in Services

In contrast to physical assets common in many industries, such as equipment that eventually wears out and materials that are eventually depleted, the intangible assets common in PSTS may gain value with each additional use. For example, the more a well-written methodology is used, the more expense it saves. Likewise, the more a professional database is licensed, the more revenue it generates. And the more critical skills are used successfully, the more honed they become.

On the other hand, some intangible assets increase in value as they reach critical mass, even if their usage rate remains the same. For example, a complete and current knowledge base produces a higher percentage of satisfied users. Likewise, a portfolio of key patents enables an enterprise to generate royalty revenue and cross-licensing agreements. And a comprehensive suite of benchmarks enables an enterprise to advise its clients about relative performance and alternative strategies.

From a TOC standpoint, high-leverage investments are modest in size but generate large Throughput for a PSTS enterprise and its clients. As in any other investment setting, however, no PSTS enterprise has unlimited investment funds. Yet ongoing investments are critical because the greatest threat to many PSTS investments is obsolescence in the face of innovations.

As noted previously, education and training are essential PSTS investments because sales depend on expertise. However, some resources contributing to investments may do so as a byproduct of delivery if deliverables and tools created to deliver services can be extended and used on later contracts. This has multiple advantages: It ensures that investments are workable, it ensures they're valuable, and it covers OE with Throughput (T) rather than requiring funding for Investment (I), so the potential leverage is high. Nevertheless, many PSTS investments require assigned resources or an acquisition because they cannot be created as byproducts.

Investment decisions need to ensure that change in net profit (ΔNP) covers both the loss of T and funding of I. Figure 9-1 illustrates several simple investment decision scenarios from a TOC perspective. To keep the illustrations simple, timing and duration are largely ignored. They would, of course, be significant in real investment decisions, particularly since benefits generally lag behind and may continue well after the investment itself has ended.

	Full-time Equivalents	Throughput per hour	Operating Expense per hour	Throughput	Investment	Operating Expense	Net Profit
Scenario #0	FTEs	T/h	OE/h	T	I	OE	NP
Billable	1,000	$100	$70	$16,000,000	$0	$11,200,000	$4,800,000
Scenario #1	FTEs	T/h	OE/h	T	I	OE	NP
Billable	970	$100	$70	$15,520,000	$0	$10,864,000	$4,656,000
Bid & Proposal (B&P)	30		$70	$0	$336,000	$0	-$336,000
Wins				$480,000			$480,000
Total	1,000			$16,000,000	$336,000	$10,864,000	$4,800,000
Δ				$0	$336,000	-$336,000	$0
Scenario #2	FTEs	T/h	OE/h	T	I	OE	NP
Billable	970	$100	$67	$15,520,000	$0	$10,398,400	$5,121,600
Research & Development (R&D)	30		$67	$0	$321,600	$0	-$321,600
Systems & Facilities (S&F)				$0	$0	$0	$0
Total	1,000			$15,520,000	$321,600	$10,398,400	$4,800,000
Δ				-$480,000	$321,600	-$801,600	$0
Scenario #3	FTEs	T/h	OE/h	T	I	OE	NP
Billable	970	$103	$70	$16,000,000	$0	$10,864,000	$5,136,000
Research & Development (R&D)	30		$70	$0	$336,000	$0	-$336,000
Intellectual Capital (IC)				$0	$0	$0	$0
Total	1,000			$16,000,000	$336,000	$10,864,000	$4,800,000
Δ				$0	$336,000	-$336,000	$0
Scenario #4	FTEs	T/h	OE/h	T	I	OE	NP
Billable	970	$100	$70	$15,520,000	$0	$10,864,000	$4,656,000
Research & Development (R&D)	30		$70	$0	$336,000	$0	-$336,000
Assets				$480,000	$0	$0	$480,000
Total	1,000			$16,000,000	$336,000	$10,864,000	$4,800,000
Δ				$0	$336,000	-$336,000	$0

160 hours per FTE per month

Figure 9-1   Investment scenarios

Scenario #0 shows a baseline of 1,000 full-time equivalent (FTE) resources generating net profit (NP) of $4.8 million per month. Without investment, however, the enterprise will either sell no more work or become less productive on the work it does sell. And if T erodes or OE rises, NP is in jeopardy, of course.

Scenario #1 shows some resources reassigned to bid & proposal (B&P), and therefore contributing to I rather than OE. The deals they win must increase T by $480,000 per month to break even. Increasing T more than this creates positive ΔNP from B&P. Less T creates negative ΔNP.

Scenario #2 shows some resources reassigned to research & development (R&D) on internal systems and facilities (S&F), so they're also contributing to I rather than OE. The S&F they create could reduce OE on the remaining billable resources, such as by eliminating some administrative tasks or taking work out of some delivery tasks. In this scenario, OE must be reduced by $800,000 per month to break even, which reduces Operating Expense per hour (OE/h) by about $3.

Scenario #3 shows some resources reassigned to R&D on intellectual capital (IC), and therefore contributing to I rather than OE. The IC they develop makes the remaining billable resources more productive, so they can generate more Throughput per hour (T/h) while their OE/h remains constant. The IC must maintain T at its present level to break even, which amounts to increasing T/h by about $3.

Scenario #4 shows some resources reassigned to R&D on assets, which generate T through license or royalty revenue instead of labor. The leverage that assets can have on ΔT is high if many licenses are sold, if they generate revenue over long periods of time, or if the ratio of T/I is large. If the asset is software, some ongoing investments in maintenance and enhancement will be required. If the asset is a patent, there may be virtually no ongoing investment, though there may be some additional OE for accounting and legal activities. Aside from their ongoing investments or expenses, these assets must increase T by $480,000 per month to break even, but this has no effect on T/h or OE/h because the assets are nonlabor revenue-generators.

Because these investment scenarios appear individually feasible, consider whether they are feasible simultaneously. They probably are not, because they would collectively decrease NP by more than $500,000 per month. The reason is simple: Diverting so many resources into investment activities leads directly to a considerable decrease in T and indirectly to a decrease in the leverage of investments tied to billable hours. Though this might be tolerable for awhile if the investments are part of a coordinated strategic program with long-term benefits, if they are independent operational or tactical investments, some might be better delayed or rejected unless their anticipated benefits significantly exceed the break-even point.

Small PSTS enterprises may make the bulk of their sales via client-initiated contacts, such as walk-ins, referrals or retainers, but larger PSTS enterprises have to make sales proactively. Hence, Investment #1, B&P, is a given if necessary to sustain T. When an enterprise uses Cost Accounting, Investment #2, R&D for OE reduction, is another likely choice because expenses are under direct control. Then again, if the enterprise uses TA, investment #3, R&D for IC, and Investment #4, R&D for Assets, are more likely choices because they both are designed to drive up T instead of drive down OE.

Clients wrestle with their own investment decisions, of course, so strategic advisors in PSTS can also view their clients' investment alternatives through a TOC lens. For example, if a client has pain points in its IT budget, core problems may be revealed when the circumstances are restated in TOC terms:

- When a client's IT projects have little or no effect on T, they probably aren't addressing that client's constraint. Moreover, IT projects expressly targeted at OE reduction are frequently symptoms of local optimization.

- When the client's IT budget is composed mostly of OE rather than I, aging IT infrastructure could be the client's constraint. And if it isn't now, it probably will be eventually.

- When a runaway project dominates the client's IT budget, I may be rising and expected T may be dropping to the point that the project's ROI is no longer acceptable, even when ignoring the sunk cost.

- When a competitor spends about the same percentage of its sales on IT as the client, yet it generates significantly higher NP, it may be using its IT for strategic advantage.

No matter whether a PSTS enterprise is facing its own strategic decisions or advising its clients on their strategic decisions, making decisions is seldom as much work as implementing them. Nevertheless, implementation is essential to close the gap between strategic vision and reality. So how do you reach agreement and follow-through to implementation? The TOC approach to change is called *buy-in*.

TOC Approach to Change

As mentioned at the beginning of this chapter, TOC fosters change by answering these fundamental questions: (1) What to change?, (2) What to change to?, and (3) How to cause the change? Previous sections covered the first two. This section covers the third.

Conventional approaches to *Change Management* are largely about changing minds and behavior, yet they often commence after the decisions that drive change have been made.[12] In contrast, the TOC approach to change covers whatever must be changed to reach the goal, so it's about more than just changing minds and behavior. It starts with careful diagnosis of core problems and then proceeds to solutions that often defy conventional wisdom. Consequently, how problems, solutions, and implementations are approached makes a huge difference in whether others buy in to change.

The TOC approach to change springs from the counterintuitive notion that the strongest force for change is resistance against change. That is, we resist change until we're convinced the situation will be improved; then there's no reason to resist. Indeed, having originally opposed change, we tend to throw our support behind change more ardently than if we had been neutral in the beginning. Hence, like the sport of judo, where a skilled player uses the opponent's strength to win the match, TOC turns each level of resistance into the corresponding phase of buy-in. Both sides are listed in Table 9-2.

Table 9-2   Levels of Resistance Versus Phases of Buy-In

Levels of Resistance	Phases of Buy-In
1. Disagreement about the problem	1. Agreeing on the problem
2. Disagreement about the direction of the solution	2. Agreeing on the direction of the solution
3. Lack of faith that the solution will yield significant results	3. Agreeing that the solution solves the problem
4. Too many side effects	4. Agreeing that the solution will not lead to significant negative effects
5. Solution is too hard to implement	5. Agreeing on how to overcome obstacles that block implementation
6. Unverbalized fear	6. Agreeing to implement

The first level of resistance is disagreement about the problem. It's human nature to believe that our own situation is unique. So it's easy to imagine reasons why someone else's solution won't solve our particular problem. Truly unique problems are quite rare, however. Fortunately, even problems that initially appear intractably complex usually stem from just one, or perhaps two, core problems. All the other pain points we feel are distractions in the sense that a solution to the core problems will relieve them, too. Moreover, the core problems are probably familiar to anyone with expertise in that specific domain.

The first phase of buy-in is therefore getting agreement on the problem. Solutions must wait. To identify core problems, the change agent has to explore cause-and-effect relationships and trace back from undesirable effects until the core problems are exposed. This is not a task that most groups can accomplish, because their members each perceive the situation somewhat differently and so are unlikely to reach consensus. However, once the change agent has identified the core problems and has shown how they connect to other pain points, a group can reach consensus on that view.

The second level of resistance is disagreement about the direction of the solution. When a core problem springs from a conflict, each side of the conflict is favored by someone. Otherwise, the direction of the solution would be unopposed. For example, consider this conflict from Chapter 4, "Resource Management." To run a profitable business delivering services on demand, one view is that it must hire-to-plan because otherwise clients will be dissatisfied by delays due to resource shortages. An opposing view is that the enterprise must hire-to-deal because it can't afford to have nonbillable resources on the bench. When faced with such a conflict, compromise usually has unintended consequences: The enterprise might hire-to-plan until resources become excessive, lay off the excess resources, hire-to-deal until a shortage develops, and then repeat the cycle—all the while falling short of the goal of running a profitable business with a stable workforce and satisfied clients.

The second phase of buy-in is therefore getting agreement on the direction of the solution. When conflicts are stated using the language in this example, breaking the conflict is done by invalidating an assumption behind a requirement ("we must...") or prerequisite ("because..."). No compromise is needed because the conflict itself then disappears. Usually, one side of a conflict can be eliminated in this manner, but in the example, the solution lies in a different direction altogether: hire-to-buffer. (Learn more about Replenishment for Services in Chapter 4). No matter how it's done, however, breaking the conflict prepares everyone to examine whether a proposed solution will really solve the core problems.

The third level of resistance is lack of faith that the solution will yield significant results. Even when the direction of the solution has been accepted, that's no guarantee that a specific solution will be effective. Hence, some skepticism is a normal and healthy reaction. Suppose, for instance, that the solution under discussion was more accurate forecasting for hire-to-plan or accelerated recruiting for hire-to-deal. Valid criticisms are that forecasting accuracy diminishes over longer horizons, while accelerated recruiting gets harder when the need for additional resources is most urgent. In contrast, the hire-to-buffer solution does not rely on either an accurate forecast or accelerated recruiting. It relies instead on actual resource consumption information and the normal recruiting process, neither of which is controversial. So it goes almost without saying that if the solution is a TOC application, some TOC education must be provided.

The third phase of buy-in is therefore agreeing that the solution solves the problem. At a minimum, the solution must be shown to eliminate the original undesirable effects by addressing the core problems; but if the solution also produces desirable effects, that's a bonus. For instance, in addition to solving the resource-management problem for services on demand, hire-to-buffer also enables projects to be scheduled on demand instead of according to availability of strategic resources. (See Critical Chain for Services in Chapter 5, "Project Management.")

The fourth level of resistance is concern that there are too many side effects. If a proposed solution creates new undesirable effects as it eliminates old ones, that's an understandable cause for concern. For example, while supporting services on demand, hire-to-buffer strives to keep an appropriate number of resources available for rapid assignment to protect against uncertainty. However, resources on the bench do not get utilization credit, so their performance evaluations could be harmed and turnover could become a problem. Change agents should welcome legitimate reservations such as this because addressing them helps polish the solution.

The fourth phase of buy-in is therefore agreeing that the solution will not lead to significant negative effects. One way to address the utilization credit objection would be to point out that average resource buffer size under hire-to-buffer is typically smaller than hire-to-plan, while time to assign resources is shorter than hire-to-deal. However, a better way to get buy-in is to ask the people raising the objection to suggest ways that the undesirable effects could be overcome. They might, for instance, observe that bench time can be used for training and staffing of internal projects. They might also note that individual resources will tend to rotate on and off the bench between assignments, so a more significant problem during periods of heavy resource demand may turn out to be how to keep individuals on the bench long enough to complete their training or internal project assignment. Accepting such insights from those who raise legitimate objections is one of the most powerful ways to get their buy-in.

The fifth level of resistance is concern that the solution will be too difficult to implement. For instance, the solution may require a change in policies and procedures, strategy, or IT. Moreover, the solution might require buy-in from a large number of people at many levels of the enterprise. Though genuine, none of these obstacles is necessarily insurmountable. At this point, the solution has already been accepted by the decision-makers, so the central question is how, not whether, to implement the solution. Nevertheless, change agents must be careful not to demand or accept answers too quickly. In light of the difficulties that may lie ahead, giving everyone 24 hours to think about implementation is far better.

The fifth phase of buy-in is agreeing on how to overcome obstacles to implementation. One way is to find prior examples where the obstacles were less onerous than anticipated. Another is to find examples where an innovative implementation approach successfully overcame the obstacles. The TOC literature and TOC consultants may provide case studies along these lines. In addition, previous chapters cover ways to alter policies, procedures, and strategy. And methods for reengineering or replacing legacy systems are readily available. Often, however, those who identify obstacles to implementation can also recommend the best ways to overcome them in their own enterprise. And this is an activity well-suited to group work. They might, for instance, authorize a pilot implementation specifically designed to overcome obstacles and thereby pave the way for the main implementation waves to follow immediately thereafter.

The sixth level of resistance, unverbalized fear, happens infrequently and only if the previous phases of buy-in were not done well enough. More often than not, the person making a complaint at this point has unique knowledge that wasn't revealed during the first phase, agreeing on the problem. For instance, previous confidential decisions might have committed the enterprise to a course of action that alters the problem, such as a merger, reorganization, or long-term contract. Whether implementation can and should proceed then depends entirely on the specifics of the situation.

If the final level of resistance never materializes or can be dealt with successfully, the sixth and final phase of buy-in is agreeing to implement. Of course, many implementation details still remain to be worked out, but this is the subject of the next chapter. Before moving on, here are some key points about the TOC approach to change:

- The natural inclination of change agents is to skip the first two phases and rush into presenting the solution. To decision-makers left unprepared by the skipped phases, however, it can look like a solution in search of a problem.

- Each phase of buy-in addresses a specific issue that can derail change. Thus, no phases can be skipped or completed out of order.

- Adequate preparation for the first three phases can easily take several days because various diagrams must be prepared, the details of which are beyond the scope of this book.

- If limited time is available for presentation, change agents should do the first two phases well, and then stop. Successfully completing those phases will leave decision-makers wanting more time later to hear the solution and discuss how it can be implemented.

As with the TOC approach to strategy seen earlier, the TOC approach to change can be used by service providers to manage their own enterprise as well as to advise clients. Therefore, how the TOC approach to change applies in services is the next topic.

Change for Services

The TOC approach to change does not require adaptation for the PSTS sector. However, the characteristics of that sector mean that PSTS professionals see change management from multiple perspectives. When working with clients, PSTS practitioners frequently fill the change agent role, but they may be called on to pursue buy-in from third parties as well as the client. And when managing their own enterprises, PSTS practitioners fill both the change agent and decision-maker roles simultaneously.

- First-order change requires buy-in by one group or enterprise, such as a client or the change agent's own enterprise. Note that the group or enterprise goal is common to all members, even though those members have different personal goals.

- Second-order change requires buy-in by groups or enterprises with a direct relationship but separate goals, such as a service provider and client, manufacturer and distributor, retailer and consumer, or utility and regulatory authority.

- Third-order change requires buy-in by groups or enterprises with an indirect relationship and different goals, such as a client's client, customer's customer, supplier's supplier, professional association, or legislative body.

The more parties are involved and the more disparate their goals and perspectives, the harder it is to get comprehensive buy-in. Moreover, selling a decision to people not involved in the decision-making can be extremely difficult. So bringing multiple parties into the TOC approach to change can increase the odds of buy-in, though it may not make sense to do so all at once.

PSTS practitioners' specific expertise can increase their effectiveness as change agents. In particular, they have an obvious advantage in identifying core problems within the domain of their expertise. And they also have the advantage of having seen previously which solutions succeeded in various circumstances. However, whether change agents are perceived as impartial depends on their own reputations as well as their sponsors'. That is, if the change agents' sponsors are known to be partisan, the change agents may have to work at affirming their own objectivity in the eyes of the other decision-makers.

During the first phase of buy-in, agreeing on the problem, PSTS practitioners know that truly unique problems are quite rare because much of their own expertise comes from having seen and solved the same problems before for other clients. So it's a bit ironic that some clients believe their problems are unique while at the same time they seek an expert for just such problems. In those rare cases where a problem really is unique, the expert may nevertheless have an edge when it comes to problem recognition, if not providing a proven solution, because the expert can eliminate a wider range of known problems. This is particularly helpful when the client is suffering from a host of pain points that obscure the core problems.

During the second phase of buy-in, agreeing on the direction of the solution, PSTS practitioners following conventional change management methods are likely to promote compromise in the face of conflict. Alternatively, they may attempt to persuade decision-makers to choose one side of the conflict without actually resolving it. In contrast, eliminating the conflict as described earlier, and thereby providing an unambiguous direction for the solution, is a signature of the TOC approach to change. However, it requires that the decision-makers be rational and open-minded enough to examine all sides of a conflict, even if they favor one side over another. Neither compromise nor buy-in will produce change if individuals are unable to accept new information and alter their positions accordingly. So this second phase of buy-in is a decision point for change agents because it tells them whether there's any point to continuing.

During the third phase of buy-in, agreeing that the solution solves the problem, clients often expect PSTS practitioners to provide evidence that a solution works. Benchmarks, statistics, simulations, methodologies, process models, and case studies can accomplish this. Nevertheless, the buy-in process can derail if influential decision-makers insist on a proof-of-concept before the solution has been polished in the later phases. Unfortunately, a premature and failed proof-of-concept project actually proves nothing because the conditions are atypical of a full-fledged implementation. Skilled change agents recognize that calls for a premature proof-of-concept may be an honest attempt to ensure success because decision-makers can be as anxious to get on with solutions as change agents are to present them. On the other hand, calls for a rapid proof-of-concept can be a disguised tactic to sabotage buy-in. In either case, skilled change agents will steer decision-makers past this pitfall.

During the fourth phase of buy-in, agreeing that the solution will not lead to significant negative effects, PSTS practitioners once again bring their experience with previous solutions. In many cases, experts know whether serious side effects are likely and perhaps how they can be avoided or mitigated. If decision-makers do not uncover side effects on their own, the change agent may need to bring them out so that they will not surface as surprises later. In addition to side effects that are obviously negative, the change agent may need to ask whether being too successful could have negative side effects. For instance, if marketing creates such a compelling offer that sales explode and production can't keep up with demand, would the newfound market success fizzle under the glare of unhappy customers?

During the fifth phase of buy-in, agreeing on how to overcome obstacles, PSTS practitioners may need to coach more than advise. As experts, they have probably seen similar obstacles to implementation overcome before, but such obstacles can be highly client-specific. What worked for one client won't necessarily work for another if the obstacles are deeply embedded in policy constraints, personal relationships, long-standing practices, or arcane organizational structures. Hence, the best thing a change agent can do at times is stand aside and let the decision-makers map their own way past obstacles to a change they have already decided is worth pursuing.

During the sixth and final phase of buy-in, agreeing to implement, PSTS practitioners must remain aware that although this signals the beginning of change, there are undoubtedly hurdles ahead. Unverbalized fear, for instance, may be a reflection of concerns coming from outside the circle of decision-makers. Opinion leaders are crucial to diffusion of innovations, yet none of them may be among the decision-makers whose buy-in has just been won. If so, gaining the buy-in of opinion leaders must be accomplished next. This may polish the solution further, but more importantly, it will start the cascade of positive chatter and role modeling necessary for change to take root.

TOC Approach to Sales

Although the previous chapter covered marketing and sales management, it deferred discussion of the TOC approach to sales to this chapter. The reason can now be easily explained: The TOC approach to sales is highly similar to the TOC approach to change. When following TOC, the steps that change agents follow to sell change to an internal audience are fundamentally the same steps that salespeople follow to sell products and services to an external audience.

Without TOC, salespeople have the same inclination as change agents: They want to present their product or service as soon as possible. Unfortunately, presenting it too early leads to objections, and the more objections customers raise, the less likely salespeople are to close sales. For their part, customers are frequently disinterested, suspicious, or perhaps even antagonistic because their previous experiences with salespeople have not been altogether positive. So even when customers perceive value in a product or service, they may resist buying it.

The TOC approach to sales is not intended for everyday sales calls where the value of the product or service being sold is comparable to competing items. It is instead intended for compelling offers designed by marketing to fulfill the enterprise strategy, as covered in the previous chapter. In a nutshell, a compelling market offer solves one or more of the customer's core problems and thereby relieves multiple pain points.

Table 9-3 summarizes levels of resistance and the corresponding phases of a sale.

Table 9-3 Levels of Resistance Versus Phases of Sale

Levels of Resistance	Phases of Sale
1. Buyers don't automatically see the value of the product/service.	1. Building rapport by confirming undesirable effects.
2. Buyers don't believe sellers understand the problems.	2. Setting the stage by confirming core problems.
3. The better the offer, the more objections buyers raise.	3. Bringing the buyer to want the product.
4. Buyers are suspicious of sellers.	4. Admitting both buyer and seller will benefit.
5. Product/service is too hard to justify.	5. Showing that product/service delivers more value to buyer.
6. Buyers may have obstacles even when they want to buy.	6. Agreeing to purchase.

- Despite a seller's enthusiasm, buyers don't automatically see the value of products or services. Thus, the seller must build rapport with buyers by using the materials prepared by marketing to confirm and discuss the undesirable effects the buyer feels.

- Buyers seldom believe that sellers really understand their problems. Thus, the seller must set the stage for the offer by using the materials prepared by marketing to confirm and discuss the core problems that lead to the buyers' undesirable effects.

- The higher the value of the product or service, the more anxious sellers are to sell, but the more wary buyers become. Thus, the seller must bring a buyer to want the product or service by showing how it solves the buyer's core problems.

- Buyers are naturally suspicious if an offer seems too good to be true. Thus, the seller must show the buyers what benefits the seller derives.

- When buyers can see why the sale is good for both parties, their resistance diminishes. Then the seller can show how the product or service delivers more value to the buyer.

- Finally, once a buyer is convinced, there may still be obstacles, such as approvals. Thus, the seller must use the list of potential obstacles prepared by marketing and work with the buyer to overcome those that apply.

The TOC approach to sales works only if marketing has created a compelling offer. Of course, even a compelling offer still has to be sold. So the TOC approach to sales requires that salespeople be trained in both the offer and how to sell it.

Impact of Strategy and Change for Services

S&C$_S$ is guided by the principle that pull works better than push in services, just as it does in manufacturing. That is, rather than pursuing an enterprise strategy that pushes the same services as competitors, pulling services via a compelling market offer is a better strategy. Likewise, rather than pushing changes before decision-makers comprehend the benefits, they are more likely to buy in to changes when they see how proposed changes solve core problems as well as many other pain points. These and other differences between conventional and TOC-based approaches to strategy and change are summarized in Table 9-4.

Table 9-4 Strategy and Change for Services

Strategy & Change for Services	Conventional	TOC-Based
Guiding principle is ...	Push	Pull
Strategic innovations address ...	Any aspect of enterprise	Constraints
Impetus for strategy is ...	Pain points	Core problems
Strategy is determined by ...	Various methods	Cause and effect
Competing mainly on price is ...	Acceptable	Not acceptable
Heart of strategy is ...	Core competency	Compelling market offers
Strategic constraints are ...	Not crucial to strategy	Deliberately chosen
Investments often target ...	Operating Expense	Throughput
Impetus for change is ...	Pain points	Core problems
Resistance to change is ...	Discouraged	Embraced
Problems are ...	Framed by change agent	Reached by consensus
Direction of solution is set by ...	Compromise	Conflict resolution
Solution is presented ...	As soon as possible	Only after groundwork is laid
Reaction to side-effects is ...	Persuasion	Polish the solution
Reaction to obstacles is ...	Persuasion	Polish the implementation
Reaction to unverbalized fear is ...	Persuasion	Redo earlier steps
Change and sales are ...	Separate steps	Same steps

Because no enterprise can escape constraints entirely, TOC strives to place them where they do the most good (or the least harm). Strategic constraints, as they are called, actually create some stability because they are known bottlenecks around which resources, projects, and processes can be managed. Physical and policy constraints can be strategic. For instance, a strategic skill group is a physical constraint, while providing services only within a particular professional, scientific, or technical realm is a policy constraint. When a service provider is ready to change strategy, it then adjusts its strategic constraints to implement the new strategy.

Strategic investments in services have different dynamics than investments in nonservices sectors. For instance, rather than wearing out or becoming depleted, some services investments grow even more valuable through repeated and intense use. On the other hand, many services investments are susceptible to rapid obsolescence and therefore have to be continually renewed. TOC may lead to different investment decisions when alternatives are viewed in terms of their impact on Throughput, and service providers can do such analysis for their clients as well as their own enterprise.

Another guiding principle of TOC says that every improvement is a change, but not every change is an improvement. This is, of course, another way of saying that improving a nonconstraint does little or nothing to help an enterprise reach its goal. Therefore, TOC achieves buy-in by showing how changes targeted at solving core problems eliminate multiple pain points. Furthermore, the steps transform decision-makers' attitudes from "Prove to me that the solution works" to "I have the information I need to prove it to myself—and others." This distinction is especially helpful in enterprises that suffer from improvement-initiative fatigue and the pervasive skepticism it spawns.

Practitioners in the PSTS sector see S&C$_S$ from the perspective of strategic advisors and change agents working on behalf of clients, as well as executives in a services enterprise grappling with their own strategy and change. Though S&C$_S$ requires no adaptation for PSTS, S&C$_S$ can enhance the other expertise PSTS practitioners already have.

Several S&C$_S$ outcomes are noteworthy:

- The TOC approach to strategy recognizes that strategy should be built around constraints because they limit what the enterprise can accomplish even if they aren't incorporated in its strategy. This approach is based on careful analysis of cause-and-effect relationships between core problems and undesirable effects. It therefore increases the odds that a change in strategy will move the enterprise toward its goal.

- The TOC approach to change follows a standard set of steps that proceed incrementally and logically toward buy-in. By embracing objections rather than discouraging them, buy-in grows progressively stronger. Hence, changes don't disappear as soon as the change agents leave. Moreover, the enterprise itself is better positioned to achieve continuous improvement via a series of changes orchestrated around its constraints.

- The TOC approach to sales follows essentially the same set of steps as the TOC approach to change. Though those steps are performed by salespeople rather than change agents, and the audience is external buyers rather than internal decision-makers, the biggest difference between the TOC approaches to change and sales is that market offers are more repeatable.

When S&C$_S$ is successful, the service provider becomes a strategic business partner with its clients. That is, each client's strategy and the service provider's strategy become aligned in ways that create more value for each party than they could attain alone or with other partners. Hence, the client should feel unequivocally that its service provider—its strategic business partner—is significantly invested in their mutual success.

Strategy is the specific way an enterprise chooses to pursue its goal, and change is how it realigns its sales and production to carry out that strategy. Once the strategy is set and buy-in to change has been attained, implementation can proceed. Technology is, of course, a part of any major change in most enterprises today. How implementation and technology apply in Theory of Constraints for Services (TOC$_S$) is the subject of the next chapter.

Summary

Strategic innovations come in many forms, including changes to products, services, markets, operations, and business models. TOC supports all forms, but it always focuses on constraints because innovations elsewhere are local optimizations that have little or no effect on the enterprise's overall Throughput. In addition, TOC directs attention to the conditions necessary for a successful enterprise because that's where core problems are found. Identifying core problems is essential to strategy because they block the enterprise from reaching its goal.

High-performing enterprises tend to adopt innovative business models, and TOC supports this in several ways. First, Throughput Accounting changes the financial model of the enterprise. Second, the TOC approach to strategy employs compelling market offers that differentiate a service provider from its competitors. Third, compelling market offers increase the value of services, so price cutting is no longer a relevant strategy. Fourth, if the market offer is constructed by breaking multiple policy constraints within the service provider's enterprise, it takes longer for competitors to catch up strategically. Finally, if the service provider's strategy is implemented by alleviating interface constraints, its suppliers and clients benefit, too.

Adopting a different strategy generally requires change, and sometimes lots of it. Whereas conventional change management discourages resistance to change, TOC embraces it. First, rather than asking decision-makers to accept a problem statement as framed by the change agent, TOC encourages decision-makers to reach consensus on the problem. Second, rather than seeking compromise on the direction for a solution, TOC resolves conflicts by uncovering invalid assumptions sustaining those conflicts. Third, rather than presenting the solution as soon as possible, TOC lays the groundwork first. Fourth, rather than reacting to potential side effects by persuading decision-makers that the solution will work anyway, TOC polishes the solution by finding ways to eliminate or minimize side effects. Fifth, rather than reacting to potential obstacles by persuading decision-makers that implementation can proceed anyway, TOC polishes the implementation by finding ways to eliminate or minimize obstacles. Finally, in the unlikely event that unverbalized fears arise, TOC repeats as many of the preceding steps as necessary.

Endnotes

1. "The Global CEO Study: Expanding the Innovation Horizon," IBM, 2006, p. 45.

2. "The Global CEO Study: Expanding the Innovation Horizon," IBM, 2006, p. 13–14.

3. Eliyahu Goldratt, *Theory of Constraints*, North River Press, 1990, pp. 3–21.

4. Bob Briscoe, Andrew Odlyzko, and Benjamin Tilly, "Metcalf's Law is Wrong," *IEEE Spectrum*, 43:7, July 2006, pp. 34–39.

5. Mehrbad Baghai, Stephen Coley, and David White, *The Alchemy of Growth: Practical Insights for Building the Enduring Enterprise*, Perseus Publishing, 2000.

6. Adrian J. Slywotzky, David J. Morrison, Ted Moser, Kevin A. Mundt, and James A. Quella, *Profit Patterns: 30 Ways to Anticipate and Profit from Strategic Forces Reshaping Your Business*, Times Business, 1999, pp. 127–135.

7. Clayton M. Christensen, *The Innovator's Dilemma: When New Technologies Cause Great Firms to Fail*, HBS Press, 1997.

8. John P. Kotter, "Why Transformation Efforts Fail," *Harvard Business Review on Change*, HBS Press, 1998, p. 1.

9. H. William Dettmer, *Strategic Navigation: A Systems Approach to Business Strategy*, ASQ Quality Press, 2003, p. 44–45.

10. David H. Maister, *Managing the Professional Service Firm*, Free Press, 1993, pp. 223–235.

11. Jena McGregor, "Most Innovative Companies," *Business Week*, May 14, 2007, p. 62.

12. Patricia K. Felkins, B.J. Chakiris, and Kenneth N. Chakiris, *Change Management: A Model for Effective Organizational Performance*, Quality Resources, 1993.

10

Implementation and Technology

Implementation puts Theory of Constraints (TOC) applications to work, and technology is a necessary enabler. If it were simply a matter of installing new technology, the technical aspects of TOC implementation would be straightforward. However, TOC implementation is no small feat, in part because technology already in use is more often an inhibitor than an enabler. In many enterprises, figuring out how to transition from legacy systems to TOC-compatible systems is the main technical challenge.

Of course, those TOC-compatible systems have to come from somewhere. In-house development requires the enterprise to have system development capability plus TOC knowledge—and that's a rare combination. Thus, the two primary sources of TOC-compatible systems are software vendors and consultants. Frequently, either software comes with consulting, or consulting comes with software.

Technical challenges are in addition to the numerous nontechnical obstacles covered in the previous chapter. Consequently, only a small percentage of the millions of readers of TOC books have implemented even one TOC application, despite acclaim for TOC and cases documenting extraordinary results.[1] What's more, after 25 years, the percentage of enterprises that have implemented every TOC application still rounds to zero. Nevertheless, three-quarters of top manufacturing plants have implemented some TOC, so implementation does pay off.[2]

In light of the inherent difficulty of implementing TOC for Goods (TOC$_G$) applications in services contexts, the dearth of services examples is understandable.[3] History notwithstanding, however, the outlook for TOC in services has never been better. For one thing, what we perceive as a slow rate of TOC adoption in a world now accustomed to "Internet time" is not at all unusual for intangible innovations. Though it can easily take a generation or more for any innovation to reach its tipping point, this is especially true when the innovation is intangible and up against a huge installed base of legacy technology. Fortunately, the TOC for Services (TOC$_S$) applications covered in earlier chapters remove some major obstacles to TOC implementation. So a TOC tipping point may be at hand as more services enterprises seek innovations they can use to compete in increasingly global markets for services on demand.

TOC has relied on technology from its inception, but TOC has also been at odds with technology. For example, TOC$_G$ opposes Enterprise Resource Planning (ERP) if it ignores the manufacturing constraint, as software packages do when they assume infinite capacity. On the other hand, TOC_G relies on software to implement Drum-Buffer-Rope (DBR). Likewise, TOC opposes Critical Path (CP) project management, in part because it does not require resource leveling. Then again, TOC relies on software to implement Critical Chain (CC).

The guiding principle behind TOC implementation and technology is simple: If technology doesn't take the enterprise toward its goal, it shouldn't be implemented. A corollary to this principle is if technology is taking the enterprise away from its goal, a better alternative should be found. For instance, it can be impractical to implement DBR and CC without simultaneously replacing ERP and CP software packages—or at least installing compatible TOC modules. Also, software developed in-house may need significant changes, because many user requirements are local optimizations that work against global optimization of the enterprise.

This chapter covers *Implementation & Technology for Services* ($I\&T_S$) from the perspective of change agents and technologists working on behalf of clients, as well as executives in a services enterprise wrestling with their own implementation and technology. As you will see, how $I\&T_S$ applies in Professional, Scientific, and Technical Services (PSTS) diverges somewhat from TOC implementation and technology elsewhere because the constraints and applications are different.

Diffusion of Innovations

Getting buy-in from decision-makers is essential for change, but their buy-in is just the jumping-off point for TOC implementation. Decision-makers are a critical part of an enterprise's formal structure, yet insofar as diffusion of innovations goes, opinion leaders are an equally critical part of its informal structure. Though decision-makers can authorize TOC implementation, there are many ways implementation can go awry if managers and workers misunderstand TOC or do not see its value. This does not mean, however, that everyone needs the same depth of understanding or appreciation of value. Opinion leaders are vital because each is at the hub of his or her own interpersonal communication network that spreads the word for or against particular innovations.

Figure 10-1 illustrates a typical innovation adoption curve.[4] The S-shape of this curve describes how innovations spread, both within a single enterprise and across multiple enterprises, though the time scale is shorter and the slope is steeper for a single enterprise.

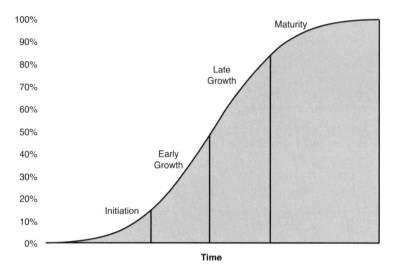

Figure 10-1   Innovation adoption

- Kicking off the Initiation stage, a small set of adopters (about 2.5 percent) known as *innovators* buy in to the innovation. Innovators include decision-makers as well as practitioners who do pilot implementations. Their judgment and experience demonstrate the practicality and value of the innovation, but innovators are rarely opinion leaders.

- Wrapping up the Initiation stage, *early adopters* (about 13.5 percent) put the innovation to work on a small scale. More importantly, however, early adopters include opinion leaders whose views are broadly influential.

- If the Initiation stage is successful, the *early majority* (34 percent) adopt the innovation during the Early Growth stage, the *late majority* (34 percent) adopt it during the Late Growth stage, and *laggards* (16 percent) may never adopt it unless forced to do so during the Maturity stage.

Innovation adoption thus reaches *critical mass*—becomes self-sustaining—when 10 to 25 percent of potential adopters accept it. This range is where the S-curve begins sweeping rapidly upward, and it agrees with the TOC rule of thumb that about 15 percent of an enterprise's employees have to buy in to TOC for it to take root.

Change agents can be innovators, early adopters, or outside experts. If change agents are not opinion leaders themselves, they increase the odds of success by seeking out "change aides" who are. The informal buzz generated by opinion leaders is more persuasive than any mass media or management communication. Thus, getting buy-in from opinion leaders is the next step toward wide adoption because it's the only way innovations reach critical mass.

Buy-in Revisited

The same steps used to get buy-in from decision-makers are used to get buy-in from opinion leaders. However, unless opinion leaders uncover truly insurmountable obstacles, which isn't likely, they can only polish the solution, hone the implementation, and carry the message to others.

As a practical matter, it may not be advisable to hold separate buy-in sessions just for opinion leaders, so those sessions may include other executives, managers, or practitioners who are themselves potential early adopters, but with less influence. In that case, their main contribution is to polish the solution and implement it in their own area, rather than carry the message elsewhere.

Although the decision to implement TOC has already been made by the time implementation kicks off, that does not mean the buy-in process with early adopters can be skipped or abbreviated, otherwise, their resistance will almost certainly derail implementation.[5]

- Executives can have a hard time at first believing that constraint management works, and then accepting that the real constraints aren't necessarily where they think, and finally realizing that the strategy they have isn't the strategy they need. Several days of dedicated TOC education and discussion, moderated by TOC change agents, are usually required to clear the clutter and refocus on constraint management.

- Managers can have a hard time trusting that less planning and control—optimizing just the constraint—can be a better approach when they've spent their careers striving for more planning and control in order to optimize every task and resource. Hands-on simulation games are a staple of TOC education and buy-in because they're an effective way to demonstrate how local optimization actually creates pain points.

- Practitioners can suffer from misalignment between their responsibility and authority. For example, practitioners in a service center are usually held responsible for customer satisfaction, yet they may have limited authority to solve customer problems, which then generates dissatisfaction. And some matrix organizations deliberately establish joint authority but separate responsibilities, which means conflict is by design. In PSTS, responsibility and authority can reside in different organizations. For instance, getting clients to meet their project responsibilities, such as providing essential resources and completing critical tasks in a timely fashion, can be a challenge because the service provider has no direct authority over the client's employees.

In addition to polishing the solution itself, another outcome from buy-in is an understanding of prerequisites that must be fulfilled. For instance, Replenishment for Services (R_S) is a prerequisite for Critical Chain for Services (CC_S). Though the buy-in sessions with decision-makers should have worked through many such prerequisites, this is a likely place for early adopters to further hone the implementation, especially if they are closer to the core problems than the decision-makers are. For example, early adopters might recognize that in order to implement R_S, the service provider's heterogeneous resource pools will have to be transformed into distinct skill groups, each composed of reasonably interchangeable resources. Likewise, early adopters may recognize that clients will apply pressure to cut the project buffer in CC_S even though CC_S cannot work without an adequate buffer.

The latter obstacle is much harder to overcome because it lies outside the service provider, but even that doesn't make it insurmountable. Rather than educate clients on CC_S, an internal implementation alternative is to minimize the number of milestones and client dependencies and then maintain dual project plans: a detailed CC_S plan for the service provider's project managers, plus a summary plan in CP format for the client's project sponsor. In this way, a service provider can adopt TOC_S even if its clients aren't ready. To the degree that CC_S delivers more projects on time and within budget, clients then reap the benefits without getting tangled in implementation details.

Managing Contracts

As an example of TOC_S implementation, Figure 10-2 shows several hypothetical services contracts. Each row represents one contract composed of projects and processes. Columns contain measures defined in Throughput Accounting for Services (TA_S).

Project or process	Duration (months)	Effort (hours)	FTEs	Revenue	T/h	OE/h	T	OE	NP	PDD
						Planned				
A	18	221,760	77	$17,800,000	$80.27	$64.30	$17,800,000	$14,259,169	$3,540,831	$9,836
B	9	38,880	27	$3,900,000	$100.31	$65.10	$3,900,000	$2,531,088	$1,368,912	$7,605
C	12	80,640	42	$7,300,000	$90.53	$72.97	$7,300,000	$5,884,114	$1,415,886	$5,900
D	36	1,244,160	216	$93,400,000	$75.07	$72.11	$93,400,000	$89,721,008	$3,678,992	$5,110
E	4	5,120	8	$700,000	$136.72	$67.79	$700,000	$347,060	$352,940	$4,412
F	6	14,400	15	$1,300,000	$90.28	$60.46	$1,300,000	$870,584	$429,416	$3,578
G	4	5,120	8	$500,000	$97.66	$70.05	$500,000	$358,651	$141,349	$1,767
H	12	80,640	42	$6,500,000	$80.61	$77.75	$6,500,000	$6,270,151	$229,849	$958
Total										$39,165

160 hours per FTE per month
20 billing days per month

Project or process	T	OE	NP	PDD	Variance	Duration (months)	Effort (hours)	T	OE	NP	PDD	Variance
	Last Month							**To Date**				
A	$988,889	$792,176	$196,713	$9,836	$0	6	73,920	$5,933,333	$4,753,056	$1,180,277	$9,836	$0
B	$433,333	$281,232	$152,101	$7,605	$0	3	12,960	$1,254,977	$825,759	$429,217	$7,154	-$451
C	$596,167	$490,343	$105,824	$5,291	-$608	1	6,720	$608,333	$490,343	$117,990	$5,900	$0
D	$2,594,444	$2,492,250	$102,194	$5,110	$0	6	207,360	$15,566,667	$14,968,455	$598,212	$4,985	-$125
E	$175,000	$86,765	$88,235	$4,412	$0	4	5,120	$717,759	$340,630	$377,129	$4,714	$302
F	$249,705	$145,097	$104,607	$5,230	$1,652	3	7,200	$676,598	$439,645	$236,954	$3,949	$371
G	$126,250	$89,663	$36,587	$1,829	$63	2	2,560	$250,000	$179,326	$70,674	$1,767	$0
H	$514,583	$522,513	-$7,929	-$396	-$1,354	9	60,480	$4,696,266	$4,749,639	-$53,373	-$297	-$1,254
Total				$38,917	-$247						$38,008	-$1,157

Figure 10-2 Managing contracts

Comparing planned Throughput (T), Operating Expense (OE), and Net Profit (NP) for entire contracts to their actual values for a particular interval of time does not reveal much because these measures are confounded with duration and timing. That is, long process contracts naturally have larger measures than short project contracts, and a project that ramps up and down has more variation over time than a steady-state process. Hence, it's difficult to manage a diverse portfolio with just information about T, OE, and NP.

Project and Process Dollars per Day (PDD) are control measures normalized for duration, however. Because PDD is a daily rate, long processes and short projects can have the same PDD. Conversely, a project that ramps up and down will have variable PDD over its lifetime, while a steady-state process will have relatively constant PDD.

Rows in the figure are sorted by planned PDD, and differences between planned and actual PDD values appear in the variance columns. Recall that projects and processes are in control when their PDD is within or rising above its normal range.

Note that the contracts with highest planned PDD are not the ones with the longest duration, highest effort, most full-time equivalent (FTE) resources, largest revenue, highest Throughput per hour (T/h), or lowest Operating Expense per hour (OE/h). They're the ones with highest NP relative to their planned durations.

Last month, the contracts in the figure collectively had a variance of only -$247/day from a planned value of about $39,000/day. Contracts F and H, however, deserve scrutiny because their individual variances are noticeably larger than the rest. Examining PDD from each contract's inception to date is one way to do this.

- Contract F has a positive but much smaller variance-to-date than last month.

- Contract H has a negative variance-to-date about the same magnitude as last month.

Hence, last month was an especially good month for Contract F. On the other hand, it was another bad month for Contract H, which appears to be chronically troubled.

Managing Resources

As another example of TOC$_S$ implementation, Figure 10-3 shows data for a couple of skill groups. Each row contains data for one working day. Columns contain either resource counts or associated dollars.

Work day	Skill group #1									Skill group #2								
	Demand	In	Out	Bench	Over	Under	RDD	ΔT	ΔL	Demand	In	Out	Bench	Over	Under	RDD	ΔT	ΔL
1	5	6	5	1	0	0	$0	$0	$0	4	2	2	0	0	2	$0	-$1,600	-$8,000
2	2	1	2	0	0	0	$0	$0	$0	0	1	1	0	0	1	$0	-$800	-$4,000
3	5	6	6	0	0	0	$0	$0	$0	0	1	1	0	0	0	$0	$0	$0
4	5	7	4	3	1	1	$280	-$400	$0	0	0	0	0	0	0	$0	$0	$0
5	6	5	5	3	1	2	$280	-$800	$0	0	1	0	1	0	0	$0	$0	$0
6	0	1	1	3	1	1	$280	-$400	$0	2	1	2	0	0	0	$0	$0	$0
7	3	4	3	4	2	1	$560	-$400	$0	0	0	0	0	0	0	$0	$0	$0
8	4	4	5	3	1	0	$280	$0	$0	0	0	0	0	0	0	$0	$0	$0
9	3	5	3	5	3	0	$840	$0	$0	0	1	0	1	0	0	$0	$0	$0
10	5	5	5	5	3	0	$840	$0	$0	0	2	1	2	0	0	$0	$0	$0
11	0	0	2	3	1	0	$280	$0	$0	5	2	4	0	0	1	$0	-$800	-$4,000
12	9	6	5	4	2	4	$560	-$1,600	$0	0	0	0	0	0	1	$0	-$800	-$4,000
13	2	4	4	4	2	2	$560	-$800	$0	0	1	0	1	0	1	$0	-$800	-$4,000
14	4	3	4	3	1	2	$280	-$800	$0	0	0	1	0	0	0	$0	$0	$0
15	0	5	4	4	2	0	$560	$0	$0	0	1	1	0	0	0	$0	$0	$0
16	6	7	7	4	2	0	$560	$0	$0	7	4	4	0	0	3	$0	-$2,400	-$12,000
17	0	5	1	8	6	0	$1,680	$0	$0	0	2	1	1	0	2	$0	-$1,600	-$8,000
18	2	2	3	7	5	0	$1,400	$0	$0	0	0	1	0	0	1	$0	-$800	-$4,000
19	3	3	2	8	6	1	$1,680	-$400	$0	0	0	0	0	0	1	$0	-$800	-$4,000
20	0	1	2	7	5	0	$1,400	$0	$0	0	0	0	0	0	1	$0	-$800	-$4,000
Total							$12,320	-$5,600	$0							$0	-$11,200	-$56,000
average	3.20	4.00	3.65	3.95	2.20	0.70				0.90	0.95	0.95	0.30	0.00	0.70			

Skill group #1:
2 upper threshold
0 target buffer
0 lower threshold
2 resupply time (working days)
$50 T/h
$35 OE/h
8 billable hours per day
0 leverage factor

Skill group #2:
5 upper threshold
3 target buffer
2 lower threshold
60 resupply time (working days)
$100 T/h
$70 OE/h
8 billable hours per day
5 leverage factor

Figure 10-3   Managing resources

Demand is the number of new resource orders received each day by the resource manager from project and process managers. *In* is resources coming back into the buffer from projects and processes and outside sources, while *out* is those resources leaving the buffer for a project or process or outside destination. *Bench* is the net number remaining in the buffer. *Over* is excess resources on the bench above the upper buffer threshold. *Under* is demand not met by assigning resources.

RDD is Resource Dollars per Day, which is calculated as excess resources times their Operating Expense per day. ΔT is lost Throughput, which is resource shortage times Throughput per day. Finally, ΔL is lost leverage, which is resource shortage times Throughput per day times the leverage factor. If the leverage factor is greater than zero, for every resource that skill group is short, the enterprise loses that many times as much Throughput because other skill groups depend on the current skill group.

Parameters are shown at the bottom of the figure. *Resupply time*, for instance, is the average number of working days required to add another resource to the skill group from outside sources.

Interpretation of this information proceeds as follows. RDD indicates whether resources are under control. That is, RDD is zero if there are no excess resources. Ideally, however, there is no lost Throughput or leverage due to resource shortages, either.

In an actual enterprise, there could be dozens, if not hundreds, of skill groups. The figure, however, illustrates the dynamics of just two contrasting skill groups:

- Group #1 is a commodity skill, so its target buffer is zero, resupply time is short, and leverage is low.

- Group #2 is a scarce skill, so its target buffer is greater than zero, resupply time is long, and leverage is high.

Turning first to Group #1, demand on Day 4 is for five resources, and there are no resources on the bench from the previous day. Seven resources come back into the buffer, but only four are reassigned to a project or process, which is one under demand. This leaves three on the bench, which is one over the upper threshold. RDD on Day 4 is thus $280, or one excess resource times eight hours per day times $35 per hour. Likewise, ΔT on Day 4 is -$400, or one resource under demand times eight hours per day times $50 per hour. Hence, if that excess resource had been assigned on Day 4, its $400 of T would have covered its $280 of OE. The other two resources on the bench are within the thresholds, so no RDD or ΔT are attributed to them.

Over the course of the working days illustrated in the figure, RDD rises steadily. The cause is more resources coming in than going out. This situation occurs naturally whenever sales are declining, such as at the end of a busy season. For a commodity skill group experiencing a rise in RDD, the resource manager would consider releasing some subcontractors.

Turning next to Group #2, demand is lumpy: It appears mainly on the first day of each week. But the skills are so scarce that lead time is lengthy, and the bench level rarely reaches the target, let alone the upper threshold. Thus, RDD is almost always zero, and ΔT is nonzero whenever resources cannot meet demand. Furthermore, because many other resources depend on this skill group, its leverage is high. On Day 16, for instance, the shortage of three resources causes $2,400 of T to be lost just on this skill group—plus another $12,000 of T for resources in other skill groups (ΔL). Unfortunately, simply hiring more resources is not an option because this skill group is a constrained resource.

Technology Assessment

If you could implement technology that would provide the information just illustrated, or any of the TOC$_S$ information illustrated in previous chapters, how would you know whether it's the right thing to do? Here are some key questions to ask about technology:[6]

- What is the power of the technology?
- What limitation does it diminish?
- What old rules accommodate that limitation?
- What new rules should be used instead?
- What changes in technology are needed to support those new rules?
- How should the change be made?

Because the information illustrated in the previous section is derived from TA$_S$, let's answer the technology questions by assuming the incumbent technology is a Cost Accounting (CA) system:

- The power of TA$_S$ is that it supports constraint management.
- The limitation of CA is that it encourages local optimization.
- The old rules of CA say that resources on the bench are an expense to be minimized.
- The new rules of TA$_S$ say that resources in the buffer protect Throughput.
- Changing from CA to TA$_S$ software would support the new rules.
- Implementing TA$_S$ rules in a legacy financial system might be possible if the old rules can be replaced.

An actual technology assessment would, of course, go much deeper, but even these simple answers are enough to show how an alternative technology can steer an enterprise toward its goal.

The TOC$_S$ applications covered in earlier chapters can be implemented in information technology (IT). Because TOC$_S$ applications are complementary, the systems in which they are implemented should interlock. Thus, the following sections provide an overview of some interlocking IT for TOC$_S$.

Resource Management System

Figure 10-4 depicts a resource management system based on Replenishment for Services (R$_S$). That system has an associated resource database in which data about individual skills and skill groups is maintained.

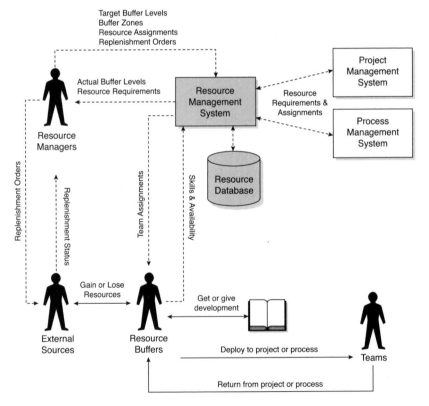

Figure 10-4   Resource management system

For each skill group, resource managers maintain data about the target buffer level, buffer zones around that target, resource assignments, and replenishment orders for additional resources. The system provides resource managers with information about actual buffer levels and resource requirements. Those requirements flow into the resource management system from project and process managers via interfaces from their management systems.

When additional resources are needed, resource managers issue replenishment orders to external sources, such as recruiters and subcontractors. They in turn keep resource managers informed about the status of those orders.

Individual resources use the resource management system to record their skills and availability. Resources arriving from external sources enter the buffer, while those leaving for external destinations, such as retirement, exit their skill group. Resources in the buffer are available for assignment to project or process teams—or to give or get resource development, such as training and mentoring. Resources deployed to a project or process, or acting as trainers, are no longer in the buffer, while resources getting trained remain in the buffer.

In summary, resource managers use the resource management system to manage resource buffers according to the rules of R_S. Resource buffer management enables projects and processes to acquire resources on demand.

Project Management System

Figure 10-5 depicts a project management system based on Critical Chain for Services (CC$_S$). That system has an associated project database in which data about multiple projects is maintained.

For each project, project managers maintain data about project plans, resource requirements, and task assignments. The system provides project managers with information about project status, task status, resource assignments, replenishment times, and resource buffer status. Replenishment information flows into the project management system via an interface from the resource management system.

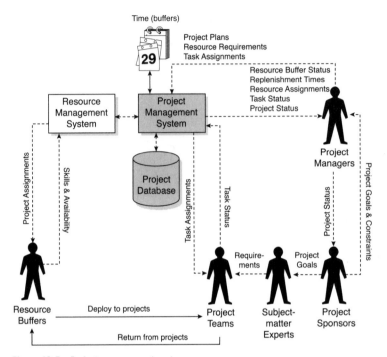

Figure 10-5 Project management system

Project managers receive project goals and constraints from project sponsors. On external projects, sponsors are clients. On internal projects, sponsors are authorizing executives. In both cases, project managers keep project sponsors informed about project status.

Project sponsors also communicate project goals to subject-matter experts. They in turn provide requirements to project teams.

Project teams are composed of resources assigned by resource managers. Team members receive their task assignments from project managers, who also record those assignments in the system. Team members use the project management system to record their task status.

In summary, project managers use the project management system to manage project buffers according to the rules of CC_S. That buffer management enables projects to be completed on time and within budget. And the interlock between project and resource management systems enables projects to be scheduled on demand.

Process Management System

Figure 10-6 depicts a process management system based on Drum-Buffer-Rope for Services (DBR$_S$). That system has an associated process database in which data about multiple processes is maintained. Each process is governed by a service level agreement (SLA).

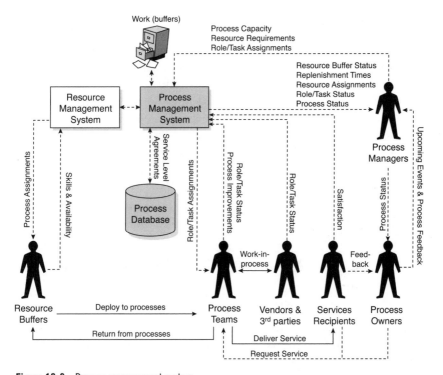

Figure 10-6 Process management system

For each process, process managers maintain data about process capacity, resource requirements, and role or task assignments. The system provides process managers with information about process status, role and task status, resource assignments, replenishment times, and resource buffer status. Replenishment information flows into the process management system via an interface from the resource management system.

Process managers receive information about upcoming events—such as new products, services, and advertising campaigns—from process owners. Process managers also receive feedback from process owners. On external processes, owners are clients. On internal processes, owners are authorizing executives. In both cases, process managers keep process owners informed about process status.

Process teams are composed of resources assigned by resource managers. Team members receive their role or task assignments from resource managers, who also record those assignments in the system. When assigned to a role rather than a task, team members themselves determine which tasks to perform. Team members use the process management system to record their role and task status, as well as process improvements. For instance, if a task can be eliminated or automated under certain conditions, that process change is entered into the system.

If vendors or third parties are involved in service delivery, work-in-process may flow back and forth with process teams. Like process teams, vendors and third parties may use the process management system to record their role or task status.

Service recipients may request service themselves, or it may be requested on their behalf by process owners. Service recipients can receive service from process teams, vendors, or third parties. Based on that service, recipients may have their satisfaction recorded in the process management system, and they may provide feedback directly to process owners.

In summary, process managers use the process management system to manage process buffers according to the rules of DBR$_S$. By adjusting capacity as needed, processes are completed according to SLAs. This, plus the interlock between the process and resource management systems, enables the process to be performed on demand.

Sales Management System

Figure 10-7 depicts a sales management system based on Marketing and Sales for Services (M&S$_S$). That system has an associated sales database in which data about multiple sales opportunities is maintained.

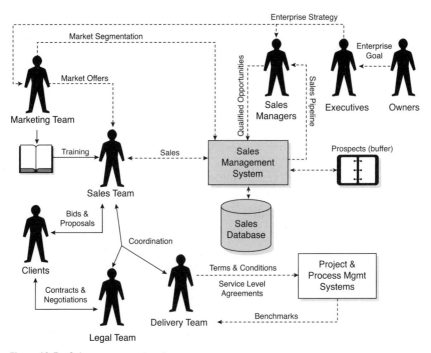

Figure 10-7 Sales management system

Owners set the enterprise goal. Executives devise enterprise strategy. Marketing teams segment markets, create market offers, and provide training on both market offers and the sales (buy-in) process.

Sales managers use the system to monitor the sales pipeline and qualify opportunities. Sales teams receive training, use the system to maintain data about opportunities at all stages of the sales pipeline, and create bids and proposals for qualified opportunities. Sales teams also coordinate with delivery teams so that bids and proposals are consistent with benchmarks derived from the project and process management systems.

Clients evaluate those bids and proposals and then decide whether to pursue contracts and negotiations. Legal teams handle contracts and negotiations for the service provider, coordinate with both sales and service delivery teams, and pass the terms and conditions for signed contracts (as well as SLAs) to delivery teams. Delivery teams enter that information into the project and process management systems.

In summary, by segmenting the market and creating compelling market offers according to the rules of M&S$_S$, marketing teams fill the sales buffer with prospects. Sales managers use the sales management system to manage the sales buffer and direct sales teams to qualified opportunities. By using the sales (buy-in) process as defined in M&S$_S$, sales teams convert qualified opportunities into completed sales.

Financial Management System

Figure 10-8 depicts a financial management system based on Throughput Accounting for Services (TA$_S$). That system has an associated financial database in which data about the entire enterprise is maintained.

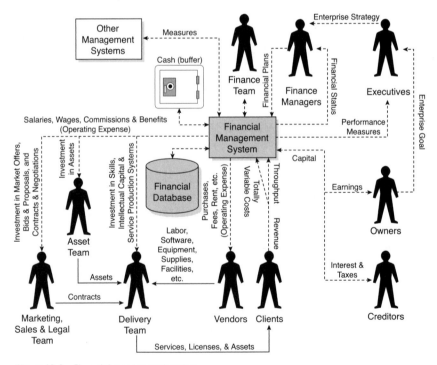

Figure 10-8   Financial management system

Owners set the enterprise goal, provide capital, and receive earnings. Creditors provide capital, receive interest, and receive taxes. Executives devise enterprise strategy and receive performance measures. Finance managers use the system to create financial plans and monitor financial status.

Operating expense is composed of salaries, wages, commissions, and benefits flowing to employees. Operating expense is also composed of purchases, fees, rent, and other payments to vendors.

Most operating expense covers the labor of service delivery teams. However, investments include market offers, bids and proposals, contracts and negotiations, assets, skills, intellectual capital, and service production systems.

In order to deliver services, delivery teams receive contracts generated through the combined efforts of marketing, sales, and legal teams. Delivery teams may also receive assets from dedicated asset development teams. Finally, delivery teams use labor, software, equipment, supplies, and facilities from vendors.

Clients receive services and assets from delivery teams. In return, clients pay fees to the service provider. Throughput is revenue (fees) minus totally variable costs, such as commissions.

Finance teams have responsibility for the financial, performance, resource, decision-support, and control measures defined by TA_S. Those measures flow via interfaces between the financial management system and resource, project, process, and sales management systems. Finance teams also do reconciliations for external reporting according to generally accepted accounting principles (GAAP).

In summary, finance managers use the financial management system to manage the enterprise's cash buffer according to the rules of TA_S. They also oversee financial measurements both for internal decision support and external reporting.

Non-Information Technology

Whereas IT is necessary for TOC implementation, it is by no means the only kind of technology that may be affected. During TOC implementation, one of the first tasks is to identify the true constraint. In most cases, that's quickly followed by the search for ways to alleviate that constraint because it governs Throughput of the enterprise. In general, any technology used to create goods or deliver services could need to be updated or replaced as a result of implementing TOC. However, most enterprises find that they have latent capacity that was hidden before they adopted TOC. Thus, they may need to turn their attention to generating more Throughput from the technology they already have.

In PSTS, various kinds of non-information technology are in wide use. For example, when scientists or their research assistants are unproductive while tending lab equipment, that lab equipment could be the constraint. If architects spend significant time building models by hand, new model-building equipment might eliminate that constraint. If technicians spend much of their time disassembling and reassembling units just to run diagnostics, redesigning those units with an external jack for diagnostic equipment might eliminate both tasks, except in cases where repairs are really required.

Of course, when an existing constraint is eliminated, another resource or task just becomes the new constraint—but with higher Throughput than before. However, when an existing constraint is alleviated but not eliminated, the increase in its capacity may be sufficient to cause other capacity-constrained resources (CCRs) to become the bottleneck at times. Therefore, it's worth determining how much spare capacity CCRs have because increasing their capacity could eliminate wandering bottlenecks.

Technology for Multiple Service Levels

Every service sector has its own versions of standard, economy, and premium service. Indeed, a single enterprise can offer a wide variety of service levels. And so it is in PSTS.

- Each client may choose a different trade-off between price, speed, and quality for a given scope of service—and clients often adjust scope to meet other objectives.

- Clients may also authorize different service levels for each class of service recipient.

- A given recipient may get different service levels based on time, place, and priority.

■ The provider may restrict service levels during peak usage periods and emergencies.

Of course, different service levels often require different technologies. For example, remote technical support requires communication technology, while on-site support may not. Priority-based service requires queue management technology, while a first-come, first-served protocol does not. Self-service requires a user-friendly interface, while professional service can rely on a power-user interface that would be incomprehensible to nonprofessionals. Ironically, "technology" sounds impersonal even though personal service sometimes means the provider uses more, not less, technology on behalf of the recipient.

Hence, when implementing TOC, the relationship between IT and non-IT has to be considered. Of course, IT can be used to optimize an IT constraint, such as scheduling supercomputers for scientific research. But IT can also optimize a non-IT constraint, such as scheduling appointments for professional services. And in some cases, IT can substitute for a non-IT constraint, such as falling back to self-service via the web when technical support is overloaded.

Continuous Improvement

Though initial TOC implementation is usually handled as a project with a due date, a successful implementation never really ends because TOC strives for continuous improvement. The key steps are as follows:

1. **Identify the constraint**—The constraint limits overall Throughput.
2. **Exploit the constraint**—The constraint should be used to its fullest extent on the optimal product or service mix, and anything nonessential should be off-loaded.
3. **Subordinate everything else**—Every nonconstraint should be able to sprint in order to keep up or catch up with the constraint, and nonconstraints should not produce anything unless it's needed to keep the constraint fully utilized (except in cases where the constraint isn't required to produce a good or service).
4. **Elevate the constraint**—Increase the constraint's capacity.

5. **Repeat**—When the constraint moves, the new constraint becomes the improvement target.

Continuous improvement is a hallmark of quality initiatives, but they are apt to be local optimizations unless directed at constraints.[7] TOC thus creates high leverage from its approach to continuous improvement by directing it onto global optimization. This has implications for applied analytics, which includes empirical data, quantitative models, and computer systems that run them:[8]

- TOC relies less on forecasting and more on root-cause analysis to predict outcomes.
- TOC relies less on quantitative models and more on aggregation to deal with random variability.
- TOC relies less on key performance indicators and more on constraint measures for management decisions.

TOC also supports an empirical approach to identifying best practices. The justification for some activities claimed as best practices in academic journals and trade publications is debatable because they are best only in local contexts. Consequently, managers of resources, projects, processes, finances, and sales can each follow so-called best practices that yield no increase in Throughput yet create pain points for other managers. In TOC, however, the criterion is clear-cut: Best practices are activities that enable the enterprise as a whole to reach its goal via continuous improvement at constraints. It can't be a best practice if it doesn't move the needle.

Improvement targets discussed so far have been mainly in PSTS because it's the sector least like the Manufacturing sector, where TOC began. PSTS therefore provides the greatest contrast. The next chapter, however, extends the discussion to other service sectors in the middle ground.

Impact of Implementation and Technology for Services

Implementation and Technology for Services ($I\&T_S$) is guided by the TOC principle that if technology doesn't take the enterprise toward its goal, that technology shouldn't be implemented. However, following this implementation principle requires a holistic view of the enterprise. Undesirable effects—pain points—felt in one part of the enterprise may be caused by problems elsewhere, so uncoordinated solutions within individual business functions may not address the core problem. Thus, successful TOC implementations usually work across traditional business functions. This and other differences between conventional and TOC-based approaches to implementation and technology are summarized in Table 10-1.

Rather than assuming authorization of implementation by decision-makers is sufficient, I&T$_S$ extends the change management process to target opinion leaders. Their buy-in is essential for any innovation to take root, including TOC$_S$. In addition, opinion leaders and other early adopters may hone the implementation beyond what decision-makers envisioned. Of course, failing to gain the support of opinion leaders—or losing it later—probably dooms the implementation.

Technology assessment is not just about technology's capability; it's also about technology's effect. Amara's Law reminds us that "we tend to overestimate the effect of a technology in the short run and underestimate the effect in the long run."[9] TOC views technology as necessary but not sufficient because the accompanying change in business rules is what thwarts or propels TOC implementation.

One of the hardest parts of TOC$_S$ implementation is getting people to stop doing things that work against the enterprise goal. Forecasting resource demand, setting universal utilization objectives, padding task estimates with contingency, balancing process capacity, allocating costs, and pushing services based on price are long-standing practices supported by technology. Thus, unplugging legacy technology and plugging in new technology are often necessary, but unless the new technology encompasses new business rules, such as TOC$_S$, it won't be sufficient for the enterprise to reach its goal.

TOC$_S$ applications are interlocking. Though this means multiple applications have to be implemented to get maximum benefit, it doesn't mean they have to be implemented all at once. For example, R$_S$ can be implemented even as the enterprise continues to use CP for project management and a conventional balanced-capacity approach for process management. CC can be implemented without R$_S$, but scheduling of multiple projects may be constrained by resources. TA$_S$ can be implemented before any other TOC$_S$ application if measurement is a core problem. And so forth.

Table 10-1   Implementation and Technology for Services

Implementation and Technology for Services	Conventional	TOC-Based
Guiding principle is ...	Implement any technology that can be justified by local optimization	Implement technology only for global optimization
Implementation depends on ...	Authorization by decision-makers	Buy-in by opinion leaders
Managing contracts is ...	Hindered by incompatible measures covering entire projects and processes of differing size and duration	Assisted by compatible measures, including PDD
Managing resources is ...	Driven by individual utilization	Guided to minimize RDD for excess resources while also minimizing lost Throughput from resource shortage
Technology assessment hinges on ...	Business benefits, regardless of location	Support for new rules that overcome a limitation
Resource management system ...	Minimizes resources on the bench	Protects Throughput with resource buffers
Project management system ...	Protects schedule with task contingency	Protects schedule with project buffer
Process management system ...	Delivers service as available, with work queues anywhere	Delivers service on demand by managing capacity based on the constraint's work buffer
Sales management system ...	Pushes prospects through the sales pipeline	Pulls prospects from the sales buffer with compelling market offers
Financial management system ...	Provides CA measures and manages cash	Provides TA measures and manages the cash buffer
Non-information technology should be ...	Upgraded or replaced if it's in scope for implementation	Upgraded or replaced only if it's a constraint or CCR
Technology should support multiple service levels ...	Because clients demand it	Because it facilitates constraint management
Continuous improvement originates ...	Anywhere	Only at constraints

The TOC approach to continuous improvement is more focused than others. Whereas conventional approaches foster local optimization wherever it can be found, TOC says the only improvement that matters is at constraints. Thus, a conventional improvement program might celebrate a 20 percent reduction in cost without recognizing that net profit didn't budge. TOC, on the other hand, would celebrate a 10 percent increase in net profit—even if cost rose by 20 percent.

Several I&T$_S$ outcomes are noteworthy:

- By recognizing that innovation adoption generally follows an S-shaped curve, TOC$_S$ implementation actively seeks buy-in from opinion leaders. Without their support, no innovation will take root, including TOC$_S$.

- TOC$_S$ can be implemented with interlocking information systems. Each additional system makes the others stronger via shared information, consistent rules, and new ways to manage constraints.

- Continuous improvement matters, but only if it's focused on the constraints that stand between the enterprise and its goal.

- TOC implementations are not easily replicated by competitors, particularly if an enterprise breaks multiple policy constraints. So if an enterprise implements multiple TOC$_S$ applications, it may have competitive advantage that's more sustainable than most.

Just as change can be the constraint on strategy, technology can be the obstacle to TOC implementation—but it usually isn't. Getting buy-in to new business rules is more often the obstacle to successful implementation.

Fortunately, TOC can solve some problems that seem unsolvable when attacked conventionally. Of course, some problems defy solutions, even by TOC. The next chapter therefore concludes with some limitations, refinements, and topics for additional research.

Summary

Implementation of TOC for Services (TOC$_S$) depends on technology—and a lot more. As with any other nascent innovation, opinion leaders have to buy in to TOC$_S$ to get the implementation rolling. Implementation reaches critical mass when about 15 percent of an enterprise, the early adopters, are committed.

The TOC approach to technology assessment naturally focuses on constraints. That is, if a technology doesn't enable constraint management, it won't enable the enterprise to reach its goal—and therefore shouldn't be implemented. Moreover, if a technology encourages local optimization, as most do, that technology may actually work against the goal.

A complete implementation of TOC$_S$ includes systems for managing resources, projects, processes, sales, and finances. Each of those systems supports management of different buffers. They interlock by sharing information for decision-making purposes and supporting a consistent set of business rules, all aimed at the enterprise goal.

In order to implement technology that can support multiple service levels, both information technology (IT) and non-IT have to be considered. When non-IT is the constraint, IT may nevertheless be able to optimize that constraint.

Implementation of TOC never really ends because it follows a continuous improvement cycle. Each trip through the cycle either improves the current constraint or reorients constraint management around the new constraint.

Endnotes

1. Dan Eckermann, "Breaking Through in a Sixty Year Culture at LeTourneau, Inc.," *TOCICO Conference*, 2005.

2. John S. McClenahen, "Manufacturing's Influential Thinkers & Doers," *Information Week*, March 1, 2006.

3. Julie Wright and Russ King, *We All Fall Down: Goldratt's Theory of Constraints for Healthcare Systems*, North River Press, 2006.

4. Everett M. Rogers, *Diffusion of Innovations*, Free Press, Fourth Edition, 1995, pp. 1–37.

5. Harold E. Cavallaro and Carol A. Ptak, *Theory H.O.W.: How Organizations Could Work*, Specialty Publishing Company, 2006.

6. Eliyahu Goldratt, Eli Schragenheim, and Carol Ptak, *Necessary But Not Sufficient*, North River Press, 2000.

7. Domenico Lepore and Oded Cohen, *Deming and Goldratt*, North River Press, 1999.

8. Thomas H. Davenport, "Competing on Analytics," *Harvard Business Review*, January 2006, pp. 1–11.

9. Roy Amara, past president of The Institute of the Future.

11

Conclusion

If Theory of Constraints (TOC) was new to you, this book has covered a wide swath of unfamiliar territory. As you now know, despite several decades of innovation and publications in more than 20 languages, TOC is still controversial because its principles run counter to many prevailing management practices. So at this point you may feel caught between the rock of conventional wisdom and the hard place of TOC. But don't worry. That's not uncommon. When the logic of TOC has you questioning what you thought you knew before, you've already taken a step or two toward breaking your own paradigm constraint, which is any way of thinking that keeps you from seeing problems and solutions objectively.[1]

If you were already familiar with TOC and now feel like your management foundation has been jostled a bit, don't be too quick to pounce on the unfamiliar parts. They're there to address specific challenges in services, not to alter how TOC has traditionally been applied elsewhere. Though the applications differ somewhat, it should be reassuring to know that TOC principles apply to enterprises delivering complex, highly customized, labor-based services as well as those producing goods.

Regardless of your prior TOC knowledge, if your own enterprise is not in Professional, Scientific, and Technical Services (PSTS), this book may have introduced some unfamiliar roles, business practices, and related issues. Though those topics may not pertain directly to your own enterprise, their introduction was necessary for adapting TOC to PSTS, which obviously required more than just a few tweaks.

Recall that PSTS was chosen for this endeavor because it's the services sector least like the Manufacturing sector, where TOC began—and it therefore provides the greatest contrast. The premise was that if TOC applications could be adapted for PSTS, TOC stood a good chance of being applied in any services sector. So it's time to review how TOC for Services (TOC_S) addresses core problems commonly found in PSTS. Then we'll look through a TOC lens at some services sectors in that vast middle ground between Manufacturing and PSTS.

This chapter also reflects on some implications of service chains and value networks, considers how internal service providers can apply TOC_S, and discusses some ways that enterprises in industrial sectors can apply TOC_S to the services they offer in conjunction with goods. Furthermore, differences in the size and reach of enterprises may affect how they view TOC$_S$. As you will see, additional refinements may be helpful in all these contexts.

Finally, some limitations and future research in TOC$_S$ will be outlined. Then we'll wrap up with a few words about the TOC community and how TOC$_S$ fits into the emerging field of Services Science, Management, and Engineering (SSME).

Theory of Constraints for Services

Figure 11-1 depicts Theory of Constraints for Services (TOC$_S$). Its interlocking applications enable constraint management for a wide range of services.

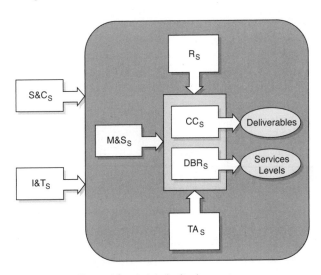

Figure 11-1   Theory of Constraints for Services

- Critical Chain for Services (CC$_S$) produces deliverables from projects.
- Drum-Buffer-Rope for Services (DBR$_S$) produces service levels from processes.
- Replenishment for Services (R$_S$) provides skilled resources.
- Throughput Accounting for Services (TA$_S$) provides key information.
- Marketing and Sales for Services (M&S$_S$) closes deals.

- Strategy and Change for Services (S&C$_S$) sets strategy and gets buy-in.

- Implementation and Technology for Services (I&T$_S$) puts TOC$_S$ into practice.

CC$_S$, DBR$_S$, R$_S$, TA$_S$, and M&S$_S$ are sufficient for steady-state but not transformation. That is, a service provider can run its business with these applications, but they do not provide a way to get from business as usual to TOC$_S$. Therefore, S&C$_S$ and I&T$_S$ first transform an enterprise to TOC$_S$ and then keep its services strategy and technology fresh.

What most differentiates TOC$_S$ from TOC for Goods (TOC$_G$) is its ability to deliver services on demand rather than just when capacity is available. When clients can choose from multiple service providers, those who deliver services on demand can have advantages in speed, quality, and value.

Professional, Scientific, and Technical Services

Table 11-1 lists the sample of PSTS conflicts introduced in Chapter 2, "Services On Demand," along with corresponding TOC$_S$ applications covered in subsequent chapters. In every case, TOC$_S$ eliminates the conflict rather than settling for a compromise. Furthermore, TOC$_S$ uses *leverage points*—where a modest change in constraint management can have a major effect on Throughput—to optimize the enterprise as a whole.

Previous chapters tended to treat PSTS as if it were a homogeneous sector. It isn't, of course. None are. Professional, scientific, and technical services each have their own characteristics, so it's appropriate to acknowledge a sample of differences and consider the implications for TOC$_S$.

Table 11-1   PSTS Conflicts and TOC$_S$ Applications

	PSTS Conflict	TOC$_S$ Application
Resource Management	Efficiency requires high utilization, but responsiveness requires resources on the bench, available for immediate assignment.	Replenishment for Services (R$_S$) uses resource buffers to maximize Throughput rather than utilization.
Project Management	Clients value projects that start and finish on time and within budget, but unique projects are inherently unpredictable.	Critical Chain for Services (CC$_S$) uses R$_S$ to schedule projects on demand and project buffers to deliver on time and within budget.
Process Management	Ongoing business processes are regulated by service level agreements (SLAs), but the service provider has little or no control over demand.	Drum-Buffer-Rope for Services (DBR$_S$) uses work buffers ahead of constraints to regulate flexible capacity, thereby meeting SLAs.
Finance and Accounting	Expense control optimizes individual contracts, but the enterprise will sacrifice future performance if it fails to invest sufficiently.	Throughput Accounting for Services (TA$_S$) provides consistent measures that put higher priority on Throughput and Investment than expense control.
Marketing and Sales	Riskier contracts increase revenue but also increase troubled projects, which leads to higher costs and lower client satisfaction.	Marketing and Sales for Services (M&S$_S$) uses compelling offers based on high-value solutions, so risky projects aren't the only way to grow.

Professional services firms, for instance, rarely exhibit economies of scale.[2] For a professional services firm organized as a partnership to grow revenue by 10 percent, it generally promotes some managers to partners, promotes some professionals to managers, and hires an additional 10 percent more professionals. If they're all billable, this increases total revenue, but revenue per partner remains largely unchanged. Hence, these firms strive to leverage their resources by boosting the ratio of professionals to partners, which increases revenue per partner—and partners are the owners—without necessarily changing revenue per professional. From a TOC perspective, however, many professional services firms are focused on resource utilization. They pay less attention to distinguishing the value they deliver—the real driver of revenue.

The vast majority of scientists who have ever lived are alive today, but science as we know it would be impossible without modern laboratories and information technology. No matter whether a scientific enterprise is profit-seeking or not, it faces technology decisions that could increase the productivity of its scientists. Yet research projects are sometimes managed without much regard for resource constraints and with considerable investment in technology whose impact on the constraint may be coincidental—or undetectable. Furthermore, although scientific discoveries cannot be scheduled, the studies that lead to them obviously can be managed as projects. From a TOC perspective, research programs thus owe some of their length to unrecognized constraints and hidden opportunities to alleviate those constraints with targeted technology.

The half-life of knowledge in technical services can be amazingly brief or prolonged. At the leading edge, new technologies are released so frequently that technicians are under considerable pressure to maintain their technical certifications, yet some clients naively demand technologists with five years of experience in technologies that are only a year or two old. At the trailing edge, successful technologies can endure well beyond the working lifetime of individual technologists, thereby creating a conundrum for firms that must convince some technologists to become experts in technologies older than they are. When nascent technologies have to interoperate with legacy technologies—and they routinely do—it can take an assortment of disparate skills to make it all work. Yet technical services firms too often treat education and training as expenses to be controlled rather than investments leading to future revenue. From a TOC perspective, technical services firms sometimes act as though technology is their constraint, when it is more likely their skilled resources or intellectual capital.

The common thread running through this sample of differences between professional, scientific, and technical services is that the enterprises often don't manage their true constraints. Thus, these are just pointed examples of core conflicts covered in earlier chapters. However, they reinforce the need for effective management of resources, projects, processes, finances, marketing, and sales—the very things that can be managed with TOC_S applications.

Asset-Based Services

As noted in earlier chapters, the PSTS sector is still dominated by labor-based services because clients often have unique requirements that can only be met by experts. Asset-based services are increasingly common, however. Such services capture expertise in knowledge bases, expert systems, and other software tools. Some services can then be delivered by the service provider's nonexpert resources, by the client's own resources via self-service, or almost entirely by the provider's automation—with the provider's experts available to handle exceptions. These alternatives thus enable the provider to offer multiple service levels at different prices, depending on the amount and type of labor used.

When services can be highly, if not fully automated, the price for those services can be much lower, of course. Yet asset-based services create additional business value for clients via compliance with standards, faster implementation, 24×7×365 monitoring, and more reliable operations. For example, information technology (IT) is increasingly handled by Managed Service Providers (MSPs). MSPs remotely monitor the client's computers, storage, networks, and other IT. MSPs also handle performance tuning, security alerts, communications outages, backups, routine maintenance, technical support, and disaster recovery.

The question then becomes whether TOC_S applies to asset-based services as well as labor-based services. Fortunately, it does. CC_S can build assets. DBR_S can deliver services via assets. TA_S recognizes the Investment (I) in assets, lower Operating Expense (OE) from assets, and Throughput (T) generated by service subscriptions instead of labor.

Service Chains and Value Networks

Previous chapters covered the relationship between a service provider and its clients, with only an occasional nod to the provider's subcontractors and vendors. When service providers collaborate with other enterprises in order to deliver services, however, there are additional implications for TOC_S.

One way service providers collaborate is to form *service chains*, which are analogous to supply chains in manufacturing and distribution. That is, each member of a service chain performs a portion of end-to-end delivery of routine services. For instance, a technical service chain may have separate providers doing return authorization, fault diagnosis, product repair, warranty replacement, recycling, and shipping. There are, however, significant differences between supply chains and service chains:[3]

- Service chains more often involve clients as active participants in production.

- Production in a service chain occurs more often at the client site.

- The specific nature of services for each client is determined closer to delivery time.

- Service chains manage perishable resources because services cannot be stockpiled.

- Service chains strive for bidirectional optimization, which means doing what's best for clients while at the same time doing what's best for the providers.

Value networks are another way service providers collaborate with other enterprises, but the activities aren't routine, and the value being created for clients isn't necessarily generated solely by service providers. Value networks can be composed of just goods producers who use digital communications and flexible processes to build custom products rather than the standard products that flow through conventional supply chains.[4] However, value networks can just as easily include service providers who handle engineering, procurement, inbound logistics, product delivery, and other services on behalf of the goods producers. Moreover, a value network can be composed of just service providers that neither produce nor handle goods, yet deliver highly customized services. For example, if a scientific research firm collaborates with professional service providers, such as engineers and attorneys, and a technical service provider that integrates scientific, engineering, and legal databases, the resulting value net is a PSTS trifecta.

Service chains and value networks can create greater value for clients than some enterprises can by themselves. Thus, service chains and value networks are formidable competitors—and their ranks are growing. However, these modes of collaboration work best when the members have a high level of coordination, rather than each operating primarily in its own best interest. Fortunately, there's nothing inherent in TOC_S which limits it to a single enterprise. Indeed, TOC_S can optimize an entire service chain or value network instead of just individual enterprises within them. Here's how:

- **Replenishment for Services (R_S)**—Shared resource buffers, if applicable.

- **Critical Chain for Services (CC_S)**—One project buffer across enterprises.

- **Drum-Buffer-Rope for Services (DBR$_S$)**—One work buffer across enterprises.
- **Throughput Accounting for Services (TA$_S$)**—Consistent measures across enterprises.
- **Marketing and Sales for Services (M&S$_S$)**—Compelling offers cover all enterprises.

This does not mean one member of a service chain or value network cannot adopt TOC$_S$ before the other members. Indeed, it may be necessary to have at least one pathfinder within the service chain or value network who can lead the others through the inevitable buy-in and implementation issues. Interface constraints in particular require resolution because they make the service chain or value network less competitive. On the other hand, service chains and value networks can pursue strategies that would be impractical for individual members.

Outsourcing and Insourcing

When a client focuses on its core competencies, it seeks new ways to get essential noncore services. IT services provides a classic example of *outsourcing*. Service providers can take over the client's software development and maintenance, data center and network operations, desk-side support, help desks, and other IT functions. Likewise, business functions such as human resources, customer relationship management, finance and administration, and procurement can be outsourced. Outsourcers sometimes transform clients' projects and processes to meet the provider's standards because that delivers more value. However, even in the most extreme cases of outsourcing, the client retains strategic activities and management oversight.

When a client focuses on its core competencies, it may also seek new ways to get core services. Distribution services provides a classic example of *insourcing*. The service provider becomes seamlessly integrated into the client's core processes because it can perform some activities significantly better than the client can itself. The client continues to run its own enterprise while monitoring the insourcer's service level performance and its impact. For instance, if the on-time delivery rate rises while inventory drops, the insourcer is creating real value for the client and its customers.

So where does TOC$_S$ fit into outsourcing and insourcing? Obviously, service providers can use it when they transform projects and processes, but clients can use TOC, too. Furthermore, clients can use the TOC approach to strategy and change and Throughput Accounting even if their service providers don't use TOC$_S$. Clients should be interested, for example, in getting service providers aligned with their strategies and measuring how those providers affect T, I, and OE.

Internal Service Providers

Another way for a client to focus on its core competencies is to reorganize internal business functions into *internal service providers*. For example, rather than funding its IT group based on a percentage of sales or some other formula and relying on core business units to negotiate for their slice of this relatively fixed pie, the client can reorganize its IT around strategic projects and expected operational service levels. Under this alternative, there is no other service provider: The transformation is internal. Thereafter, the internal service provider is expected to manage its service delivery capability based on the value it can deliver to the enterprise, which is precisely the purpose of TOC$_S$.

Sometimes external service providers are also their own internal service providers. For instance, IT service providers can run their own IT infrastructure, and payroll service providers can process their own payroll. If those service providers are separate business units within a larger enterprise—and are measured accordingly—the enterprise is in effect outsourcing to itself. This may not seem profound or particularly significant at first, but clients of the external service provider generally view this as an expression of confidence. Thus, a common question during the sales cycle is, "If your enterprise doesn't buy its own services, why should we?"

So is TOC$_S$ really usable by internal service providers? Yes, because they have many of the same core problems as external service providers. Indeed, if internal clients have the option to choose external service providers instead of the interval provider, that internal service provider even has marketing and sales conflicts. It has to demonstrate repeatedly that it is at least as proficient and efficient as its external competitors, and TOC$_S$ can point the way.

Services Sectors Most Like PSTS

PSTS was chosen as the proving ground for TOC_S because it exhibits the greatest contrast with Manufacturing, where TOC originated. Recall that PSTS is unique even among services sectors because it's the only sector where:

- The primary output is services, but sales are made on expertise.
- Workers are typically assigned to serve specific clients.
- The degree of customization for specific clients is extremely high.
- Reliance on intellectual capital is quite high.
- Repeatability of processes is relatively low.

Now it's time to consider other services sectors. As noted in Chapter 2, the Information, Educational Services, and Health Care and Social Assistance (HCSA) sectors are most like PSTS in the sense that they too require workers with higher education and specific experience. Yet each sector is unique:

- The Information sector includes publishing, recording, broadcasting, and software.
- Educational Services includes primary through graduate and professional schools.
- HCSA includes medical and welfare services.

Let's begin by exploring TOC_S applications most likely to be generally usable. Throughput Accounting (TA), for instance, encompasses financial, performance, resource, decision-support, and control measures. TA_S recognizes that PSTS measures Throughput and Investment in a different manner than goods producers do, but nothing in TA_S prevents it from being used in other services sectors. For example, the Information, Education, and HCSA sectors all generate Throughput via deliverables and service levels. And they all invest in service production systems, skills, and intellectual capital. However, as defined in Chapter 7, "Finance and Accounting," Resource Dollars per Day (RDD) depends on R_S to quantify excess resources. So RDD has to be calculated another way if R_S is not in use. Fortunately, just counting unassigned resources is a simple alternative.

Critical Chain (CC) is another TOC application that is broadly usable. Any sector—services or not—can use CC to manage projects. Rather than scheduling multiple projects around availability of a strategic resource, however, CC for Services (CC_S) enables multiple projects to be scheduled independently if R_S provides additional resources on demand. For instance, the software industry within the Information sector is heavily project-based, and the job market for IT skills is flexible enough to accommodate R_S. On the other hand, employment contracts and union rules can make R_S less viable in Educational Services. And the tight job market for skills in HCSA can make it even less amenable to R_S. Therefore, because Educational Services and HCSA less often deliver their services via projects, they are less likely to use CC_S externally and more likely to use it internally, such as on projects to develop a new curriculum or health care program.

Some form of DBR can be used in every sector where processes must be managed. When capacity is rigid, the original DBR application uses that capacity as effectively as possible, regardless of whether the enterprises deliver goods or services. When capacity is relatively flexible, as it must be in any enterprise delivering services on demand via a process, DBR_S adjusts capacity to maintain service levels as demand fluctuates. For instance, as the publishing, recording, and broadcasting industries move to the web, customers can receive books, videos, and music on demand. Likewise, when software vendors deliver software as a service, subscribers get software on demand. Educational Services can use DBR_S if courses are offered on demand, which can be done via self-learning programs. It remains to be seen, however, whether HCSA can make practical use of DBR_S. With demand for HCSA skills frequently outstripping supply, flexible capacity is problematic.

Thus, among standard TOC applications, R_S is the application that is not readily usable in every services sector because job markets and other resource constraints will not always support it. However, when resources are plentiful and easily assimilated, services can be delivered on demand without R_S. The enterprise just gets more resources as needed, and the constraint lies elsewhere.

Finally, $M\&S_S$ is not a standard TOC application because every effective marketing program is unique in some way. Ironically, that makes $M\&S_S$ broadly usable. Even enterprises with excess demand, such as those in HCSA, can establish their marketing and sales programs to serve just specific market segments because they cannot serve all segments well.

Services Sectors Less Like PSTS

Having considered TOC_S for services sectors most like PSTS, it's time to look at some of those less like PSTS. Financial Services and Public Services each offer pure services, but they are less customized than services from any of the sectors discussed in the previous section. Wholesale and Retail Services are as close to the goods end of the spectrum as any service sectors, and they too are much less customized.

For reasons discussed in the previous section, any services sector can use TA_S and $M\&S_S$. How R_S, CC_S, and DBR_S apply in sectors less like PSTS varies, however.

Financial Services includes the banking, insurance, and securities industries, which have large back-office operations amenable to R_S and DBR_S, such as mortgage processing, insurance underwriting, and stock trading. Of course, this sector has its own internal projects that can be managed with CC_S, but it also finances projects in other sectors. If borrowers use CC to deliver more projects on time and within budget, that could affect lending by Financial Services.

Public Services can always use traditional multiproject CC, but not CC_S unless R_S is available—and it's not always practical with public or unionized employees. Likewise, Public Services have large back-office operations, but they aren't as amenable to DBR_S if it too relies on R_S. However, traditional DBR_G, with its emphasis on effectively using rigid capacity, can be used. And when Public Services processes have flexible capacity via technology, such as automatic road tolling and self-serve parking, even DBR_S can be used.

Retail Services are goods-based, of course, but also include installation, personal shoppers, extended warranties, walk-in repair or replacement, and many other services. Wholesale Services are likewise goods-based, but can include inventory and logistical management services upstream to manufacturers and downstream to retailers. Retail and Wholesale Services are rarely, if ever, delivered as projects, though these service providers do manage their own internal projects. R_S and DBR_S are possible, but variations in demand for Retail and Wholesale Services are dominated by the business cycle and seasons, thereby diminishing the need for services on demand. Yet there are exceptions, such as natural disasters and product launches for popular consumer products, both of which generate spikes in demand for goods and related services.

Overall, even sectors less like PSTS can use some TOC_S applications. It hinges on whether they are called on to deliver services on demand and whether external or interface constraints prohibit flexible capacity.

Industrial Sectors

Services are increasingly provided by enterprises whose core offering is goods rather than services. For example, services are available from manufacturers of aircraft engines, mining machinery, medical imaging equipment, computers, and networking devices. In addition to maintenance, repair, and operation (MRO), those services can include financing, installation, and training.

Such enterprises may generate substantial services revenue even though their core business is manufacturing. Services are offered as an adjunct to goods for many reasons:

- Commoditization of products compresses profit margins.
- Complex products can require equally complex services.
- Independent service providers may not have the necessary expertise or tools.
- Remote monitoring can anticipate some failures before they occur.
- Computer software is required for scheduling or performing services.
- Optimal operations benefit from monitoring and tuning beyond customers' capability.
- Preventive maintenance costs customers less than breakdowns and repairs.
- Customers receive value through automatic upgrades and longer product life.
- Safety certification or resale value depend on verifiable services.
- The customer is relieved of removal and recycling responsibilities.
- Services can generate more profit than the goods to which they apply.

Construction is an industrial sector that can nevertheless make use of TOC_S in its core offerings. Its flexible labor markets make it amenable to R_S, and its time-critical projects make it suitable for CC_S. Furthermore, when construction supply chains must deliver perishable materials, such as cement or sod, DBR_S may be usable as well.

So is TOC_S usable in industrial sectors? It is if their services have to be delivered on demand. In selected cases they do, but in many cases, they do not.

Sector Overview

Table 11-2 compares the sectors discussed in preceding sections. At one end of the spectrum, PSTS delivers highly customized services. At the other end, Manufacturing produces goods using highly repeatable methods. In between are the other sectors.

Table 11-2 Theory of Constraints for Services

● Goods o Services	● Repeatable o Customized	Sector	R_S	CC_S	DBR_S	TA_S	$M\&S_S$
o	o	PSTS	■■■■	■■■■	■■■■	■■■■	■■■■
o	●	Information	■■■	■■■	■■■	■■■	■■■
o	●	Education	■■	■■	■■	■■■	■■■
o	●	HCSA	■	■	■	■■■	■■■
o	●	Financial	■■	■	■■	■■	■■
o	●	Public	■	■■	■	■	■
●	●	Retailing	■■	■	■■	■	■
●	●	Wholesaling	■■	■	■■	■	■
●	●	Construction	■■	■■	■■	■	■
●	●	Manufacturing	■	■	■	■	■

The table also indicates how likely each TOC_S application is to be used in each sector. The wider each bar, the more likely that application is to be used in that particular sector. Sometimes there's little need for an application because the sector delivers few, if any, services on demand. Other times one TOC_S application depends on another that's not always practical.

Overall, applications from either TOC_S or TOC_G can be applied in every sector, regardless of where it appears on the goods-services and repeatable-customized continuums. However, other factors affect how TOC_S is used. They are the subject of the following sections.

Enterprise Size

Enterprises are often classified by size for marketing and service delivery purposes, but there is no standard set of thresholds between classes. Table 11-3 shows how enterprises and employment in the U.S. are distributed across one set of thresholds. Small and medium businesses (SMB) clearly account for the majority of both enterprises and employment—and this is true in other countries as well. Therefore, similarities and differences between SMB and large enterprises (LE) are examined next for potential impact on TOC_S.

Table 11-3   Enterprise Size

Size	Employees	Enterprises	Employment
Small	<500	99.66%	50%
Medium	500–2,500	0.27%	12%
Large	>2,500	0.07%	38%

Source: "Statistics About Business Size," U.S. Census Bureau, 2003, http://www.census.gov/epcd/www/smallbus.html.

Enterprises in SMB and LE typically have the same goal: profitable growth (or the equivalent in whatever other goal units apply). They also must cope with the same level of external complexity because they operate in the same environment. For instance, enterprises of all sizes must contend with regulation, inflation, and competition.

Nevertheless, small and medium enterprises do differ from large ones:

- SMB organizations are composed of fewer layers, so they are less complex internally.
- Everyone fills multiple roles.
- Sales and delivery cycles are shorter.

- There is no excess capacity.
- SMB enterprises cannot recover as readily from problems.

Thus, employees in SMB enterprises often describe themselves as under intense pressure, with little margin for error.

When service providers fall under SMB, they tend toward highly specialized, boutique firms. Due to that specialization, practitioners have less diverse skills, but skill levels tend to be higher. Therefore, there are fewer opportunities for partners and senior practitioners to gain leverage by delegating tasks to junior resources. Furthermore, everyone does both sales and service delivery.

When clients fall under SMB, they expect the same skills and quality from their service providers that LE clients receive—but lower fees and faster results because it's less common for SMB clients to engage PSTS service providers. Thus, SMB clients expect smaller, leaner, shorter contracts. Moreover, SMB clients experience "fee fatigue" faster, so there are fewer follow-on contracts.

So what are the implications of enterprise size for TOC_S? SMB providers can use TA_S and $M\&S_S$ to make the most of their existing capabilities, but it's harder for SMB providers to use CC_S and DBR_S because R_S isn't as practical. That is, SMB providers can have a harder time delivering services on demand because overtime and part-time employees are their principal means of creating flexible capacity. On the other hand, SMB clients can benefit from service providers that use TOC_S because it's tailor-made for smaller, leaner, shorter contracts with high business value.

Enterprise Reach

Enterprises can be classified by their geographic reach: local, regional, national, multinational, and global. They also can be classified according to whether they serve developed or emerging markets—and whether their services emanate from developed or emerging markets. It works both ways. Most service providers seek to operate from strong bases of clients in their home markets. However, service providers in emerging markets exploit their cost advantages and vast labor pools to serve clients in developed markets. And service providers in developed markets exploit their deep skills and technical advantages to serve clients in emerging markets.

Nothing in TOC_S favors enterprises with a particular reach or base. It is worth noting, however, that interest in TOC_G has been growing faster in emerging markets lately. Given the rise of services around the world, it remains to be seen whether interest in TOC_S will follow the same path. However, highly skilled resources are hard to find in every market, but especially in emerging markets, so implementation may not necessarily align with interest.

Having shown that TOC_S is usable in sectors beyond PSTS and in enterprises of various sizes and reach, it should be acknowledged that TOC_S does have limitations. That is the subject of the next section.

Limitations

Every management approach has limitations, including TOC_S. Of course, knowing the limitations is as important as knowing the approach itself. Here are some examples.

First, TOC_S does not have an application for services delivered without a defined project or process. Yet in PSTS this situation does happen because no client hires an expert to solve a mundane problem. Sometimes all a client can do is describe undesirable effects, and it's up to the service provider to frame the problem and trace its cause. Other times the client has misdiagnosed the problem, and it's up to the service provider to reframe the problem and reorient the client. Sometimes, however, a client really does have a unique problem, and the service provider has to figure out a solution without a roadmap.

Experienced practitioners draw on previous cases, of course, but the solution may require experimentation, improvisation, or invention. Scientists typically see many failed experiments before a success. Professionals must improvise for their clients in response to the actions of third parties. Technicians have to invent solutions when unprecedented problems occur. In time, a standard solution may evolve, but once it does, the most skilled practitioners generally move on to new frontiers.

Second, TOC_S does not say much about development of new service offerings. $M\&S_S$ provides some guidance about what the market values, and TA_S provides some guidance about which services would likely enable the provider to reach its goal, but service offering development requires an inspired blend of marketing, management, and engineering. Service offering development is not entirely covered by $M\&S_S$ because it requires collaboration with service delivery experts. And service offering development is not directly analogous to new product development because complex services are intangible and considerably less repeatable than manufacturing. Once a new service offering is developed, people still have to learn how to sell it and deliver it, which is sometimes a voyage of discovery in itself.

Third, TOC_S does not say much about quality assurance and risk management. In PSTS, quality is subjective, and risks are many. Moreover, because clients are actively involved in service delivery, not only is risk management not entirely under the service provider's control, but clients themselves are the source of some risks. TA_S can quantify the costs and benefits of particular outcomes, but it doesn't predict which outcomes are more likely. Service providers document lessons learned to avoid repeating mistakes, but anytime resources are assigned to projects or processes they find unfamiliar, that organizational learning has to be reinforced. Furthermore, if clients don't fully understand a particular solution or are trapped in a conflict, they may try to drive their provider down a path that the provider knows will not end well.

Fourth, TOC_S cannot create absolute stability when clients need services on demand, but it can create the flexibility necessary to deliver services on demand. Floating constraints are strenuously avoided in TOC_G, but they can be inescapable in TOC_S. Like a boat that rights itself in rough seas, however, TOC_S creates dynamic stability—the capability to return to a steady state after disruption rather than sinking into chaos.

Fifth, TOC_S can be difficult to implement for many reasons, including external and interface constraints that refuse to be managed. Scarce skills raise the cost of acquiring resources. Unions, work councils, and patronage raise the cost of releasing resources. Small size can make any unutilized resources unaffordable. As these conditions become more pronounced, the optimal buffer size for R_S eventually drops to zero, even for constrained resources, and the enterprise is forced to revert to services as available rather than services on demand. Fortunately, R_S isn't always necessary because not all skills are scarce, and there are other ways to alleviate resource constraints.

Finally, TOC in general is optimistic regarding change. It contends, with good reason, that many problems that seem unsolvable are actually solvable via buy-in and other elements of the TOC Thinking Process (which is beyond the scope of this book). An implicit assumption, however, is that participants are rational, tolerant, and sincere. If they aren't—or their enterprise is dysfunctional in other ways—problems aren't so readily solvable. Thus, PSTS practitioners must ask themselves whether a particular problem is solvable within the client's time frame and budget, whether the solution will have positive and lasting impact, whether the client will be satisfied with the solution, and whether factions within the client's enterprise or its trading partners will conspire to thwart the solution. By these criteria, PSTS practitioners encounter unsolvable problems more often than they'd like.

Research

Limitations are a ready source of research questions, as are issues discussed in previous chapters. In addition, some research questions spring from general business issues. Here are a few examples.

First, if R_S as defined in Chapter 4, "Resource Management," isn't practical, can it be extended to manage fractional rather than whole resources? That is, rather than hiring practitioners full-time to deliver services on demand, under what conditions might practitioners and a service provider agree to an on-demand employment arrangement? This would differ from seasonal employees, who work full-time for only a short period with no benefits. It would also differ from part-time employees, who work less than full-time for less than full benefits. And it also would differ from subcontractors, who work for a different enterprise altogether.

How would the employment contract and working conditions have to be altered to attract highly skilled PSTS practitioners who want to work less than full-time but are flexible about when they do it? Would retainers be sufficient? Could one enterprise manage resource buffers for the benefit of multiple service providers? Would members of a service chain or value network be more open to this arrangement? Technology that enables remote work means location matters much less. And with healthy retirees becoming one of the fastest-growing segments of the population in developed countries and some enterprises anticipating a severe "brain drain," fractional resources activated on demand isn't necessarily a far-fetched notion.

Second, how should DBR$_S$ be implemented? How and when flexible capacity should be adjusted depends on the process being managed. For instance, it's not likely that DBR$_S$ would be implemented quite the same way for benefits processing, technical support, online booksellers, web universities, and cement delivery. Likewise, how flexible capacity should be adjusted depends on how service level agreements are written, how much flexibility is provided by technology rather than labor, and whether the conditions driving changes in capacity are normal or abnormal. Who makes capacity adjustment decisions is also a source of variation. In some cases it may be the local service center manager, but for globally integrated service providers, not all capacity decisions can be made locally. Just as service delivery can follow the sun, so can primary responsibility for global adjustments.

Third, can TOC be used to define sensible stopping rules that kick in well before diminishing returns become painfully evident? It really is possible to have too much of a good thing. With enterprises subject to increasing legal and regulatory compliance issues, striking the right balance on controls can be difficult without an indicator to know when enough is enough. For instance, some enterprises find it difficult to answer these simple questions. How many and what type of business controls are sufficient? Are controls optimizing nonconstraints? Have business controls become the new constraint that keeps the enterprise from reaching its goal? Would fewer, simpler, better-placed controls actually be stronger? Thus, it's worth studying whether TOC can reveal anything about the optimum level of business controls.

Finally, empirical studies of TOC$_S$ can steer practice, research, and education. How many TOC$_S$ implementations are there? Do they meet unanticipated barriers? What are the quantifiable benefits? How are enterprises using TOC$_S$ for continuous improvement of services? Are innovators using it in new ways? Where has TOC$_S$ been incorporated into college curriculums? Where has TOC$_S$ been offered in corporate training programs? How is it being taught? What improvements in services skills are employers seeing?

TOC Community

The TOC community includes practitioners, consultants, academics, and software vendors. They expand the limits of TOC by conducting research, inventing solutions, and putting innovations to use.

Like other communities, the TOC community has its own distinctive concepts, terminology, and diagrams. Many of those concepts, but only some of that terminology, and none of those diagrams were covered in this book. The reason is straightforward: For many readers, covering in one volume all the standard TOC_G applications, the intricacies of PSTS and services on demand, and the adaptations required by TOC_S is tough enough without using unfamiliar terms and strange diagrams.

If you want to delve deeper into TOC, you need to understand more of its terms and all of its diagrams. Bookstores sell an assortment of TOC publications, many of which are referenced in this book's endnotes. And a web search is a good way to find websites, discussion groups, blogs, products, and services pertaining to TOC.

In addition, here are some professional organizations whose members have TOC interests:

- **APICS**—Association for Operations Management
- **IEEE**—Institute for Electrical and Electronics Engineers
- **PMI**—Project Management Institute
- **TOCICO**—Theory of Constraints International Certification Organization

These organizations publish journal articles and conference proceedings on TOC. Such publications are a good source of information from enterprises using TOC.

Finally, colleges and universities offer courses covering various TOC topics. Both instructor-led and self-learning programs for practitioners are available from commercial sources, too.

Services Science, Management, and Engineering

Services Science, Management, and Engineering (SSME) is an emerging multidisciplinary academic field and research area. Its purpose is to study, improve, and teach services innovation. Its reference disciplines include

- Computer science and engineering
- Information technology
- Management of business and public affairs
- Operations research
- Industrial engineering
- Behavioral and social sciences
- Economics

These disciplines have been around for decades, but they didn't come together to concentrate on services until recently.[5]

Whether SSME will ever be recognized as a separate discipline remains to be seen. After all, it took three decades for the National Science Foundation to treat Computer Science as a distinct field.[6] For now, however, what matters is that practitioners and academics from multiple disciplines are collaborating on SSME. What's more, the real-world problems and opportunities driving SSME make it a noteworthy development.

Indeed, SSME represents a significant turning point because most of what is known today about innovation comes from breakthroughs in the production of goods, not delivery of services.[7] Yet as this book illustrates, manufacturing innovations are not easily adaptable to services. At some point, the analogies become tenuous, and eventually they break down completely. Hence, most members of the SSME field believe services are overdue for their own innovations.

Paradoxically, every business, not-for-profit, and governmental enterprise consumes services, and the majority provide services as well. Yet few universities offer degrees in SSME, and few businesses conduct services research. The trend is growing, however. Universities are incorporating SSME into their research and curricula because they recognize that their students need new skills to compete in services-dominated economies. Likewise, businesses are conducting services research because they recognize it as critical to their own and their clients' success—and they're actively hiring graduates with SSME skills.

Final Thoughts

Although the boundaries of SSME are vague and may remain so indefinitely, TOC_S clearly fits at the heart of SSME because it addresses core problems in services. As TOC_S and other areas of SSME make progress, each should benefit from discoveries made elsewhere. This book covers mostly the management aspects of TOC_S, so ample opportunities will exist for TOC_S research and engineering. For instance, much of the technology needed for TOC_S in some services sectors has yet to be invented, let alone implemented.

As TOC_S becomes more widely known, the need to explain how and why it differs from traditional TOC_G should diminish. This will be a milestone because when stripped to its essential elements, TOC_S provides simple solutions to some vexing problems when clients want services on demand.[8] In a world of increasing complexity, TOC_S makes services management simpler because managing constraints is the key to reaching the goal.

Summary

Professional, Scientific, and Technical Services (PSTS) was chosen as the proving ground for Theory of Constraints for Services (TOC_S) because it's the services sector least like the Manufacturing sector, where traditional TOC for Goods (TOC_G) began. Though professional, scientific, and technical services each have their unique aspects, TOC_S is usable throughout PSTS, including both labor-based and asset-based services. TOC_S is also usable when enterprises form service chains and value networks, when clients opt for outsourcing or insourcing, and when enterprises establish their own internal service providers.

Furthermore, TOC_S is usable in other services sectors, ranging from those most to least like PSTS. And just as enterprises in services sectors offering highly repeatable services can use TOC_G to deliver services as available, enterprises in industrial sectors can use TOC_S to deliver goods-related services on demand.

Neither enterprise size nor geographic reach are limiting factors: Enterprises large or small, local or global can use TOC_S. The current limitations of TOC_S spring more from the attributes of services that have no counterpart in industrial enterprises. In time, however, more of the unique attributes of services will likely be covered because both the TOC community and the larger Services Science, Management, and Engineering (SSME) field are focusing their practice, research, and teaching on services as never before.

Whether acknowledged or not, constraints are what keep an enterprise from reaching its goal. That fact frequently gets lost in complex solutions to a seemingly limitless array of complex problems. Thus, TOC_S is ultimately the quest for a few simple solutions that each dispel many complex problems.

Endnotes

1. Lisa Scheinkopf, *Thinking for a Change: Putting TOC Thinking Processes to Use*, St. Lucie Press, 1999.

2. David Maister, *Managing the Professional Service Firm*, Free Press, 1993.

3. James A. Fitzsimmons and Mona J. Fitzsimmons, "Service Supply Chain Management," *Service Management*, McGraw-Hill, 1994, Chapter 15.

4. David Bovet and Joseph Martha, *Value Nets: Breaking the Supply Chain to Unlock Hidden Profits*, John Wiley, pp. 2–7.

5. Linda Dailey Paulson, "Services Science: A New Field for Today's Economy," *IEEE Computer*, 39:8, August 2006, pp. 18–21.

6. Henry Chesbrough and Jim Spohrer, "A Research Manifesto for Services Science," *Communications of the ACM*, 49:7, July 2006, pp. 35–40.

7. Mary Jo Bitner and Stephen W. Brown, "The Evolution and Discovery of Services Science in Business Schools," *Communications of the ACM*, 49:7, July 2006, pp. 73–79.

8. Bill Jensen, *Simplicity: The New Competitive Advantage in a World of More, Better, Faster*, Perseus Books, 2000.

PART IV

Appendixes

A

Resource Optimization

Chapter 4, "Resource Management," covered the basic method for buffer sizing and buffer management under Replenishment for Services (R_S). For many skill groups, the intuitive approach presented in that chapter works well. If the buffer level doesn't reliably synchronize supply with demand, manually tweaking the thresholds between buffer zones or the buffer size itself can be sufficient to tune R_S until the buffer level is just right.

The basic method, however, omits several factors that can affect the financial consequences of resource buffers. If the objective is to optimize financial performance, rather than just use a resource buffer to synchronize supply with demand, those additional factors can be brought into scope.

This appendix discusses how to optimize resource buffers under R_S. While adjusting buffer size to accommodate net consumption during resupply time, the optimization method may skew the thresholds defining buffer zones to maximize revenue and minimize cost during buffer management. However, even an optimal buffer relies on judgment by resource managers, so this appendix concludes with actions that resource managers can take to improve service levels.

Replenishment for Services

In a nutshell, here's the basic method of R_S:

1. Cluster resources into skill groups based on their primary skill code. Members of each skill group should be reasonably substitutable for each other.
2. Set the buffer size for each skill group to its net consumption during average resupply time with adjustment for unreliability of resupply. A rule of thumb is to add one standard deviation of resupply time to average resupply time.
3. Establish buffer zones around the buffer size. A rule of thumb is to make the normal zone one standard deviation of net consumption above and below the buffer size, with warning zones one standard deviation on each side of the normal zone.
4. Perform buffer management by increasing or decreasing resources whenever the buffer level strays into or beyond a warning zone and there's reason to believe it will not return to the normal zone by itself.

5. Consider resizing or regrouping whenever buffer management alone is insufficient.

Buffer optimization replaces the rules of thumb in steps 2 and 3. Otherwise, the steps are unchanged.

There are, of course, several assumptions behind basic R_S. Most of those assumptions are justified because they keep the method simple. Simplicity is a precious trait when introducing a management method. And simplicity has ongoing value if it makes that method both effective and easy to use.

Nevertheless, if R_S can be improved by altering assumptions, that may be worth doing, even if it makes the method more complicated. Fortunately, the complicated bits of optimizing R_S can be kept separate from the simple bits, which is why this optimization topic is relegated to an appendix.

Assumptions

Perhaps the most obvious assumption underlying basic R_S is the normality assumption. References to averages and standard deviations implicitly assume that net consumption and resupply time have approximately normal distributions. Of course, either one will naturally deviate from normal at times, but resupply time is more likely to be positively skewed because it's lower-bounded at zero. Thus, it's more like a lognormal distribution. Whether violations of the normality assumption are significant enough to matter is a question that can be answered only with respect to a specific skill group over an interval of time, but experience suggests that for the majority of skill groups, it just doesn't matter.

The normality assumption also underlies the rule of thumb for setting buffer zones. That is, buffer zones can be calibrated for different levels of sensitivity by making them wider or narrower, depending on how much of the normal distribution they are intended to cover. Of course, narrowing the buffer zones makes R_S more sensitive during buffer management even if the underlying distributions aren't strictly normal.

Another implicit assumption, however, is that buffer zones should remain symmetric around the buffer size whenever their widths are adjusted. This assumption is inherited from normal distributions, which are symmetric, but thresholds between zones do not have to be equidistant from the target buffer size. They are that way in basic R_S because it does not have enough information to specify a better alternative.

Suppose, however, that depleting the buffer for a given skill group has a substantial impact on revenue and profit (T and NP in Throughput Accounting), but the cost of each resource on the bench (OE in Throughput Accounting) is relatively small in comparison. Raising the buffer size would protect revenue and profit, but it would also increase the bench cost. On the other hand, keeping the buffer size where it is, while narrowing the shortage zone and widening the excess zone, might protect revenue and profit without increasing bench cost as much. The question then becomes what should the buffer size and thresholds be?

Hence, the assumption behind basic R_S most likely to yield suboptimal buffers is that decisions about buffer size and buffer zones are revenue- and cost-neutral. They aren't. Allowing the buffer to become depleted occasionally for one skill group may be optimal, while for another skill group the buffer should be sized and zoned so it will rarely, if ever, be depleted—assuming sufficient resources can be obtained when R_S calls for more.

Cost Factors

Having recognized that having too many resources does not necessarily cost the same as having too few, it's easy to assume that having too many resources costs more than having too few. But this assumption is not necessarily true either when the impact on revenue is considered.

In a profit-seeking enterprise, the revenue a resource can produce is generally higher than its labor cost. Likewise, in a governmental or not-for-profit organization, the value produced by a resource should be higher than its labor cost. There are exceptions, of course, such as new resources who haven't reached their full potential and net-negative producers who drag down their team's performance. Nevertheless, for an entire skill group, revenue or value lost due to insufficient resources can be converted into opportunity cost, which is typically higher than labor cost.

If several resources are available, but they depend on a resource that is unavailable, the revenue or value lost on those dependent resources represents a leverage cost. When it occurs, leverage cost for a resource (Throughput per hour, T/h, for the leveraged resource plus all dependent resources in Throughput Accounting) can be many times larger than its opportunity cost (just T/h for the leveraged resource).

If a service provider has insufficient resources to achieve a service level agreement (for example, percentage of calls answered within 20 seconds or percentage of transactions completed without error), penalty cost may be incurred. Such a cost can be nonlinear with respect to resources. That is, penalty cost often moves in steps, and repeated occurrences may increase the penalty at each step.

For a given resource type, hiring cost and severance cost are rarely the same. Moreover, for many resource types, their resupply time is short enough that their hiring and severance costs are substantially greater than their labor and opportunity costs.

Collectively, these cost factors mean that an optimal "no action" zone around the target buffer size is likely to be asymmetric. And as the zone becomes more asymmetric, the optimal target buffer size itself may move away from average net consumption during time to resupply. This bias thus compensates for differences in cost.

Noncost Factors

Several factors determine the conditions under which the costs just outlined occur. Some of those factors are under resource manager control, but others are not.

Attrition (loss of resources through resignation, retirement, or death) decreases severance cost but increases hiring cost. Unfortunately, attrition and net consumption are positively correlated. So unless attrition drops to zero, net consumption greater than or equal to zero results in ongoing hiring cost. On the other hand, attrition naturally decreases capacity during periods of negative net consumption. Hence, the effect of attrition can be detrimental or beneficial to resource management.

Transfers, if feasible, move resources between skill groups and thereby alleviate imbalances. If the skill groups are highly compatible, transfers may impose little or no cost. But to the degree that the skill groups are incompatible, transfers can lead to transfer cost in the sending and/or receiving skill group, due to retraining and perhaps relocation. From a resource management perspective, however, the overall effect of transfers is often beneficial, despite the cost.

Full-time equivalents (FTEs) can be substantially different from resource head count, so optimization models are often built with FTEs. For example, each of three resources working half-time represent a head count of three, but only 1.5 FTEs. Conversely, each of three resources working 25 percent paid overtime represent 3.75 FTEs. However, each of three resources working 20 percent unpaid overtime may nonetheless represent only 3.0 FTEs if overtime is inherent in their jobs, as is generally the case with salaried positions.

Optimization Model

An *optimization model* is a set of mathematical formulas that can be solved to determine the inputs that maximize or minimize an objective, subject to constraints. Inputs exert their influence on the objective via computations, which are in turn governed by parameters.

In this appendix, the optimization model is implemented as follows:

1. Objective = minimize total expected cost
2. Inputs = target buffer size, upper threshold, lower threshold
3. Constraints = lower threshold ≤ buffer size ≤ upper threshold
4. Parameters
    a. Excess resource cost rate (OE/h in Throughput Accounting)
    b. Shortage cost rate (T/h in Throughput Accounting)
    c. Transfer cost rate
    d. Leveraged resource cost rate (T/h for leveraged + dependent resources)
    e. Severance cost rate
    f. Hiring cost rate
    g. Penalty cost formula
    h. Distribution of net consumption
    i. Distribution of time to resupply
    j. Attrition during average time to resupply
    k. Transfers during average time to resupply
    l. Warning width as percent of distance from buffer size to threshold

Typical effects of changes in parameters are summarized in Table A-1. Note that some parameter changes can diminish or amplify the effects of other parameter changes, so the combined effect cannot be deduced from the table. It has to be calculated.

Table A-1   Typical Effects of Changes in R_S Parameters

Parameter	Effect
Average net consumption increases	Buffer size increases
Standard deviation of net consumption increases	Thresholds widen
Attrition increases (supply decreases)	Buffer size increases
Time to resupply increases	Net consumption during resupply time increases
Shortage cost > excess cost	Buffer size and thresholds shift to avoid shortage cost
Leverage cost > shortage cost	Buffer size and thresholds shift to avoid leverage cost
Severance cost > hiring cost	Buffer size and thresholds shift to avoid severance cost
Incoming transfers increase	Buffer size decreases
Outgoing transfers increase	Buffer size increases

Optimal Buffer Sizing for Nonconstrained Resource

Consider a skill group with the following characteristics:

- Resources are readily available, so this skill group is never a constraint on the enterprise.
- Average time to resupply is ten working days and is very reliable.
- Net consumption during resupply time is approximately normally distributed with average of 1 and standard deviation of 5.
- Attrition is 1, but potential transfers from other groups is 2.
- Shortage costs more than excess.
- Severance costs more than hiring.
- Leverage and penalty costs are zero.
- Buffer size and thresholds are constrained to integers.

Figure A-1 shows several kinds of information for this skill group:

- For each level of net consumption, stacked bars show costs against the left axis.

- The line shows the probability for each level of net consumption against the right axis.

- On the horizontal axis, the small triangle indicates the optimal buffer size is 2, the filled circles indicate the thresholds are 7 and −6, and the diamonds indicate the warning levels are 5 and −3. Hence, the target buffer does not equal average net consumption, and the thresholds are not symmetric around the target.

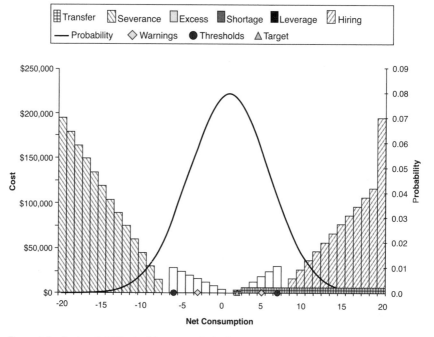

Figure A-1   Cost-probability chart for nonconstrained resource

Note that large changes in net consumption have high cost, yet low probability. This relationship generates an entirely different pattern in Figure A-2.

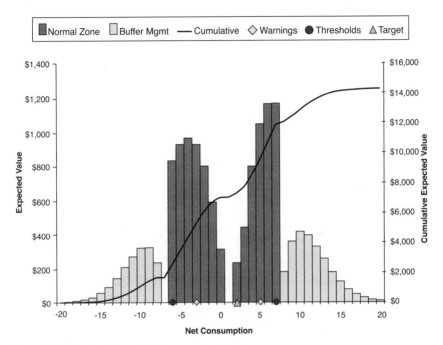

Figure A-2   Expected value chart for nonconstrained resource

This figure shows expected values, which are computed as cost times probability for each level of net consumption:

- Dark gray bars in the middle are the normal or "no action" zone.
- Light gray bars on the left and right are the buffer management zones that correspond to increases or decreases in capacity.
- The line shows cumulative expected value against the right axis.

The buffer size and thresholds shown in the figure are optimal because they minimize the expected value of all costs. So long as the assumptions underlying the model hold, net consumption should fall in the normal zone about 84 percent of the time, and there will be excess about 6 percent of the time and shortage about 10 percent.

Figure A-3 shows the probability that various buffer levels will occur. Note that the thresholds and warnings are rotated around the buffer size because buffer levels move in opposition to net consumption, as illustrated in Figure A-2.

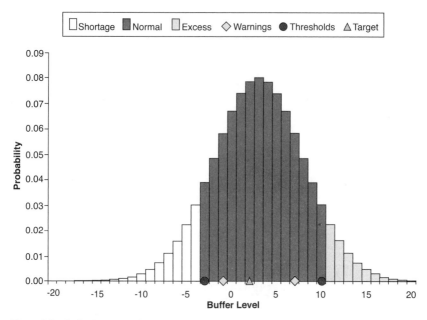

Figure A-3   Buffer level chart for nonconstrained resource

A resource manager would consider reducing resources if the actual buffer level rose above 10 and consider increasing resources if it fell below −3. A *negative buffer level* means there are outstanding requisitions that cannot be fulfilled immediately. Thus, this solution tolerates resource shortages (buffer levels between −1 and −3) about 15 percent of the time.

Optimal Buffer Sizing for Constrained Resource

Now consider a skill group with these characteristics:

- Resources are not readily available, so this skill group is a constraint on the enterprise.
- Mean time to resupply is six weeks, yet very reliable.
- Net consumption is normally distributed with average of 1 and standard deviation of 5.
- Attrition is 1, but transfers from other groups are not feasible.
- Shortage costs more than excess.

- Leverage costs are much greater than shortage costs, but penalty costs are zero.
- Severance costs more than hiring.
- Excess and shortage costs are higher than those for the nonconstrained resource.
- Buffer size and thresholds are constrained to integers.

Figure A-4 shows the optimal buffer size is 4, and the thresholds are 4 and −1. Therefore, as before, the target buffer size does not equal average net consumption, and the thresholds are not symmetric around the target. Moreover, in this case, the upper threshold coincides with the target buffer, thereby indicating a strong bias against shortages because they cost far more than the buffer.

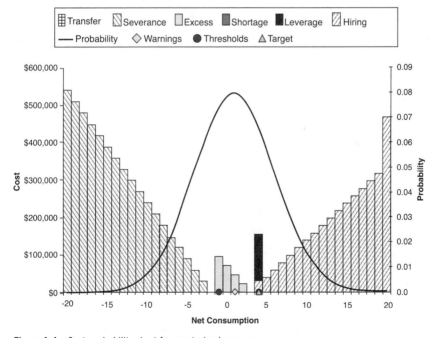

Figure A-4   Cost-probability chart for constrained resource

Figure A-5 shows expected values, which are computed as cost times probability for each level of net consumption:

- Dark gray bars in the middle are the normal or "no action" zone.
- Light gray bars on the left and right are the buffer management zones that correspond to increases or decreases in capacity.
- The line shows cumulative expected value against the right axis.

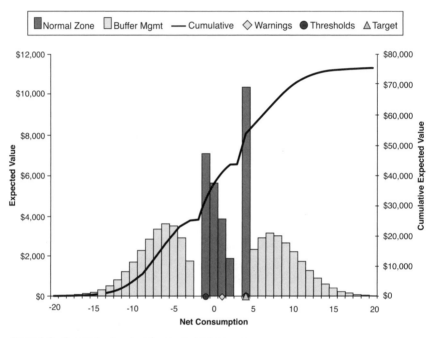

Figure A-5 Expected value chart for constrained resource

So long as the assumptions underlying the model hold, net consumption should fall in the normal zone about 45 percent of the time, and there will be excess about 31 percent of the time and shortage about 24 percent. This assumes that it's possible to acquire as many resources as needed, which is a tenuous assumption if the skill group is a resource constraint.

Figure A-6 shows the probability that various buffer levels will occur. Remember that the thresholds and warnings are rotated around the buffer size relative to Figure A-5 because buffer levels move in opposition to net consumption.

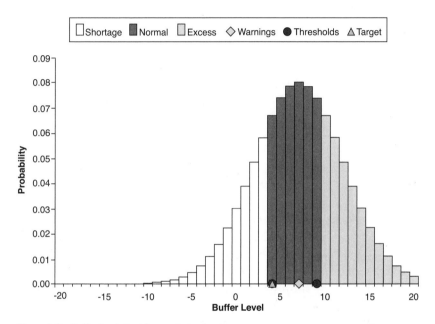

Figure A-6   Buffer level chart for constrained resource

The resource manager would consider reducing resources if the actual buffer level rose above 9 and consider increasing resources if it fell below 4. Hence, *shortage* in this case does not mean "zero resources." Indeed, unlike the previous example for a nonconstrained resource, which tolerated some negative buffer levels, this solution does not even tolerate some positive buffer levels because the cost of shortages is quite high.

Recall that unassigned resources do not sit idly on the bench. If the enterprise could obtain enough of this constrained resource to meet the optimal buffer size, resources not currently assigned would be engaged in investment activities, such as getting training, giving training, developing intellectual capital, mentoring other resources, or working on internal projects.

Resource Management Notes

Deciding whether to increase or decrease resources is not generally automated in R_S because the resource manager has to judge whether changes are transient or enduring and then determine the best course of action. This does not, however, represent a dramatic change from what resource managers already know. For instance, a resource manager may be aware of ongoing market forces or upcoming strategic initiatives that haven't yet fully affected net consumption.

Ideally, no opposing resource decisions occur in quick succession, and skill group capacity ratchets up smoothly as the enterprise grows. So the best course of action is often a repeat of whatever the action was during the previous period. Turning points are crucial, however.

When net consumption flips from positive to negative, or vice versa, R_S picks up that signal via a buffer level that strays and stays outside the normal zone. R_S thus differs from hire-to-plan by refocusing resource managers' attention on the services market and job market rather than the plan and budget. R_S differs from hire-to-deal, which tends to be focused on local practices or business units rather than global skill groups, by providing actual market data in decision-impelling formats. And R_S differs from supply-demand matching, which tends to match demand to supply rather than supply to demand—a crucial distinction.

One way to minimize regret when making resource management decisions is to require the actual buffer level to stay beyond the warning level for more than one buffer management decision cycle if the skill is not critical. If the deviation is random, the next buffer level is more likely to bounce back toward its mean than to stay beyond the warning level.

Another way to minimize regret is to increase or decrease resources just enough to get the buffer level back into the normal zone. The statistical phenomenon known as *regression to the mean* may then recenter the buffer level on its own without further management intervention.

Finally, increasing or decreasing resources are not the only possible actions. Expediting, substitution, and overtime may all be viable alternatives while assessing whether a deviation is transient.

Summary

The basic rules of thumb included in Replenishment for Services (R_S) are sufficient whenever the financial impact of resource buffer sizing and management is relatively small. When that impact is potentially large, however, optimization can be better than rules of thumb. One of the ways optimal buffer zones differ from those based on rules of thumb is optimal zones can be asymmetric, thereby steering buffer management to have more or fewer resources than symmetric zones would indicate.

Optimization is only as good as the parameters and assumptions behind it, so it's important not to overengineer R_S. Even so, the examples in this appendix illustrate how optimization can yield buffer sizes and zones that are considerably different from those based on the basic rules of thumb, so their financial impact could be substantial.

Optimization is not a technique every resource manager must master. It can be done by computer software and then inserted into the R_S steps where the rules of thumb are. Optimization can also be done strictly for educational purposes. In any event, it should be done only if it adds value.

B

Process Simulation

Chapter 6, "Process Management," covers Drum-Buffer-Rope for Services (DBR$_S$). Though it compares a few basic capacity management scenarios for an entire process, it does not explore the dynamic behavior of elements within that process. It thus treats the process itself as a black box. Fortunately, the basics of DBR$_S$ can be appreciated without an understanding of internal process dynamics.

In case you want to probe a bit deeper, however, this appendix contains some DBR$_S$ simulations. In effect, this appendix opens the lid a bit and shines some light inside the black box covered earlier. Though much simpler than actual processes, the simulations are realistic enough to show how the elements of a process can interact. Nonetheless, the concepts underlying the simulations are complicated enough to relegate this topic to an appendix.

This appendix concludes with notes about simulating real processes. Those notes include a general approach to consider as well as some pitfalls to avoid.

DBR for Services

The essential elements of DBR$_S$ are as follows:

1. The constraint ultimately limits what any process can yield, regardless of whether that constraint is recognized by the service provider, client, or service recipients.
2. In addition to internal and external constraints, service providers may also be subject to interface constraints, which govern how they interact with individual service recipients and with other enterprises, such as clients and subcontractors.
3. The constraint may shift among external, interface, and internal locations during the normal course of selling and delivering services on demand.
4. When a service provider must deliver services on demand, its capacity has to be elastic enough to accommodate a reasonable amount of unanticipated change.
5. DBR$_S$ balances flow rather than capacity and turns the push for utilization into the pull of explicit or implicit service level agreements (SLAs).

6. Unbalanced capacity simplifies process management by using the constraint to trigger capacity changes and by letting the constraint dampen volatility at downstream tasks.

7. Buffer sizing must consider all the constraints embodied in the SLA, which typically includes cycle time, cost, and quality.

8. Buffer zones must be inset within the buffer thresholds determined by the SLA to allow sufficient lead time for capacity management. Those buffer zones are bidirectional because they must trigger both increases and decreases in capacity as needed.

9. Routine capacity management is performed by scheduling capacity in anticipation of predictable demand patterns. Nonroutine capacity management is accomplished when the buffer level unexpectedly strays into a red zone and there's reason to believe it will not return to the green zone by itself.

10. When the constraint sprints, it achieves a flow rate above the typical maximum. It is often necessary for capacity constrained resources (CCRs) to sprint in order to keep up. It may even be necessary for some nonconstraints to sprint, too.

11. Process improvement anywhere other than the constraint and CCRs generally doesn't increase how much the process produces, but it may raise quality or lower cost.

12. Strategic constraints can maximize the value of services to clients, which ultimately maximizes the service provider's net profit.

This appendix explores rigid versus elastic capacity. Then, for elastic capacity, it compares balanced versus unbalanced scenarios. It shows how the constraint limits what the process overall produces, even when there are queues everywhere.

Simulation Methods

Role-playing games are a staple of TOC education. In such games, people assume roles in which they must act according to prescribed rules, while dice or game spinners simulate uncertainty. For example, during one game, the role might be an operations manager striving to maximize utilization in a factory with balanced capacity but variable demand, as determined by a roll of the dice. The next game might be a manager striving to minimize cycle time in a factory with unbalanced capacity but the same variable demand. Lessons learned then come from comparing the rules and results.

Pure computer simulations are likewise a staple of TOC research. In such simulations, computer software acts according to prescribed rules. Although not as useful for experiential learning, computer simulations have the advantage of being fast and repeatable, which enables controlled experiments across a wide range of scenarios.[1]

Simulations (as shown in Figure B-1) may also contribute to decision support. That is, if decision-makers can run simulations that show the possible outcomes of alternative decisions, they may make better decisions. This is particularly true when TOC is being introduced, but it's also true when unfamiliar decisions arise.

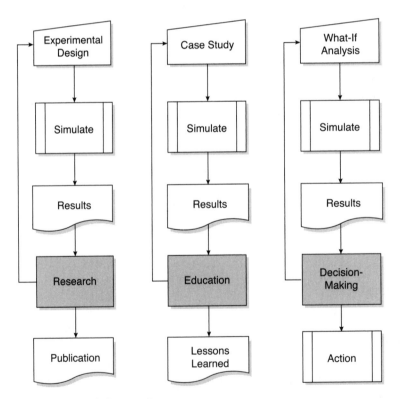

Figure B-1   Simulation contexts

System Dynamics is a specific computer simulation method well-suited to observing changes over time, such as those that characterize services on demand. A System Dynamics model is composed of graphic symbols with finite difference equations behind them. The graphics depict pipes with valves that govern flows between blocks. The flows can represent whatever a researcher wants, such as service requests being handled through a process. The blocks also can represent whatever a researcher wants, such as activities or queues. Running the model with various equations and parameters allows researchers to compare outcomes. This is the method used in the following sections.

Single-Activity Simulation

Figure B-2 is a simple simulation model with a single activity and two capacity management rules. The flow path can be read as follows:

1. Service requests enter the model from the cloud on the left.
2. Requests flow into the queue, where they wait until capacity is available.
3. If the queue grows long enough, some service requests balk (exit into the cloud at the top without processing).
4. Flow from the queue into the activity is governed by capacity.
5. Time spent in the activity is governed by service time.
6. Completed requests exit the model into the cloud on the right.

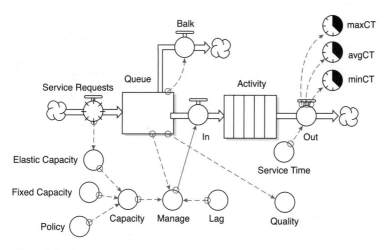

Figure B-2 Single-activity simulation model

Policy determines which capacity management rule applies:

- **Elastic**—Adjusts based on the volume of service requests.
- **Rigid**—Changes only by management decision.

Parameters include:

- **Lag**—Time between a change in requests and a change in capacity.
- **Service time**—Periods spent performing the activity.

Outcomes include:

- **Queue size**—Number of requests waiting for processing.
- **Cycle time**—Queue time plus service time.
- **Quality**—Errors per 100 requests.

In a simulation model such as this, so long as new items are entering the model, the queue never falls entirely to zero. Each time period is divided into multiple ticks of a simulated clock, but each item spends at least one tick just passing through the queue block.

A cycle time clock starts when each service request enters on the left and stops when it exits on the right. Cycle time thus includes both queue time and service time.

Quality declines when the queue becomes excessive due to pressure to reduce cycle time. That is, haste makes waste.

Figure B-3, which was generated by the simulation model in the previous figure, compares a rigid capacity scenario to a flexible capacity scenario. Service time is constant at three periods. The simulations start empty and idle, so they take three periods to warm up. The lag parameter is constant at one period, so capacity adjustments occur in the period following a change in demand.

Service requests rise and fall in a sine wave every 10 periods, which makes it easy to observe how changes in the queue and completed requests lag behind. For the first 20 periods, requests average 80 per period and then rise suddenly to 100 per period. An abrupt change such as this is useful for observing whether a model restabilizes and how long it takes to do so.

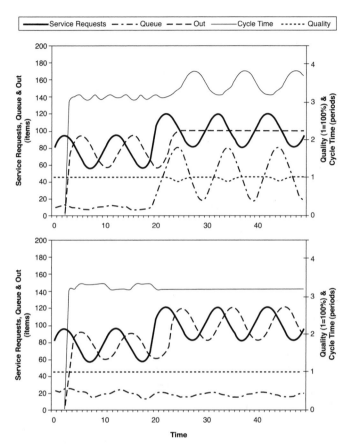

Figure B-3   Rigid versus elastic capacity

In the rigid capacity scenario at the top, the process can handle a maximum of 100 requests per period. Incoming requests are within capacity through Period 20, so the queue is small and cycle time is stable at just slightly more than service time. Once incoming requests begin to exceed capacity, however, the queue fluctuates widely, and so does cycle time, which then includes more queue time in addition to service time. Furthermore, whenever the queue becomes excessive, quality dips due to pressure to reduce cycle time.

In the elastic capacity scenario at the bottom, capacity adjustments are triggered by changes in incoming requests. Consequently, the patterns are consistent throughout the entire scenario, despite the sudden rise in average incoming requests after Period 20. The queue is stable, and so is cycle time. Moreover, cost is lower for the first 20 periods because there is no excess capacity. And quality does not suffer because the queue never becomes excessive.

Multi-Activity Simulation

Figure B-4 is a more complicated simulation model composed of four activities similar to the one just seen but with only one capacity management rule: elastic capacity. Capacity limits on each activity, however, can be balanced or unbalanced.

The flow paths can be read as follows:

1. Service requests (SR) enter the model from the cloud on the upper left.
2. Requests flow into a queue (Q1).
3. Flow into the activity (A1) is governed by capacity management (CM1).
4. If queue time (SRwait) becomes excessive, some requesters balk (SRbalk), but others opt for self-service (SRself).
5. Time spent on the requests is governed by service time (ST1).
6. Some requests are completed at this activity (SRdone).
7. Transactions (XA) enter the model from the cloud on the lower left.
8. They flow through another queue (Q2) and activity (A2), but without balking or self-service.
9. Service requests and transactions merge in Q3 and are processed in A3.
10. Erroneous items are reworked (XArework).
11. Items pass into Q4 and are completed in A4.
12. Completed items exit the model into the cloud on the right.

Policy determines which capacity limits apply:

- **Balanced**—Each activity has just enough capacity to keep its queue in check.
- **Unbalanced**—One activity is the constraint, and all other activities have sprint capacity.

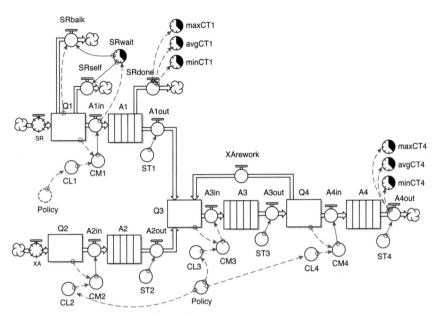

Figure B-4   Multi-activity simulation model

Parameters include:

- **Service times**—Constant at 1, 2, 3, and 1 periods for Activities 1 to 4, respectively.

Outcomes include:

- **Queue size**—Number of requests waiting for processing.
- **Cycle time**—Queue time plus service time.

Figure B-5 compares balanced and unbalanced capacity scenarios. As before, the simulations start empty and idle, so they take several periods to warm up.

As in the previous simulation, service requests average 100 per period but rise and fall in a sine wave every 10 periods. Transactions do the same over 20 periods. About a third of the remaining service requests merge with transactions at Q3.

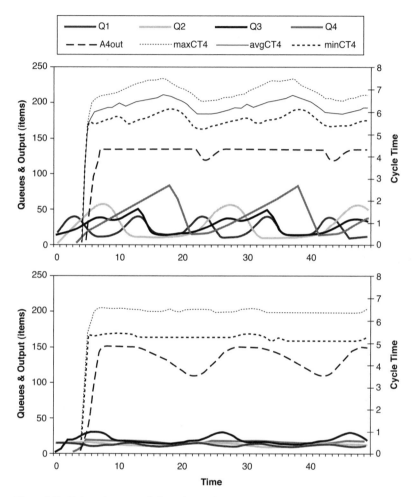

Figure B-5   Balanced versus unbalanced capacity

In the balanced capacity scenario at the top—conventional capacity management—every activity develops a queue whenever the number of incoming items exceeds its capacity limit. However, those queues peak at different times because items move in waves and take time to work their way through the process. The capacity limits for Activities 1 through 4 are 100, 110, 140, and 135 items per period, respectively. Though it is hard to infer from the chart, Activity 4 is actually the constraint, so the process overall produces a maximum of 135 items per period. Thus, improving any of the other activities—reducing their service time—would just create a bigger queue ahead of the constraint. Overall cycle time is variable, ranging from 5.25 to 7.5 periods.

In the unbalanced capacity scenario at the bottom, DBR_S, the capacity limits for Activities 1 through 4 have been raised to 120, 120, 150, and 160 items per period, respectively. Activity 3 is the new strategic constraint, so the process overall produces a maximum of 150 items per period. However, none of the activities' base capacities have changed: They all rely on sprinting when necessary to keep up or catch up. This is accomplished through overtime, flextime, cross-training, and other methods discussed in Chapter 6. Only the constraint is unable to meet all demand. Thus, it occasionally develops a modest queue. Overall cycle time is stable, ranging from 5.25 to 6.5 periods.

In this unbalanced capacity scenario, A3 is the drum. The buffer is all work items ahead of the constraint, so it includes Q1, Q2, and Q3, plus whatever is in process in A1 and A2. The constraint rope is within an information system that monitors the buffer level relative to the buffer zones and triggers capacity management as appropriate. The service level rope is also within an information system, but it signals how work should be done on the constraint. In an actual process, for instance, it might prioritize items based on how they will affect service levels.

Hence, the unbalanced capacity scenario eliminates most queue time and thereby smoothes cycle time even when demand for service fluctuates. It relies on every activity other than the constraint to have either spare or elastic capacity. In contrast to the balanced capacity scenario, where queues are everywhere, the constraint is the activity most likely to have a queue in the unbalanced capacity scenario. An unexpected change in the buffer signals the need for capacity management. In this simulation, however, the model tolerates an occasional queue at Q3 because it subsides naturally without adversely affecting cycle time.

Simulating Real Processes

Real processes can be considerably more complex than the previous example, if for no other reason than they contain a lot more than four activities. However, real processes can be especially difficult to study if they contain random variability that masks underlying relationships.

For instance, noise in the inputs and exponential service times would make the previous simulation more realistic, but much harder to understand. Yet in the end, the result would likely just be more capacity to cover the random variation or a change in the SLA to tolerate a certain amount of extreme values. If quantifying the necessary capacity or negotiating suitable SLA terms are the objectives, such enhancements are certainly warranted. But they might not contribute much to a basic comparison of alternative capacity management policies, which is why they are simplifying assumptions here.

An approach to simulating real processes worth considering is to start with the simplest practical simulation, and try various enhancements, but retain only those that create genuine insights. For example, more than 90 percent of cycle time in real processes can be queue time rather than service time. If so, shrinkage of most queues would have an even more dramatic effect on cycle time than shown previously.

One pitfall to avoid is simulating behavior that is not present in the real process, such as a vicious cycle where things spiral out of control. For instance, it's easy to simulate a queue that grows without limit, even though this is impossible in a real process. As seen previously, *balking* means refusing to join a queue. In addition, *reneging* means leaving a queue before service is completed. In a real process, both phenomena limit the growth of queues if the activities themselves don't.

Another pitfall to avoid is omitting critical behavior that is present in the real process, such as a virtuous cycle where feedback and motivation keep things under control. For instance, people can work smarter when they see a queue growing—or they can cut corners. Variable productivity and quality in a services enterprise are beyond the scope of this appendix, but they are often intangible factors quite worthy of consideration.

A final pitfall to avoid is overlooking potential side effects or unintended consequences. For instance, if unions or work councils oppose flexible capacity, imposing it without first getting their buy-in would be unlikely to produce all the anticipated benefits and could create thorny problems.

Summary

Simulations show that when demand for services is variable, flexible capacity outperforms rigid capacity in terms of speed, cost, and quality. Furthermore, simulations show how unbalanced capacity can simplify capacity management and outperform balanced capacity.

Simulations are not, of course, the same as real processes. Yet it may not be necessary to simulate real processes in all their complexity to gain useful insights into process management. Indeed, a guiding principle of TOC is the more complex the problem, the simpler the solution must be.

Endnote

1. Michael Schrage, *Serious Play: How the World's Best Companies Simulate to Innovate*, Harvard Business School Press, 2000.

C

Throughput Accounting for Software

Chapter 3, "Theory of Constraints," summarizes essential elements of Throughput Accounting for Goods (TA$_G$), as applied in the Manufacturing sector. Chapter 7, "Finance and Accounting," covers Throughput Accounting for Services (TA$_S$) as applied in the Professional, Scientific, and Technical Services (PSTS) sector. For comparison, this appendix summarizes Throughput Accounting for Software. As explained in Chapter 2, "Services On Demand," the Software industry is part of the Information sector according to the North American Industry Classification System (NAICS), but any enterprise can have software projects.

All three versions of TA follow the same fundamental principles, but they implement them in ways appropriate for each sector. Consequently, enterprises that have business units in more than one sector can use TA throughout. For example, manufacturers increasingly offer services around their products, software vendors can offer their software as either a product or service, and PSTS enterprises more and more augment their services with software. Thus, opportunities to apply TA across sectors are plentiful.

This appendix covers Throughput Accounting for Software at two levels: software engineering and software business. Software engineering is done in software projects, which can create software for internal use or for sale. Software business includes research and marketing in addition to software engineering, so it applies to enterprises that produce software for sale.[1]

Throughput Accounting for Software Engineering

Throughput Accounting for Software Engineering (TA$_E$) differs from TA$_G$ because software engineering is mostly intangible, while manufacturing is mostly tangible. Even though software engineering and PSTS services are both largely intangible, TA$_E$ nevertheless differs from TA$_S$ because software is vastly more automated and reusable than labor-based services.

TA$_E$ has these financial measures:

■ **Throughput (T)** is the rate of cash generated through delivery of working code into production, assuming a constant level of investment in consecutive projects. It is computed as sales price minus direct costs, such as packaging, delivery, installation, training, support, and networking.

- **Investment (I)** is all money invested in software production systems plus money spent to obtain ideas for client-valued functionality. It thus includes software development tools and requirements gathering. For a one-time project, however, its I is not constant, so I is subtracted from T at the end.

- **Operating Expense (OE)** is all money spent to produce working code from ideas. It is primarily direct labor of software engineers, but it also includes selling, general, and administrative (SG&A) costs.

The following performance measures are computed exactly the same way for goods, services, and software even though each sector generates T, I, and OE differently:

- Net Profit: $NP = T - OE$
- Return on Investment: $ROI = NP / I$

As in TA_G and TA_S, the way to maximize NP and ROI in TA_E is to increase T while decreasing I and OE. This is done in software engineering by gathering requirements rapidly yet accurately, creating software that customers value, and eliminating waste, which is composed of requirements and functions that are discarded before software enters production.

Like TA_G and TA_S, TA_E reverses the usual management priorities from OE, T, I to T, I, OE. However, TA_E also has these software production measures, which have no direct counterparts in TA_G or TA_S:

- Production Quantity: Q = client-valued functions delivered in working code
- Inventory: V = ideas + functions in development + completed functions
- Average Cost Per Function: $ACPF = OE / Q$

Note that Q, V, and ACPF correspond to T, I, and OE, respectively.

Like TA_G and TA_S, TA_E is a radical alternative to Cost Accounting (CA), which focuses more on OE than T or I. As each software engineering task is performed, CA uses time sheets to add the cost of those tasks to the recorded value of the software being produced. So the longer a project lasts and the more effort it consumes, the more CA values the software asset. This creates no financial inventive for early completion, even though the business value to the client of undelivered software tends to go down with time.

In contrast to CA, but consistent with TA_G and TA_S, TA_E does not record value added. It simply records I at the beginning of the project and T at the end. TA_E dispenses with time sheets because effort is a fixed cost captured in OE. Thus, the longer a project lasts and the more effort it consumes, the more TA_E increases its OE and decreases its T. This creates incentive to complete projects on time or early because that maximizes NP.

TA_E also provides a different viewpoint on some common circumstances in software engineering:

- When turnover occurs, CA just measures the cost of replacing lost software engineers. TA_E captures this cost in OE, but TA_E also measures the loss of T on the constraint, which can be many times larger because it is output lost by the entire organization.

- When hiring occurs, TA_E sees no increase in T unless the hiring is for the constrained resource. That is, hiring a nonconstrained resource increases OE without increasing T.

- When outsourcing occurs, it decreases OE, but it may also shift which resource type is the constraint. If the constraint is outsourced, the decrease in OE may also decrease T.

- When projects are constrained by schedule, budget, resources, and scope, each constraint needs a buffer to protect it from uncertainty, but buffers increase OE without increasing T. Formal methodologies and process maturity certifications attempt to reduce uncertainty and thereby reduce buffer sizes, but methodologies and certifications themselves increase OE.

Translated into TOC terms, one of the great controversies in software engineering is whether the net difference in OE due to methodologies and certifications is a favorable or unfavorable change. Proponents of each side can support their position with examples because portfolios of projects react differently, depending on their objectives, size, complexity, resources, and other factors.

When a software engineering project produces software for internal use or implements a software package for internal use, its T is zero or negative because the project itself generates no cash. This does not mean, however, that such a project is useless. The business case instead considers the impact of the project on business units:

- Change in Net Profit: $\Delta NP_{BU} = \Delta T_{BU} - \Delta OE_{BU}$

If the software enables business units to increase their NP by increasing their T or decreasing their OE, the business case is obviously favorable. For example, internal projects to implement TOC software generate no T, yet they're routinely justified by their impact on ΔNP.

There are situations, however, where ΔNP is negative and the business case still justifies the project. For example, regulatory compliance is not discretionary, and even an internal software project with negative ΔNP may be the best alternative when compared to manual methods and the punitive consequences of noncompliance.

Many organizations face two challenges. First is to identify internal software projects where ΔT is overestimated and ΔOE is underestimated. Such projects may appear to have positive ΔNP, when in fact they are doomed before they start. Second is to identify internal software projects where projected ΔNP is legitimate but unexpected delays and scope changes erode ΔT and inflate ΔOE, thereby turning ΔNP from positive to negative while the project is underway. Conventional risk management tends to focus on ΔOE, but TA_E emphasizes that ΔT usually has more impact.

Throughput Accounting for Software Business

Throughput Accounting for Software Business (TA_B) is broader than TA_E because it covers sales and research in addition to software engineering. Moreover, there are variations on TA_B when a business sells its software as a product or service. Of course, selling software is itself a misnomer whenever a vendor sells licenses to use its product rather than own the product itself.

For software sold as a product, financial measures for TA_B are somewhat different from TA_E:

- **Throughput (T)** has sales commissions and subcontractor fees subtracted from it because they are totally variable costs (TVC).

- **Investment (I)** includes research to generate original ideas unless the business relies entirely on clients for ideas. It can also include physical inventory consisting of computer media and documentation.

- **Operating Expense (OE)** also includes training and support unless they are TVC.

For a software product, assuming the release currently being sold (r) was developed during the prior time period (t–1) and prior releases are no longer sold, these performance measures apply:

- Net Profit: $NP_t = T_t - OE_{t-1} = T_r - OE_r$
- Return on Investment: $ROI_t = (T_t - OE_{t-1}) / I_{t-1} = (T_r - OE_r) / I_r$

For a software product developed and sold over multiple periods, engineering lifetime (EL) generally starts and ends earlier than product lifetime (PL), but performance measures still apply:

- Net Profit: $NP_{PL} = T_{PL} - OE_{EL}$
- Return on Investment: $ROI_{PL} = (T_{PL} - OE_{EL}) / I_{EL}$

When a business sells its software as a service, the vendor provides more of the computing infrastructure for its software. That is, the vendor may host the software on its own servers and allow customers to use it via the Internet. Rather than purchasing a software release and installing it on their own servers, customers then pay one price for the software and infrastructure based on their usage.

From an accounting standpoint, this is analogous to selling a product over time rather than all at once because the service is largely automated rather than labor-based. Thus, the following financial and performance measures apply to a business selling software as a service:

- Throughput: T = Total Sales − Total Direct Costs
- Investment: I = Investment in ideas and tools
- Operating Expense: OE = Overhead + Infrastructure

To understand a particular release of software as a service, additional measures are needed. *New subscribers* are those who start their subscription with a particular software release (r). *Saved subscribers* are those who would have ended their subscription but are retained because they find that release sufficiently attractive. *Lifetime revenue per subscriber* is revenue over all periods during which a subscriber uses that release. Thus, the following measures apply to a particular release of software as a service:

- Sales: S_r = (New subscribers + Saved subscribers) × Lifetime revenue per subscriber
- Throughput: $T_r = S_r$ − Total Direct Costs$_r$

Regardless of whether software is sold as a product or service, the same decision-support measures apply in TA_B as well as TA_G and TA_S:

- Throughput per Constraint Unit: T/CU = (Revenue − TVC) / Constrained resources
- Change in Net Profit: $\Delta NP = \Delta T - \Delta OE$

A normal decision made with T/CU concerns which requirements to include in a release. A major decision made with ΔNP concerns which products to develop, enhance, or withdraw.

Summary

Throughput Accounting for Goods, Services, and Software all follow the same guiding principles even though each sector generates T, I, and OE differently. For instance, they all recognize that T should have higher priority than OE, and they all optimize production around the constraint.

Table C-1 summarizes accounting differences between internal and external software engineering projects and between a software business selling software as a product versus a service. While software engineering is project-oriented, a software business is more than just software engineering. Despite the differences, the TA measures are consistent in the sense that a good software engineering decision is also a good business decision.

Table C-1 Throughput Accounting for Software Engineering and Software Business

Throughput Accounting For...	Software Engineering (TA$_E$)		Software Business (TA$_B$)	
	Internal	External	Product	Service
Throughput is ...	Zero	Cash from code	Cash from code	Cash from code + infrastructure
Investment is mainly ...	Ideas + tools	Ideas + tools	Ideas + tools + inventory	Ideas + tools
Operating Expense is ...	Labor	Labor	Labor + SG&A + training + support	Labor + SG&A + training + support + infrastructure
Production metrics are ...	Q, V, ACPF	Q, V, ACPF		
Major decisions depend on ...	ΔNP	ΔNP	ΔNP	ΔNP
Optimization is done via ...	T/CU	T/CU	T/CU	T/CU

Endnote

1. David J. Andersen, *Agile Management for Software Engineering: Applying the Theory of Constraints for Business Results*, Prentice-Hall, 2004, www.agilemanagement.net.

Index